Food for Life

Food for Life

Delicious & Healthy Comfort Food from My Table to Yours!

LAILA ALI

with LEDA SCHEINTAUB

St. Martin's Press

New York

FOOD FOR LIFE. Copyright © 2017 by Laila Ali. All rights reserved. Printed in the United States of America. For information, address St. Martin's Press, 175 Fifth Avenue, New York, N.Y. 10010.

www.stmartins.com

Designed by Susan Walsh
Photographs by Matt Armendariz and Allen Cooley

The Library of Congress Cataloging-in-Publication Data is available upon request.

ISBN 978-1-250-13109-6 (hardcover)
ISBN 978-1-250-13110-2 (ebook)

Our books may be purchased in bulk for promotional, educational, or business use. Please contact your local bookseller or the Macmillan Corporate and Premium Sales Department at 1-800-221-7945, extension 5442, or by email at MacmillanSpecialMarkets@macmillan.com.

First Edition: January 2018

10 9 8 7 6 5 4 3 2 1

To Curtis Jr. and Sydney: You are my inspiration to use the
power of food to stay at my best for you!

Dad, you are an angel . . . and I know you are
comfortable at home in heaven,
eating a warm slice of my sweet potato pie with a scoop
of vanilla ice cream on top.
This book is for you!

CONTENTS

INTRODUCTION:
FOOD FOR THOSE WHO WANT IT ALL!

Boxing was my first love, but before I ever got into the ring, I was cooking! And today I am just as competitive in the kitchen as I was as a professional boxer. Okay, I take that back, but only because nobody has ever tried to knock my head off in the kitchen! Still, I've always wanted my food to be impressive—so good that people would talk about my meals long after they were over. And to this day, I have a passion for throwing down in the kitchen. That's why I jumped at the opportunity to compete on Food Network's hit show *Chopped* and walked away as the winner twice! I've cooked with Rachael Ray, Emeril, and Paula Deen and on *The Chew*. I've even cooked some of my famous Oven-"Fried" Chicken for Steve Harvey on his daytime talk show. And I wrote this book to share with you my favorite recipes, dishes inspired by my love for creating nutritious, winning meals.

Getting into the Kitchen

When we were growing up, my parents led a healthy lifestyle—both exercised regularly and neither smoked cigarettes or drank alcohol. Even though they were often on the go, they made sure my sister and I ate fresh, home-cooked meals. Now, that might sound like my parents prepared the meals, but we actually had a cook! And when my parents separated, I had to separate from those meals. I was always an independent person, and so at the early age of nine, I decided to get in the kitchen and teach myself how to cook. My first recipes were as simple as spaghetti and scrambled eggs, but by trial and error, over time I expanded my repertoire to include more complex dishes

such as seafood gumbo and stewed chicken and gravy, which to this day are favorites among my friends and family. I remember having a good appetite as a kid. To be honest, I was borderline greedy for food. I was that kid who would go over to their friends' houses and raid their refrigerators and pantries looking for something good to eat. I'm not quite sure why I was always on the hunt for food, but needless to say, I liked to eat!

Setting Myself Apart from the Competition

Many people assume that my success in boxing was automatically passed on to me from my dad. Actually, the truth is, I didn't learn how to harvest those boxing "genes" and build on the healthy fitness and eating habits my parents instilled in me until I was eighteen and became a boxer myself.

As I got serious about the sport, I set out to learn how the food I ate affected my performance. You see, as a boxer, I had to weigh in before each fight. So I needed to pay close attention to my food intake. But to make it as an elite athlete, I knew I had to take it to the next level. The meals I ate needed to help me become stronger and quicker and enable me to think more clearly. Once I learned the impact nutrition had on my performance, I became unstoppable! I didn't eat oatmeal, eggs, and green smoothies because I loved the taste (though I did what I could to make them tasty!) but rather so I could fuel my body. The food I ate allowed me to get the most out of my training and set me apart from the competition. It helped me make my mark in the ring: I became a four-time undefeated world champion boxer with twenty-four wins—twenty-one of them knockouts—and zero losses.

Fighting for an Honest Meal

For close to a decade I fought professionally by choice. But nowadays, each of us has to fight just to get a good, honest meal to the table. It isn't as simple as it was in the past, because food isn't as nutritious as it used to be. Produce is sprayed with chemicals that pollute our bodies. The same food

that was grown a couple of generations ago doesn't contain the same nutrition. Food manufacturers are putting health claims on junk food, and most of us are confused by all the misleading information out there on how we should be eating.

God put perfect foods on this planet to give our bodies everything we need to be healthy and to heal ourselves when we get sick. But ever since we started tampering with our food, what we consume has been making us sick. Much of what we are eating is more food-like than food. Consuming toxic ingredients, processed foods, and genetically modified grains and produce is not moving us in the right direction. We are going downhill fast, and our health is suffering. Major diseases, including heart disease, stroke, diabetes, and cancer, are on the rise, and we have the highest infant mortality and lowest life expectancy rates of all the developed nations. More than a third of American adults are obese—and that jumps to 50 percent of African Americans and more than 40 percent of Latinos.

A Simple Plan to Feed My Family

When I became a mother, armed with these statistics, I set out with a simple plan: I would feed my family nourishing and wholesome yet delicious meals. My kids would grow up with an appreciation for real food and have every opportunity to be strong and succeed in life, and my husband

and I would have the energy to make that vision a daily reality. I've never been one to hop on to food fads, trendy diets, or any one rigid way of eating. There are so many ways to approach the food we put on our plates, from veganism and vegetarianism to Paleo, low-carb, and elimination diets. There's so much information out there, and it seems to change all the time—who can sort through it all? But there *is* one thing we all can agree on: we should be eating as much unprocessed, whole food as possible. Nobody will argue that adding more fresh veggies to your diet isn't good for you. So even though I live a busy life with multiple businesses to manage, I have made a promise to myself: to make home-cooked meals for my family a reality and a priority.

Bringing My Passion into the Kitchen

After my last fight, I took some time to meditate on how I could continue to share my love for living a healthy lifestyle. My dad cared deeply about making a difference in the world, and he taught me to always try to do the right thing for the right reason and to treat everyone with kindness, love, and respect. In my motivational speaking around the country and internationally, I tell people that we all have what it takes inside to become champions in our lives. I encourage people to work harder and smarter if they want to reach their goals. But it's difficult to focus on success when you're feeling run-down, stressed out, depressed, overwhelmed, and devoid of energy! It's hard enough just to get by and finish the day. We aren't meant to live our lives that way. We should be full of energy and vitality and facing life with a winning attitude. So I decided to bring my passion for fighting into the kitchen, and that's how *Food for Life* was born.

Food for Your Life

Food for Life is my story told through the meals I put on the table each and every day. The star of the story is nourishing food, and the hero is you taking control of your health. The happy ending is a life filled with vitality: a clearer mind, satisfying sleep, healthy digestion, and more energy overall. All this adds up to you becoming the confident and strong person you are meant to be!

When we pump up our meals with nutrition rather than focusing on what we *can't* eat, we tend to be more successful and satisfied. For example, when you drink a superfood-packed shake in the morning, you're getting more nutrition in that drink than some people get in a whole week out of the food they eat. And when you start your day with the right foods, you're more likely to make better choices for the rest of the day. Then when you allow yourself a cheat meal, you won't beat yourself up but rather get right back on track. It's pretty simple—it's not a gimmick, promise, or plan—but this balanced approach to food works for me, and that's how I live my wonderfully full life as an athlete, businesswoman, and mom.

Many of today's chronic illnesses, in particular heart disease and diabetes, have their roots in lifestyle choices, and they can also be alleviated by lifestyle choices. And there's nothing more powerful than choosing to eat clean and healthy food. Many of us eat mindlessly just to fill our stomachs. Processed foods made with refined sugar, refined flour, and other empty-calorie ingredients leave us less than satisfied, and then we tend to overeat and crave more of those empty calories.

In my experience, small changes over time have the greatest impact, and weight loss is often a natural side effect. And as you go deeper, instead of craving sugar, you'll start to crave food that's good for you! Portion control is still important, but you won't have to count calories or carbs to know how much to eat. You'll find you're satisfied with less, emphasis on *satisfied*! The more real food you add to your meals, the less room there is for anything second best. You'll break up with junk food and start a lifelong affair with healthy, clean, fresh food.

Food for Life Recipes

We all love to eat, and there's no denying the strong emotional connection we have to food: food can be nostalgic and comforting, and it can provide a connection to family and friends. But to me, the nutritional connection is equally important, and uniting the two was my prime motivation in putting together this book. I strive to cook food that satisfies on every level: food for life, for those who want it all!

In this book, I've given you more than one hundred of my favorite real-life recipes, meals that I make for my family and that you can easily incorporate into your own life. Whether you're new to cooking, a busy parent feeding a family, or ready to take control of your health, these recipes were created for you! It's food that's healthy for you, but you'd never mistake it for "health food." That's because nutrition is king in my kitchen, but flavor is queen, and I won't sacrifice one for the other in my cooking.

We begin with Set the Tone: Victorious Breakfast Recipes, featuring the superfood shakes that fuel my workouts, make-ahead gluten-free muffins, eggs poached in salsa to spice up your morning meal, and more.

From the first meal of the day to the first course, First Impressions: Standout Soups and Salads includes innovative recipes for packing the veggies into soups and salads as well as my personal takes on Caesar and Cobb salads.

In a hurry? Make It Snappy: Quick, Luscious 30-Minute Meals takes the pressure off. Flavorful stir-fries, perfectly seared steak and salmon, healthy egg-fried rice, and my dad's favorite burger will get you through the week with grace.

Been There, Done That: Delicious

Make-Ahead Dishes gives you time when you need it most: just before dinner, when you'd rather be kicking back with the family. Recipes include pulled beef with barbecue sauce, several satisfying chicken dishes, and a protein-rich vegetarian chili. This chapter also introduces my Super-Sassy Seasoning, a lively knockout spice blend that appears in recipes throughout the book.

Cut to the Chase: Comforting One-Pot Suppers is one more way to have it all: all in one pot! This recipe highlights two special, passed-down Louisiana-style family favorites: jambalaya and gumbo.

Talk of the Town: Tantalizing Crowd-Pleasers gives you the tools to entertain in style. Starting with a gluten-free flatbread to live for and two dips—one with dairy and one dairy-free—to serve with it, and moving on to kebabs, stuffed mushrooms, and my famous oven-"fried" chicken, you'll be breaking new ground in party food.

Picky . . . Not Tricky! Easy Kid-Pleasing Foods will make it a cinch to satisfy the choosiest of kids, with updated versions of pancakes, mac and cheese, fries, and spaghetti and meatballs, and even spaghetti for breakfast!

Worthy Complements: Delectable Side Dishes brings serious flavor to the plate and pulls together a meal with finesse. Recipes include a vibrant, light creamed spinach and my West Coast take on Southern greens, coconut black rice, and a simple way to perfect brown rice.

On the Move: Easy, Satisfying Snacks means no more impromptu (i.e., unhealthy) snacking: making energy bars, granola bars, or spiced nuts and seeds in advance enables you to stay the course in between meals.

Next Level, Please! is just that: nutrient-rich recipes including bone broth, sauces spiked with veggies, and a trio of ferments to take your cooking to the next level of nutritious eating while silently or boldly taking your recipes a step further.

You don't want to give up desserts? Neither do I, and in Sweet Benefits: Scrumptious, Unbelievably Wholesome Desserts, you'll find my takes on classics including German chocolate cake, red velvet cupcakes, and sweet potato pie. All my desserts happen to be naturally gluten- and refined sugar–free, truly delivering on my promise to satisfy those who want it all!

Food for Life Ingredients

The recipes in my book are based on whole foods, whole grains, nutrient-rich ingredients, and healthy fats and oils, and they never call for refined sugar. All of the good stuff and none of the bad!

Choosing organic is like health insurance to me: the cost up front may be higher, but my family's lifelong health is worth it. When it comes to meat and dairy, going organic is extra important, as factory-farmed meat and dairy are often treated with hormones and antibiotics and fed pesticide-laden foods, none of which I want passed to my children's growing bodies! If you eat beef, choosing grass-fed beef is the best choice, as it's higher in heart-healthy, immune-boosting omega-3 fatty acids than factory-farmed beef.

By whole grains, I mean brown rice, black rice, quinoa, and millet instead of white rice or pasta. When purchasing pasta, choose a whole-grain or gluten-free variety. Whole grains are superior because they contain the intact bran and germ of the grain, providing the protein, fiber, vitamins, and minerals that refined grains do not. Refined grains can cause blood sugar spikes, while whole grains can hold your blood sugar steady and keep you satisfied beyond the end of a meal. I like to soak my whole grains before cooking them, which makes them more digestible and even more nutritious. See page 219 to learn how to soak your grains.

Nutrient-rich ingredients are the healthiest ingredients. From the spirulina, chlorella, and maca supplements that turn my smoothies into superdrinks to the concentrated veggies I pack into my secret sauces and the turmeric I sprinkle in just about everything, my aim is to make every recipe as nutrient-rich as possible. Next Level, Please! sidebars pepper the pages with ways of adding even more nutrition to your recipes, like a sprinkle of mineral-rich dulse seaweed in your meatballs or a strip of kombu for your pot of beans. An entire Next Level, Please! chapter is dedicated to upping the nutrition to a higher level yet—

with recipes for bone broth, super-nutritious sauces, and a foray into fermentation. I love how ferments help with digestion and provide an impressive probiotic power-punch!

When shopping for oils, look for the words *unrefined* or *extra-virgin* on the label. All other vegetable oils, including canola oil, are refined, which means they are stripped of flavor, color, and nutrients. I favor extra-virgin olive oil and coconut oil in my cooking for their heart-supportive qualities. I use healthy amounts of grass-fed butter for flavor, and sometimes I'll cook with ghee (clarified butter), as it withstands higher heat than plain butter.

You'll notice that my recipes don't specify fat percentages for dairy. I'll leave that to your personal preference, but know that getting quality fat into your diet is crucial for brain, heart, and overall health, and a low-fat diet can deprive a growing child of essential nutrients. Fat adds flavor and satisfaction, filling us up without the need for seconds and thirds. See page 284 for more information on fats.

Even dessert can fit into a healthy lifestyle! For me that means my treats are made with whole grains and unrefined sweeteners such as honey and maple syrup rather than processed wheat and table sugar. Many people are gluten-free these days, and although I'm not, I don't feel my best after indulging in gluten-heavy desserts. For that reason, the entire dessert section is gluten-free, and not only that, the gluten-free flour

FOOD *for* LIFE

If you want your food to taste great every time, pack it with flavor! The following simple tips will help bring out the flavor in your food and satisfy your taste buds. **Number one, don't skimp on the salt.** The purpose of the salt in my recipes isn't to make your food salty, but to bring out the natural flavors of the food. Once you minimize your consumption of processed foods, you'll have reduced your salt intake by a ton, so don't be afraid to use it judiciously in your cooking. **Second, load up on herbs and spices:** they play an important supporting role in your cooking, making the star of the dish really shine. **Third, make citrus your friend.** Lemon and lime and their zests not only act as alkalizing forces in your body, they make flavors really pop, which is why I use them liberally, even in unlikely places like smoothies, energy bars, and desserts. If your food tastes like it needs a little something, more times than not citrus will do the trick! If you've gone a little too far with the citrus, add salt to balance things out, and likewise add citrus if your food tastes too salty. And speaking of taste, remember to always taste your food as you cook and make adjustments to the salt, spices, and citrus accordingly. Ingredients, especially produce and meat, range widely in quality and flavor, and no recipe turns out the same way twice. That's the beauty of cooking. Trust and honor your sense of taste and you'll become a better cook!

I favor is free of the common binders—xanthan gum and guar gum—that contribute to digestive issues for many people. I know you will be pleased with the results!

Now let's fill your fridge and pantry with your foods for life!

Food for Life Shopping List

Whether it's simply making a few changes to your current shopping habits or doing a full cleanout of your pantry, preparing your kitchen will enable you to make the most of the *Food for Life* recipes. The guiding principle is simple: clean your fridge and pantry of processed and packaged foods with unpronounceable ingredients and replace them with fresh, whole foods. When you've stocked the basic ingredients for breakfast, lunch, and dinner, you're much more likely to make meals at home! The shopping list that follows will have you covered for the recipes in this book, but there's no need to go out and buy everything at once. Start with pantry ingredients—these will be used often throughout the book—and build from there; then shop fresh for fruits, veggies, dairy, seafood, and meat as you need them.

GRAINS, PASTA, AND BREAD

Barley
Black rice
Brown rice
Corn tortillas
Millet
Quinoa
Rolled oats (not instant)
Whole-grain or gluten-free spaghetti and noodles
Whole-grain or gluten-free bread crumbs
Whole-grain, sprouted wheat, or gluten-free bread

BEANS, SOY, AND PROTEIN SUPPLEMENTS

Adzuki beans (dried or canned)
Black beans (dried or canned)
Black-eyed peas (dried, frozen, or canned)
Chickpeas (dried or canned)
Edamame (fresh or frozen)
Miso paste (refrigerated)
Tofu
Whey powder or other protein powder

NUTS AND SEEDS

Almonds
Cashews
Chia seeds and chia flour
Flaxseeds and flax meal
Hazelnuts
Macadamia nuts
Nut butters
Peanuts
Pecans
Pine nuts
Pistachios
Pumpkin seeds (pepitas)
Sesame seeds
Shredded coconut (unsweetened)
Walnuts

DRIED FRUIT

Dates
Dried cranberries (unsweetened)
Raisins

OILS AND VINEGARS

Cooking spray (extra-virgin olive oil or unrefined coconut oil)
Extra-virgin olive oil
Toasted sesame oil
Unrefined coconut oil
Apple cider vinegar
Balsamic vinegar
Red wine vinegar
Rice vinegar
Sherry vinegar
White wine vinegar

CONDIMENTS, SAUCES, AND PASTES

Anchovy paste
Canned tomatoes and tomato puree
Capers
Clam juice
Coconut milk
Dijon mustard
Extra-virgin olive oil mayonnaise (egg-based or vegan)
Fish sauce
Gochujang (Korean chile paste)
Hot sauce
Mirin (rice wine)
Olives
Sriracha sauce
Sun-dried tomatoes
Tahini (sesame seed paste)
Tamari or soy sauce
Tomato paste
White wine
Worcestershire sauce

SEA VEGETABLES

Dulse seaweed granules (in a shaker)
Kombu seaweed
Nori seaweed

DRY SEASONINGS

Allspice (ground)
Bay leaves
Black peppercorns
Cardamom (ground)
Cayenne pepper
Celery seed
Chipotle chile (ground)
Cinnamon (ground)
Cloves (ground)
Coriander (ground)
Cumin (whole seeds and ground)
Curry powder
Dill (dried leaves and whole seeds)
Fennel seeds
Garlic powder
Ginger (ground)
Italian seasoning
Marjoram
Matcha tea powder
Nutmeg (whole seeds for grating)
Onion powder
Oregano
Paprika (smoked and sweet)
Parsley
Pink peppercorns
Red pepper flakes
Rosemary
Sea salt (fine and flaky)
Turmeric (ground)

BAKING AND SWEETENING INGREDIENTS

Almond extract (pure)
Vanilla extract (pure)
Almond flour or meal
Almond milk
Baking powder
Baking soda
Cocoa powder (unsweetened)
Cornstarch or arrowroot powder
Dark chocolate
Dark chocolate chips
Gluten-free flour blend (preferably Steve's GF Cake Flour)
Quinoa flour
Whole wheat flour
Orange flour water
Honey
Maple syrup (pure)
Molasses
Raw sugar
Stevia
Unrefined brown sugar

SUPERFOOD SUPPLEMENTS

Spirulina powder
Chlorella powder
Maca powder

FRESH FRUITS

Apples
Avocados
Bananas
Blueberries
Grapefruits
Lemons
Limes
Oranges
Raspberries
Strawberries
Other seasonal fruits

FRESH HERBS

Basil
Chives
Cilantro
Dill
Mint
Oregano
Parsley
Rosemary
Tarragon
Thyme

FRESH VEGETABLES

Artichoke hearts (jarred)
Arugula
Beets
Belgian endive
Bell peppers (red, orange, green)
Bok choy
Broccoli
Butternut squash
Carrots
Cauliflower

Celery
Collard greens
Corn
Cucumber
Eggplant
Fennel
Garlic
Ginger
Green beans
Green, red, and napa
    cabbage
Jalapeños
Jicama
Kale
Leeks
Mushrooms (button,
    cremini, shiitake,
    portobello)
Mustard greens
Parsnips
Peas
Potatoes
Radishes
Red, yellow, and white
    onions
Romaine lettuce
Scallions
Serrano chiles
Shallots
Snow peas
Spaghetti squash
Spinach
Sweet potatoes
Swiss chard
Tomatillos
Tomatoes

Turnips
Zucchini

MEAT AND FISH
Beef for stewing and
    stir-fries, steak,
    chuck roast
Canned tuna
Chicken breasts, thighs,
    wings, and whole
    chicken
Chicken or beef bones
Crabmeat
Fresh salmon and other
    fish
Ground beef
Ground lamb
Ground turkey
Lamb chops, leg of
    lamb
Sausage meat
Scallops
Shrimp
Turkey bacon
Turkey leg

DAIRY AND EGGS
Blue cheese
Cheddar, Jack, Gruyère,
    and other melting
    cheeses
Feta cheese
Goat cheese
Mozzarella cheese

Parmesan cheese
    (grated or in a
    chunk)
Ricotta cheese
Buttermilk
Cage-free eggs
Cream
Cream cheese
Grass-fed butter
Milk
Sour cream
Yogurt (Greek and
    regular)

BEVERAGES
Coconut water
Green tea
Rooibos tea

Food for Life Tools and Equipment

The *Food for Life* recipes were designed to make healthy cooking simple, with no special equipment required. Having some basic tools and equipment will bring ease to your cooking. Here's what I recommend:

- Chef's knife and paring knife
- Cutting board
- Heatproof spatula
- Whisk
- Measuring spoons
- Measuring cups (dry and liquid)
- Mixing bowls
- Cheese grater/microplane grater
- Vegetable peeler
- Handheld citrus press
- Garlic press
- Instant-read thermometer
- Fine-mesh strainer
- Colander
- Stockpot
- Saucepans: small, medium, large (a Dutch oven is also useful)
- Skillets: large and small (cast iron is great)
- Sauté pan
- Roasting pan
- Baking sheets/cookie sheets
- Stand mixer or handheld mixer
- Blender/immersion blender
- Food processor
- Baking dish
- Cake pans (8- or 9-inch)
- Loaf pan (9-inch)
- Springform pan (10-inch)
- Muffin pan (12-cup)
- Pie plate (9- or 10-inch)
- Wire cooling rack
- Timer

Start Where You Are

Whether you're a busy parent, an on-the-go-single person, or an athlete looking for foods to fuel your performance, my hope is that *Food for Life* will help you take control of your health while bringing a level of enjoyment and satisfaction to your food that will inspire and excite you! Start wherever you are, even if it means something as simple as blending a smoothie for breakfast or making one fresh home-cooked meal a week. And by the time you've tried a handful of recipes, you just may be convinced that home cooking is worth the effort. We all want to eat flavorful, satisfying food that the whole family can get excited about. We want it all . . . and you *can* have it all!

Set the Tone

VICTORIOUS BREAKFAST RECIPES

When you start the day with a healthy breakfast, you're much more likely to keep it up for the rest of the day. But when it's a doughnut at the desk or a bagel behind the wheel, you are headed in the wrong direction! These breakfast recipes are nutritious and hearty while remaining light, like my breakfast casserole that packs in the greens and calls for sweet potato instead of bread (page 15). My chicken and egg tacos (page 33) make use of leftover chicken, perfect for when you only have a few minutes to spend in the kitchen. Whipping up a shake is one of the quickest ways to get a head start on meeting your daily nutritional needs. It also gives your digestive system a break because the blender does the "chewing" for you! I count on my shakes to replenish me after a good workout, and I've included two of my favorites—my go-to green shake (page 21) and a shake for the coffee lover in you (page 25). And if you're up for something totally new, sip on a bowl of miso soup (page 37) for a light and warming breakfast boost! Don't forget to check out two of my kids' favorite breakfast treats—pancakes and blueberry muffins—in the Picky, Not Tricky chapter (pages 171 and 173). Yes, breakfast sets the tone for the day, and it can even set you in the direction of a victorious lifestyle!

CHARD, CHEDDAR, AND SAUSAGE BREAKFAST CASSEROLE

This dish gets me excited about eating breakfast! If you like "soul food" the way I do, this recipe is for you. It's comforting and packed with flavor, and it fills you up without weighing you down. Most breakfast casseroles call for a large amount of bread, making them carb-heavy. To lighten up my casserole, I use antioxidant-rich sweet potato and load it with greens. Because I love sweet potatoes so much—both for their flavor and health value—I look for unexpected ways to add them to recipes, and I especially enjoy them for breakfast, even in my oatmeal (see page 29)!

Another thing that's great about this casserole is that you can assemble it the night before or bake it in advance, then put slices in the toaster oven to reheat for a quick or on-the-go breakfast. Or you can serve it with a salad, quiche-style, for lunch or dinner. My Simple Red Cabbage Salad (page 59) and Avocado, Asparagus, and Artichoke Salad (page 67) are two nice accompaniments. *Serves 8*

Extra-virgin olive oil cooking spray
1 pound loose breakfast sausage
1 medium yellow onion, finely chopped
12 large eggs
1 teaspoon sea salt, or to taste
¾ teaspoon garlic powder
¼ teaspoon ground turmeric
¼ teaspoon cayenne pepper
1 medium to large sweet potato (about 8 ounces), peeled and coarsely grated on a box grater
8 ounces cheddar cheese, coarsely grated (about 2 cups)
1 small bunch Swiss chard, stemmed, leaves cut into ribbons
4 scallions, white and green parts, trimmed and thinly sliced

OPTIONAL TOPPINGS
Avocado slices
Hot sauce
Sliced scallions
Green Salsa (page 28)
Roasted Tomato Salsa (page 34)

Preheat the oven to 375°F. Coat an 8 by 10-inch casserole pan with cooking spray.

Heat a large skillet over medium-high heat. If you are using turkey, chicken, or another lean sausage meat, add a generous coating of cooking spray. If it's a fatty sausage, skip the oil. Add the sausage and cook, breaking it up with a wooden spoon, until it starts to release a little fat, about 5 minutes. Add the onion and cook, stirring often, for 10 to 15 minutes more, until the sausage and onion are well browned. Transfer to a plate to cool.

Beat the eggs in a large bowl. Beat in the salt, garlic powder, turmeric, and cayenne, then stir in the sausage mixture, sweet potato, all but ½ cup of the cheese, the chard, and the scallions. Pour the mixture into the prepared casserole, cover with aluminum foil, and bake for 20 minutes, or until starting to set. Remove the foil, sprinkle evenly with the remaining ½ cup cheese, and bake for 15 to 20 minutes more, until the center is set and the casserole is lightly browned and bubbling on top. Let sit for 5 to 10 minutes, then slice and serve.

Swap It Out

- For the chard, use a similar leafy green such as collards, kale, spinach, or beet greens.
- Instead of scallions, try another fresh herb such as dill, cilantro, or parsley, or a combination.
- Use any melting cheese you already have in the fridge or you've been wanting to try. Pepper Jack will add a little spice.
- Use fresh sausage; there are so many varieties to pick from, including hot Italian, caraway, and roasted red pepper. Simply remove the meat from the casing and crumble it into the pan.
- Add ½ cup fresh or thawed frozen peas or corn along with the vegetables.

- Add a bell pepper, any color. Chop it and cook it with the onion.

WHERE'S THE PORK?

Because my father was Muslim, I grew up without pork in my household. Then one day when I was a teen, I ate a slice of pepperoni pizza, not knowing pepperoni was a pork product, and I enjoyed it. I don't eat pork now—other than the occasional pepperoni pizza—because I'm just not used to eating it. If pork is part of your diet, feel free to swap it into your breakfast casserole or any of my recipes calling for beef or any type of ground meat.

Next Level, Please!

- Double up on the greens by adding a handful of fresh arugula leaves to your plate. Dressing is optional; while some salad mixes are ho-hum without oil and vinegar, in-season arugula, ideally picked locally, is so full of flavor that it needs no adornment.
- Chop the chard stems and save them to add to your next pot of Very Veggie Broth (page 248) or blend them into a batch of hummus (page 228).

CINNAMON, CARROT, AND MACA MUFFINS

Muffins have a special place in my heart. I especially enjoy eating them sitting on my patio in the morning with a steamy cup of coffee. These potent, gluten-free breakfast muffins get a boost from maca powder to energize you in the morning. See the sidebar on the next page to learn about this exciting superfood. You can make them ahead of time or whip up the batter for baking the night before, then pop them in the oven when you get up and enjoy the warming smell of cinnamon spice wafting through the house as you get ready for your day. I like to make a double batch, freeze them, and thaw for a quick breakfast or snack. *Makes 10*

Unrefined coconut oil cooking spray (if not using paper liners)

1 cup cup-for-cup replacement gluten-free flour blend, such as Steve's GF Cake Flour

2 teaspoons maca powder

1 teaspoon ground cinnamon

½ teaspoon ground ginger

¼ teaspoon ground allspice

¾ teaspoon baking powder

¼ teaspoon baking soda

¼ teaspoon sea salt

2 large eggs, at room temperature

½ cup (1 stick) plus 1 tablespoon unsalted butter, melted and still warm

½ cup liquid honey

1 teaspoon pure vanilla extract

1 teaspoon grated lemon zest

1½ cups (6½ ounces) shredded carrots

½ cup raisins

½ cup chopped walnuts

Preheat the oven to 350°F. Line 10 cups of a 12-cup muffin pan with paper liners or grease them with cooking spray.

Sift the gluten-free flour blend, maca, cinnamon, ginger, allspice, baking powder, baking soda, and salt into a medium bowl.

In a separate medium bowl, whisk the eggs, then gradually pour in the warm melted butter and whisk to combine. Add the honey and whisk until the ingredients are blended. Add the vanilla and lemon zest and whisk to combine.

Pour the dry mixture into the wet mixture and stir with a wooden spoon until just combined. Add the carrots and stir briefly to combine, then add the raisins and walnuts and stir until well blended and the batter has a loose consistency. (At this point, the batter may be covered with plastic wrap and stored in the refrigerator overnight. Allow the batter to come to room temperature before baking fresh in the morning.)

Fill the muffin cups to ¼ inch from the top (these muffins don't rise very much) and bake for 20 to 25 minutes, until the tops are golden brown and just firm to the touch and a cake tester inserted into a muffin comes out clean. Remove the muffin pan from the oven and place it on a wire rack. Release the muffins by running a small metal spatula or knife along the inside edge of each muffin cup, then place the muffins on the rack to cool completely.

The muffins will keep, wrapped in plastic wrap, at room temperature for up to 3 days or in the freezer for up to 2 months.

Swap It Out

Substitute coconut oil for the butter to make these muffins dairy-free. Melt the coconut oil and let it cool until just warm before whisking it into the eggs.

MAKE MINE WITH MACA

Maca is a plant that comes from high in the Andes mountains, where it has been used as a food and medicine for thousands of years. What I like best about this superfood is that it's an adaptogen, meaning that it helps us naturally adapt to the stressors in our lives. It is mineral- and nutrient-rich and high in antioxidants, and it contains more calcium than milk. It also helps restore hormonal balance and gives us more stamina and energy—who couldn't use that! (Note that physicians do not recommend maca for people with hormone-sensitive conditions such as breast cancer, ovarian cancer, or prostate cancer, and it is recommended that pregnant and nursing mothers avoid it, as there isn't sufficient evidence as to whether it is safe for them.)

You'll generally find maca in powder form (liquid and supplements are also available). It has an earthy, nutty, slightly sweet and mild taste, making it easy to add in small amounts to pretty much any recipe without being detected. You can sprinkle it into muffin batter, as we do here, use it in your smoothies, mix it into breakfast cereal and energy bars (page 237), and even add it to desserts (see my recipe for Cocoa Maca-Roons on page 283)!

GREEN POWER SHAKE

I remember the first time I drank a green protein shake. It was more than eighteen years ago, at the beginning of my boxing career. My nutrition coach mixed up some bland-tasting protein powder, green powder, and water in a shaker cup and handed it to me. Those shakes became a part of my everyday meal plan, and while they were nutritious, they gave me absolutely nothing to look forward to! Happily, protein shakes and smoothies don't have to be boring and uninspiring anymore, thanks to a greater availability of fresh ingredients and some innovative mixing and matching. This recipe transformed my morning smoothie from a chore to something special to wake up to!

1 cup plain kefir, homemade (page 254) or store-bought
½ cup water
1 scoop whey or other natural protein powder
½ small ripe avocado, peeled and chopped
1 tablespoon honey or maple syrup, or to taste (optional)
½ to 1 teaspoon spirulina or chlorella powder (see sidebar, on page 22)
Large handful of fresh or frozen spinach or kale leaves, torn into pieces if using fresh
1 teaspoon fresh lemon juice, or to taste
Small pinch of sea salt, or to taste
Handful of ice cubes

In a blender, combine all the ingredients except the ice. Blend, starting on low speed and finishing on high speed, until smooth. Add the ice and blend again, starting on low speed and finishing on high speed, until smooth, adding more water if your shake is too thick.

Swap It Out

Swap in coconut water or maple water (see page 250) for the water for their mildly sweet flavor and electrolyte content.

SUPER GREENS TO THE RESCUE!

With toxic chemicals lurking in our food, environment, and even our bodies, we need to fight back with everything we've got. Spirulina is one of my favorite toxin-busting blue-green algae! It is grown in either fresh water or salt water via sunlight and is one of the richest sources of easily assimilated nutrition of *any food*! Now *that's* a true superfood! This algae offers complete protein and a host of B vitamins, making it particularly appealing for vegetarians. And it is so potent that it has been used by the World Health Organization in its programs to feed malnourished children.

Chlorella is another superfood champion. Primarily composed of cleansing chlorophyll, chlorella has been shown to assist with heavy metal (mercury and lead in particular) detoxification while strengthening the immune system, cleansing the body, and stimulating the growth of friendly bacteria for improved digestive health. It also contains high levels of the antioxidant beta-carotene.

Supplementing with both spirulina and chlorella is a concentrated way of packing in the greens and a powerful adjunct to your daily dose of veggies. Use either or both in your smoothies; you can also take them in supplement form. They even make their way into snacks—you'll love them in my Clean Green Energy Bars (page 237)!

MY THREE-PART SMOOTHIE FORMULA

When you've got my three-part smoothie formula down—1) a good source of protein, 2) a healthy fat, and 3) a nice handful of greens—your smoothie becomes endlessly adaptable. Superfood add-ins such as spirulina, chlorella, and maca will take your smoothie to the next level. Make sure to use an all-natural brand of protein powder, preferably without sweetener, and adjust the amount up or down based on your size and activity level. When I've got more veggies or fruit in the fridge than I can eat, I chop them up and blend them or freeze them to add to my smoothies. A tip for the tastiest green smoothies: include a little lemon juice to offset the grassy taste of the greens and a pinch of sea salt to make the flavors pop.

COLD-BREW COFFEE: FOR THOSE WHO WANT IT ALL!

Recent science has revealed that coffee is high in antioxidants and heart-protective factors. It gives a sensation of energy and can even help us feel happy. One concern with coffee is its acidity, but this is easily remedied when you cold-brew your coffee. A second concern is that coffee is a mild diuretic, so if you're a coffee drinker, consider drinking additional water throughout the day to avoid dehydration. Cold-brewing brings down the acidity of your coffee by half, and if you start with a good organic low-acid coffee like I do, you'll already be ahead of the game. Cold-brewing coffee results in a smoother, sweeter brew that's kind to your stomach and equally perfect served over ice, heated on the stovetop, or added to a smoothie.

You can cold-brew your own at home with no special skills or equipment required (and if you don't have the time, you now can find the prepared concentrate in many grocery stores). Simply use cool water instead of hot and leave the grounds to soak overnight before straining. This recipe can easily be doubled or tripled and made with caffeinated or decaf coffee. *Makes 4 cups*

1 cup very coarsely ground coffee (your coffee may be cloudy if you use fine grind)
4 cups cool water

Spoon the coffee into a jar or pitcher with a lid or the bottom of a French press.

Slowly add the cool water to thoroughly moisten the coffee. Cover the jar or put the top on the French press (but don't press down on the plunger).

Refrigerate for 12 to 24 hours (the longer it sits, the more concentrated it will be).

If your coffee is in a jar, pour the coffee through a coffee filter, a nut-milk bag, or a mesh strainer lined with cheesecloth into another jar. If you're using a French press, press down on the plunger and pour the coffee into a jar.

Cover and refrigerate for up to 2 weeks. Add directly to your smoothies in small amounts or dilute with water at a 1:2 or 1:3 ratio and serve either over ice or gently heated on the stovetop.

Next Level, Please!

Freeze cold-brew coffee in ice cube trays. Pop the cubes into your iced coffee or add them to your smoothie for a thicker, slushy drink.

COFFEE LOVER'S SMOOTHIE

It's no secret that I am a coffee lover! I enjoy the taste, with or without the caffeine. So I just had to create this recipe for all my coffee-lovin' folks! This smoothie—packed with nutrition and spiked with low-acid cold-brew coffee—is the best of both worlds. See the recipe on page 23 to learn how to make your own cold-brew concentrate—you'll be surprised at how easy it is! *Serves 1*

¾ cup water

¼ to ½ cup cold-brewed coffee concentrate (page 23)

1 scoop whey or other natural protein powder (I like chocolate flavor with my coffee smoothie)

1 tablespoon no-sugar-added almond butter or other nut butter

1 tablespoon unsweetened cocoa powder (optional)

1 tablespoon honey or maple syrup, or to taste (optional)

1 tablespoon flax or chia seeds

½ teaspoon maca powder (optional; see page 20)

Large handful of fresh or frozen kale, spinach, romaine lettuce leaves, or other greens, torn into pieces if using fresh

Handful of ice cubes

In a blender, combine all the ingredients except the ice. Blend, starting on low speed and finishing on high speed, until smooth. Add the ice and blend again, starting on low speed and finishing on high speed, until smooth, adding more water if your smoothie is too thick.

FROZEN FRUITS AND VEGGIES

The farmers' market is one of my favorite places to pick out seasonal produce, and there's nothing quite like a garden-picked tomato or freshly harvested greens. But when I need to make a meal in a hurry, frozen veggies come in handy! We tend to think that frozen produce is less healthful than fresh, but sometimes the opposite can be true. Packaged produce is typically frozen just after picking, at the peak of ripeness when nutrition is at its height. Vegetables are blanched (cooked in water briefly; fruit isn't) before they are frozen, which means there's a slight loss of vitamins and minerals. But, on the other hand, much of our fresh produce is picked *before* it's ripe, so those fruits and veggies aren't able to reach their full vitamin, mineral, and antioxidant potential. They ripen as they travel across the country, arriving far from fresh by the time they make it to your kitchen. Freezing vegetables is my solution to vegetables that are about to turn, and then they can be on standby to fortify smoothies, broth, soups, and other dishes.

GREEN SALSA–POACHED EGGS

I've had my share of eggs over the years. Because eggs are a great source of high-quality protein, vitamins, and minerals, I've been eating them regularly for a good part of my life. But plain scrambled or poached eggs just don't do it for me. That's why I appreciate a good fresh salsa to accompany my eggs. This festive Mexican-inspired breakfast is quick to put together, and I love the bold, tart flavors! If you make the salsa in advance, this dish can be on the table in less than ten minutes. Poaching eggs in water can be a little fussy to get just right, but when you poach your eggs in salsa, you're pretty much guaranteed success. Just make sure to poach the eggs gently over low heat so the whites don't break apart. And for ease of cooking, crack each egg into a small ramekin before adding them to the salsa. *Serves 2*

1 cup Green Salsa (recipe follows) or good-quality store-bought salsa
4 large eggs
Sea salt
Whole-grain toast
½ avocado, peeled and sliced
Extra-virgin olive oil (optional)
Chopped fresh cilantro leaves

Pour the salsa into a medium skillet and bring to a simmer over medium heat. Crack each egg into a small ramekin or teacup and gently lower them one by one into the salsa, evenly spacing the eggs around the skillet. Season the eggs lightly with salt. Reduce the heat to low, cover the pan, and poach the eggs for about 5 minutes, until the whites are just set and the yolks are cooked to your liking. Set the eggs and salsa atop toast slices. Add the avocado, sprinkle the avocado with a pinch of salt, then drizzle with olive oil if you like and finish the dish with a sprinkle of cilantro.

Swap It Out

- Use a jarred tomatillo salsa as a timesaver; check ingredients lists and choose a brand without any additives or added sugar.
- Use a Roasted Tomato Salsa (page 34) in place of the green, or try my Secret Red Sauce (page 265).

Green Salsa

Tomatillos are the base of many Mexican dishes and the star of the green salsa we enjoy at our favorite Mexican restaurants. They are a relative of the tomato but smaller and green in color, with a naturally tart flavor and a papery husk that is removed before using. It's surprisingly easy to make your own salsa, and the rewards are freshness and a spice level that you get to control—serranos will generally pack a greater punch than jalapeños, and if you leave the seeds in, you'll have an additional blast of heat. This salsa has a fresh, bright taste to it; for a deeper, slightly smoky flavor, try the variation below using roasted tomatillos. Note that from-scratch salsa can separate in the jar; just give it a stir before using. *Makes about 2½ cups*

1 pound fresh tomatillos
2 or 3 fresh serrano or jalapeño chiles, stemmed and chopped
1 small yellow onion, chopped
3 garlic cloves, quartered
¾ cup chopped fresh cilantro
1¼ teaspoons sea salt, or to taste

Peel off and discard the papery husks from the tomatillos; rinse them well. Coarsely chop the tomatillos and place them in a blender. Add the remaining ingredients and blend until chunky or smooth to your liking. For the Green Salsa–Poached Eggs, go for a smooth, soupy consistency; for a chip- or vegetable stick–dipping consistency, chunky is your goal. Add a little water if needed to achieve the desired consistency. Taste and add more salt if needed. If you're not using your salsa right away, pour it into a jar, cover, and refrigerate for up to 1 week.

Swap It Out Variations

- **Roasted Tomatillo Salsa:** Preheat the broiler. Place the peeled and washed tomatillos, whole chiles, and garlic (unpeeled) on a broiler pan. Broil about 4 inches from the heat, turning once, until the tomatillos are softened and slightly charred, 6 to 8 minutes. (Alternatively, you can roast the tomatillos on a super-hot cast-iron skillet for about the same amount of time.) Peel the garlic and transfer the contents of the pan, including any juices that the tomatillos have released, to the blender along with the cilantro and salt and blend as directed above.
- **Creamy Tomatillo Salsa:** Blend an avocado into the salsa (do not heat this variation).

PECAN SWEET POTATO PIE OATMEAL PARFAIT

I was never a big fan of oatmeal until I added my beloved sweet potato to the mix. Now I'm smitten with my morning bowl of oats. For creamier, less firm oats, combine the oats with the water and then bring to a boil. For everyday breakfast fare, go ahead and serve the oatmeal in a regular bowl instead of parfait cups or jars, with or without the yogurt topping. *Serves 2*

¾ cup water, or dairy or nondairy milk, or a combination
½ cup rolled oats
2 tablespoons fruit juice–sweetened dried cranberries or raisins
½ teaspoon ground cinnamon, or to taste
Pinch of sea salt
½ cup mashed sweet potato (see sidebar, page 31)
1 tablespoon pure maple syrup, or to taste
½ teaspoon pure maple extract (optional)
½ teaspoon pure vanilla extract
½ cup plain Greek yogurt
¼ cup chopped toasted pecans (page 261)

Pour the water into a medium saucepan and bring to a boil over medium-high heat. Add the oats, cranberries, cinnamon, and salt, return to a boil, then reduce the heat and simmer for about 5 minutes, stirring only once or twice, until the oats begin to soften and the liquid thickens. Stir in the sweet potato and cook for about 2 minutes, until smooth and heated through. Add a little water if the oatmeal thickens too much. Turn off the heat and stir in the maple syrup, maple extract (if using), and vanilla. If you've got the time, cover and set aside for 5 minutes to absorb excess moisture and to bring all the flavors together.

To assemble the parfaits, pour one-quarter of the oatmeal into each of two parfait bowls or Mason jars. Top each with one-quarter of the yogurt, followed by one-quarter of the pecans. Repeat the layering, starting with oatmeal and ending with pecans. Serve immediately, or, if using Mason jars, cover and pop into your bag to take to your a.m. destination.

Swap It Out

- Make it a pumpkin pie parfait by substituting 100 percent pure pumpkin puree (not pumpkin pie filling) for the mashed sweet potato. Or try mixing in my Pure and Simple Squash Puree (page 212).
- Add 1 teaspoon grated lemon zest or a drop of pure lemon extract to your yogurt; the tang of the lemon plays perfectly against the sweet maple syrup. A dash of freshly grated nutmeg is another tasty addition.
- Use walnuts instead of pecans and add a sprinkle of sesame, flax, or chia seeds. Read more about these super nuts and seeds on page 233.

Next Level, Please!

- Set up your oats for soaking the night before. Soaking is a traditional practice to make grains more digestible that a new generation of home cooks is starting to rediscover. It requires a little advance thinking but almost no work (read more about the practice on page 219). Place the oats in the pan you're going to cook them in, add water to cover by a couple of inches, cover with a dishtowel, and leave till the morning. Drain and proceed

with the recipe, reducing the amount of water in the recipe to ½ cup.
- Swap out some of the maple syrup for stevia—adding a little stevia pumps up the sweetness while keeping blood sugar in check, and when balanced by the maple syrup, the taste of the stevia becomes barely noticeable.

HOW TO STEAM SWEET POTATOES

Peel a few sweet potatoes and cut them into roughly 1-inch chunks. Place them in a steamer basket set over a pot filled with a couple of inches of simmering water. Cover and steam until tender when poked with a knife or fork, 20 to 30 minutes. Remove from the steamer, let cool, then process in a food processor until smooth. You won't need more than a small sweet potato to yield ½ cup puree, but don't stop there. Set some chunks aside for your carb portion of lunch or dinner tonight, then puree the rest and freeze for future oatmeal breakfast parfaits. To freeze: Line a baking sheet with parchment or waxed paper. Scoop the sweet potato puree into a ½-cup measuring cup and empty it onto the baking sheet. Repeat with the remaining puree. Place in the freezer and freeze for 1 to 2 hours, until solid, then pop into a freezer bag or container and store in the freezer.

CHICKEN AND EGG BREAKFAST TACOS

Sometimes I come up with recipes just by using leftovers; this is one of them. It's a great way to enjoy the remains of last night's barbecue or roast. Just shred the meat (save the bones for Basic Bone Broth, page 245), put it in the refrigerator, and you're halfway to breakfast. Or poach some chicken (see page 94), shred it all, and store in the freezer as a super-fast source of protein. If you don't have time to make salsa from scratch (it can be made a day or two ahead), a good-quality jarred brand can be substituted. *Makes 6 to 8 tacos (about 3 cups filling)*

4 large eggs
Pinch of ground turmeric
Sea salt
1 cup shredded cooked chicken (page 94)
½ cup fresh or thawed frozen corn kernels
1 tablespoon extra-virgin olive oil
1 cup loosely packed fresh baby spinach leaves
½ cup Roasted Tomato Salsa (recipe follows) or good-quality store-bought tomato salsa, plus more for topping
Freshly ground black pepper
6 to 8 corn tortillas, warmed

In a large bowl, beat the eggs until light and foamy. Add the turmeric and ½ teaspoon salt and beat again. Stir in the chicken and corn.

In a large skillet, heat the oil over medium heat. When it starts to sizzle, add the egg and chicken mixture. Cook for about 30 seconds, until the eggs begin to set, then, using a heatproof spatula, gently fold the eggs and continue to fold until the eggs are set. Stir in the spinach for about 45 seconds, until wilted, then add the salsa and cook, stirring, for a few seconds to warm it up. Taste and season with salt and pepper if needed. Stuff into the tortillas, top each with a little salsa, if you like, and serve.

Swap It Out

- Use another meat, such as last night's lamb or beef roast.
- Use crab instead of the chicken for a special-occasion breakfast.
- Add varied-colored heirloom cherry tomatoes.
- Add fresh herbs such as mint, cilantro, basil, or even Thai basil.
- Add avocado slices.
- Add thinly sliced fresh chiles, with or without the seeds, for extra spice.
- Serve with Green Salsa (page 28) instead of the Roasted Tomato Salsa.
- Stir some chimichurri (page 155) in at the end (skip the salsa), after the eggs come off the heat.
- Finish with a sprinkle of Parmesan cheese.

Roasted Tomato Salsa

Roasting gives a depth of flavor to tomatoes, taking your salsa-making skills up a notch. Use this salsa in recipes from scrambled eggs to spaghetti squash. *Makes about 1 quart*

1 or 2 jalapeños, stemmed
4 garlic cloves
½ small white onion
2 pounds small round or medium plum tomatoes
Sea salt
½ cup chopped fresh cilantro

Preheat the broiler.

Set the jalapeños, garlic, onion, and tomatoes on a broiler pan. Broil for about 5 minutes, until darkened in color with a few blackened spots. Turn and broil on the other side until darkened with a few blackened spots on the second side and the tomatoes are softened, 3 to 4 minutes. Peel the garlic. Transfer the jalapeños, garlic, and onion to a food processor and pulse to chop the ingredients. Add the tomatoes along with any juices from the pan and process to break down the tomatoes into salsa consistency, as smooth or chunky as you like. Season with salt, add the cilantro, and pulse for a couple of seconds to incorporate. If you're not using your salsa right away, pour it into a jar, cover, and refrigerate for up to 1 week.

SKILLET SMASHED ROSEMARY POTATOES AND EGGS

This fragrant dish is a perfect way to impress your friends and family at Sunday brunch; it becomes a weekday dish when you boil the potatoes the night before (it's easy—when you're making potatoes for another dish, just throw a few more into the pot). Fragrant rosemary elevates this simple skillet dish to something special (and see the sidebar on the next page for rosemary's remarkable memory-boosting properties). Since this recipe uses a fair amount of oil, make sure it's a good-quality one; my favorite is unrefined coconut oil (it can add a slight coconut taste to the dish; if you'd prefer a more neutral oil, use extra-virgin olive oil). Think of this dish as a healthier version of hash browns! Serve with a side of fresh arugula to lighten up the plate. *Serves 2*

6 small unpeeled new potatoes (about 3 inches in diameter)
Sea salt
¼ cup unrefined coconut oil
4 large eggs
½ cup cherry tomatoes, halved or quartered if large
¾ teaspoon minced fresh rosemary
Coarsely ground black pepper

Put the potatoes in a medium saucepan, add water to cover, and season well with salt. Bring to a boil over high heat, then reduce the heat to maintain a high simmer and cook for about 10 minutes, until the potatoes are tender (a sharp knife poked through the center of a potato should meet no resistance). Place in a colander and leave for about 5 minutes to drain excess water.

Working with one potato at a time, place the potatoes on a cutting board and smash them with the bottom of a heavy skillet to about ½ inch thick. Transfer each smashed potato to a plate. Try to keep the potatoes whole, but it's fine if they break apart a bit (in fact, it's very likely they will!); everything will come together in the finished dish.

In a 10- to 12-inch cast-iron skillet, heat the oil over medium heat. Arrange the potatoes over the pan in a single layer and cook until the bottoms are well browned and crisp, about 5 minutes. Scoop out indentations in between the potatoes and crack the eggs directly into your chosen spots. Arrange the cherry tomatoes over the potatoes (not over the eggs), sprinkle with salt, and drizzle 1 tablespoon water all around the sides of the pan (this will help to steam the eggs and keep the potatoes from sticking to the bottom). Cover and cook until the eggs are done to your liking, about 5 minutes for medium runny.

Uncover the pan and sprinkle with the rosemary and some pepper. Place the pan on a trivet at the table and serve directly from the pan.

Swap It Out

- Search out heirloom potatoes of various colors at your farmers' market, from Adirondack red to purple Peruvian and Inca gold.
- Use any fresh herbs, such as thyme, oregano, or sage.
- For a smoky finish, sprinkle with a touch of smoked paprika.

REMEMBER ME, ROSEMARY

In addition to its prowess in the kitchen, rosemary can also clear the head and restore memory. In fact, it recently has been shown to work with memory as well as ginkgo biloba. So while you're fixing up your breakfast skillet, toss a sprig of rosemary into a teacup, pour in some boiling water, and steep for about 5 minutes. Then enjoy with your breakfast while you bring your mind into focus and set forth into your day. Rosemary can also settle your stomach and help your body digest fatty foods, which may be why you often see it paired with lamb (as it is in my seared lamb chop recipe on page 141).

ANYTIME MISO SOUP

You're probably wondering why I've included a soup recipe in my breakfast chapter. Well, let me tell you why you should add soup to your morning rotation. While soup is not typically considered breakfast food in this country, it is in many others, notably in Asian countries. Miso soup for breakfast gets your day jump-started with live and active cultures, something totally different from yogurt or kefir, and it replaces popping a probiotic supplement in the morning. And, of course, you can enjoy miso soup any time of the day.

My miso soup can be made with bone broth or the traditional Japanese way, with a simple dashi broth. Based on two superfoods—kombu seaweed and bonito fish flakes—dashi takes less than ten minutes to make and provides a mild, comforting flavor base. Both kombu and bonito can be found in Asian food stores and some natural foods stores. Read more about kombu on page 39. *Serves 2 to 3*

6 cups Basic Bone Broth (page 245), Very Veggie Broth (page 248), good-quality store-bought broth, or water
1 (4-inch) piece kombu (if using water)
1½ cups bonito flakes (if using water)
6 to 8 tablespoons miso paste

PROTEIN ADD-INS
1 cup cooked shredded chicken (page 94)
½ cup small-diced firm tofu or drained silken tofu
1 cup cooked chickpeas (page 107), edamame, or other bean
6 ounces fresh white fish, cut into cubes or flaked

VEGGIE ADD-INS
Chopped or shredded leafy greens such as chard or spinach

Sliced or chopped scallions or leeks
Thinly sliced shiitake or other mushrooms
Thinly sliced radishes or baby turnips
Sheet of nori seaweed, torn into pieces, or handful of dried wakame seaweed

FLAVORING FINISHES
1 (1-inch) piece fresh ginger, juiced (see Note on the next page)
1 teaspoon toasted sesame oil
Splash of chile oil, thinly sliced fresh chiles, or a sprinkle of cayenne pepper
Splash of fresh lemon or lime juice

If you're using bone broth, pour it into a large saucepan and bring to a simmer. If you're making dashi stock, combine the water and kombu in a large saucepan and bring to a bare simmer over medium-high heat. Remove from the heat, fish out and discard the kombu, add the bonito flakes, and stir gently. Cover and steep for 5 minutes. Strain through a fine-mesh sieve into a new pan, pressing gently on the flakes to extract all their liquid, and discard the bonito flakes. You can make the dashi in advance; it will keep in an airtight container in the refrigerator for up to 5 days.

Reheat the bone broth or dashi and turn off the heat. Put the miso paste in a fine-mesh sieve and, using the back of a spoon, press the paste through the sieve into the broth, discarding any large grains that don't pass through (for a rustic miso soup, simply whisk in the miso). Stir in whichever protein and veggie add-ins you like and cook until heated through. Pour into bowls and serve with your choice of flavoring finishes.

NOTE: Finely grate a small piece of ginger (no need to peel it first) and squeeze it in the palm of your hand to extract the juice.

Swap It Out

- Include vegetables you have on hand—leafy greens, green beans, corn, anything that calls to you from your crisper drawer.
- Instead of scallions, seek out seasonal local relatives such as garlic scapes or wild leeks.
- Miso comes in a variety of flavors, from mild white miso to yellow to red; experiment with them all to find your favorite. The darker the color, the stronger the miso tends to be. Most miso is based on soy; if soy isn't part of your diet, try chickpea miso.
- Vegetarians can omit the bonito flakes and use Very Veggie Broth.

Next Level, Please!

- Choose miso from the refrigerated section of your supermarket or natural foods store for guaranteed live and active cultures. You'll be making a definite upgrade from opening a packet, which contains zero live and active cultures. Plus, live tastes a million times better! The key to keeping it live is not to boil the miso; add it at the very end, after the other ingredients have been cooked.
- Use dashi as a quick fish or seafood stock stand-in.
- Use dashi in place of water to cook rice, quinoa, or any other grain.

NO RECIPE REQUIRED! SEVEN SIMPLE BREAKFAST SUGGESTIONS

1. Sprouted wheat bread or To Live for Flatbread (page 153) with 10-minute Nut Butter (page 260)

2. Berries with ricotta or cottage cheese drizzled with flax oil and sprinkled with cinnamon

3. Open-face turkey bacon, avocado, and sprout sandwich

4. Last night's rice or quinoa, heated up like oatmeal with milk, nuts, and maple syrup

5. Half a sweet potato spread with 10-minute Nut Butter (page 260)

6. Leftovers from dinner with a poached egg on top

7. Sliced hard-boiled egg over arugula drizzled with olive oil and sprinkled with salt and pepper

MOTHER NATURE'S MSG

MSG, or monosodium glutamate, is a chemical that was extracted in a lab over a hundred years ago by a Japanese chemist in search of the perfect savory (umami) flavor. And where did he find it? In seaweed! A substance called glutamic acid was isolated from seaweed, sodium was added, and MSG was born. But this chemical form of glutamic acid acts differently in the body, with possible health risks ranging from headaches and flushing to long-term neurological problems. And if that's not enough, consider this: MSG has been used to induce obesity in lab animals. I say no thanks to that! Instead I cook with kombu—known as the "king of seaweed"—for its pure and natural savory flavor. Adding a strip of it to soups or stews or a pot of beans helps soften them and make them more digestible. Kombu can be found in natural foods stores and Asian markets.

First Impressions

STANDOUT SOUPS AND SALADS

We all know how important first impressions are. So when the first course comes out, I like to make it a showstopper! Soup is a healing food, especially when you start with a from-scratch base such as my Basic Bone Broth (page 245) or Very Veggie Broth (page 248). My chicken noodle soup (page 45) will stand up to a nasty cold, while my vegetable soup (page 43) is a celebration of any season you serve it in. And my carrot and sweet potato soup (page 49) is one of my absolute favorites. I like to eat something raw with every meal, so salads are part of my everyday life. Raw vegetables have their enzymes intact, adding vibrancy to your meals and keeping your digestion in good working order. I never get bored with salads, and I've included some of my favorites in this chapter, including a succotash salad made with edamame (page 70), a simple red cabbage salad (page 59) that I serve with many of my mains, a stunning heirloom tomato salad (page 61), and a tuna and pickle salad (page 73) that provides live and active cultures with every bite! Soups and salads are a great way to get in a lot of veggies, and with so many mix-and-match options, they allow for a lot of creativity in the kitchen. Good looks, good taste, and good health—that's the impression I want you to make when you place your first dish on the table!

VERY VEGGIE SOUP

While soup is a comfort when it's chilly out, a light spring or summer soup satisfies without weighing you down. And a big pot of veggie soup is a quick, healthy dish I love to make for my whole family. The recipe is never exactly the same because I use different veggies each time I make it, depending on what's in season. This soup gets its lush green color from a generous amount of cilantro, and it puts the stems to use, too! For those who don't care for cilantro, spinach can be swapped in. Sometimes I'll add avocado slices to my bowl for a dose of healthy fats. Add shredded turkey, chicken, or chickpeas, crumble in some tofu, or top with a poached egg and your veggie soup turns into a satisfying one-bowl meal. *Serves 4 (makes about 6 cups)*

2 teaspoons extra-virgin olive oil
1 small onion, finely chopped
1 medium carrot, finely chopped
1 medium celery stalk, finely chopped
Sea salt
2 garlic cloves, minced
1 (½-inch) piece fresh ginger, peeled and minced (optional)
½ teaspoon red pepper flakes, or to taste
1 quart Very Veggie Broth (page 248), Basic Bone Broth (page 245),
2 sprigs fresh thyme
1 bay leaf
Freshly ground black pepper
½ red, orange, or yellow bell pepper, chopped
½ cup small cauliflower florets
½ cup chopped green beans
1 small zucchini, chopped
½ cup corn kernels (from 1 small ear of corn)
½ cup thinly sliced or shredded green or red cabbage
2 cups chopped fresh cilantro
1½ tablespoons fresh lemon juice, plus more to taste

In a large saucepan, heat the oil over medium-low heat. Add the onion, carrot, and celery and a pinch of salt and cook until the vegetables are starting to soften but not lose color, about 10 minutes. Add the garlic, ginger (if using), and red pepper flakes and cook for about 2 minutes, until aromatic. Add the broth, thyme, and bay leaf, season with salt and black pepper, increase the heat to high, and bring to a simmer. Reduce the heat to medium-low, cover, and cook for 10 minutes. Add the bell pepper, cauliflower, and green beans and cook for 3 minutes, or until starting to soften. Add the zucchini, corn, and cabbage and cook for 2 minutes more, or until all the vegetables are crisp-tender. Remove and discard the thyme sprigs and bay leaf.

Scoop out 1 cup of the broth and transfer it to a blender. Add the cilantro and blend until smooth with no flecks of green remaining. Return the blended mixture to the soup and add the lemon juice. (Don't cook after returning the blended cilantro to the pan to keep its vibrant green color.) Taste and add more salt, pepper, and/or lemon juice if needed. Spoon into bowls and serve.

Swap It Out

- **Vegetables that cook in more or less the same time are easy swaps. Here are some to get you started:**
  Broccoli for the cauliflower
  Asparagus for the green beans
  Peas for the corn
  Leeks for the onion
  Fennel for the celery

Next Level, Please!

- Add miso to your soup for a probiotic boost: After the soup is done, remove a small amount of broth from the pan, put it in a cup, and whisk in the miso until it has dissolved. Return the miso mixture to the pot, but do not heat the soup further (this keeps the miso's enzymes live). Read more about miso on pages 37–38.
- Add a little Secret White Sauce (page 263) to the soup.

INFLAMMATION-BUSTING CHICKEN NOODLE SOUP

Now *this* soup is the real deal! There's no doubt it's tasty, but it's also just what you need in your culinary arsenal to help knock out germs and strengthen your immune system. Just what makes it inflammation-busting? A base of bone broth, for starters, then a good sprinkle of turmeric, one of nature's most powerful anti-inflammatories (read more about turmeric on page 50), and lots of nutritious veggies. But what really takes it off the charts is lots and lots of garlic! Roasting mellows the bite of the garlic and brings out its natural sweetness, so you can really load up on it. Take that, flu season! *Serves 4 to 6*

2 quarts Basic Bone Broth (page 245) made with chicken bones

2 pounds bone-in chicken breasts or thighs

Sea salt

Cloves from 3 heads Toaster Oven Roasted Garlic (page 47)

¾ teaspoon ground turmeric

2 carrots, parsnips, or turnips, peeled and chopped

1 large tomato, chopped (optional)

About 4 cups leafy greens, such as spinach, stemmed beet greens, chard, or kale, chopped or torn into bite-size pieces

4 ounces cooked rice vermicelli or other thin noodles

Tamari or soy sauce, fish sauce, or a combination

Fresh lemon or lime juice

Chopped fresh herbs, such as scallions, cilantro, mint, or dill

Sliced fresh jalapeño, serrano, or other chile, or a hit of hot sauce

Pour the broth into a large saucepan and bring to a boil over medium-high heat. Add the chicken and season with salt. Reduce the heat to medium-low, cover, and cook until the chicken is cooked through, 20 to 25 minutes. Transfer the chicken to a plate to cool, then pick the meat off the bones and shred it with two forks or your fingers.

While the chicken is cooling, remove 1 cup of the broth from the pot and pour it into a blender. Add the roasted garlic and blend until smooth.

Add the turmeric and carrots to the broth in the pot and cook until the carrots are softened, about 5 minutes. Add the tomato (if using) and cook for 1 minute, then add the greens and cook for another minute or two, until wilted. Return the chicken to the pot and add the noodles and blended garlic. Season with the perfect amount of tamari and lemon juice for your taste. Spoon into bowls, top with your choice of herbs and chiles, and serve.

Swap It Out

- This is my go-to chicken soup recipe, and it's widely open to interpretation and reinvention every time you make it, for a slightly different soup every time. The basics are a base of bone broth, plus a firm vegetable such as carrot or parsnip, leafy greens, and flavorings such as tamari, fish sauce, and citrus. Then the final product is entirely up to you!
- If you've got chicken left over from last night's roast, shred it and skip the poaching.

Next Level, Please!

- After you've removed the chicken meat from the bones, save the bones to include them in your next batch of Basic Bone Broth.
- Shake a sprinkle of dulse granules into your soup. Read more about this flavor- and nutrition-enhancing seaweed on page 76.
- Poach two batches of chicken; shred and store one batch in the freezer to have ready for recipes that call for cooked chicken, such as my Chicken and Egg Breakfast Tacos (page 33) or Cheddar Chicken Enchilada Skillet (page 135).
- Add a little Secret White Sauce (page 263) to your soup.

TOASTER OVEN ROASTED GARLIC

Roasted garlic adds a depth of flavor to your dishes, from soups to salad dressings to mashed potatoes. It's simple to make, and you can roast several heads at a time and store them in the fridge to use whenever you like. And you don't even have to turn on the oven—you can roast your garlic right in a toaster oven. But you certainly can use the oven if you want to make multiple heads of roasted garlic at a time.

Garlic heads (as many as you wish)
Extra-virgin olive oil

Preheat the toaster oven to 400°F. Peel the papery outer skin from the garlic heads, leaving the cloves intact. Cut ¼ to ½ inch off the top of each garlic bulb to expose the top of the cloves. Place each head on a square of aluminum foil, drizzle lightly with oil, and wrap it up. Place in the toaster oven and roast for about 45 minutes, until the garlic is completely softened and lightly browned. Remove from the toaster oven, open the foil, and let cool until you can handle it easily. Squeeze the garlic from the skins. If not using right away, store in a covered container in the refrigerator for up to 1 week.

CURRIED CARROT AND SWEET POTATO SOUP

This soup is often on the menu when I have friends over for dinner! It's easy to prepare and visually striking, and the flavors are equally impressive.

The secret to a fresh-tasting curried soup is a light hand with the curry powder and just the right amount of coconut milk for a rich but not overly heavy texture. Curry powder typically gets its golden color from one of my favorite spices, turmeric. I add a little extra turmeric for its amazing health benefits and to enhance the orange in the vegetables. Serve this soup piping hot, at room temperature, or lightly chilled. I usually make extra, because it tastes even better the second day, after the flavors have had some time to mingle. It freezes well, too! *Serves 4 to 6*

2 tablespoons extra-virgin olive oil, plus more for drizzling
1 large red onion, chopped
2 garlic cloves, chopped
1 (1-inch) piece fresh ginger, peeled and finely chopped
½ teaspoon ground cumin
½ teaspoon ground turmeric
Pinch of cayenne pepper (optional)
1 teaspoon mild curry powder
8 ounces carrots, cut into ½-inch-thick slices
1 large sweet potato (about 12 ounces), peeled and cut into ½-inch chunks
5 cups Very Veggie Broth (page 248), Basic Bone Broth (page 245), or good-quality store-bought broth
¾ cup unsweetened coconut milk
1½ teaspoons sea salt, plus more to taste
1 teaspoon grated orange zest
3 tablespoons fresh orange juice
1 teaspoon grated lime zest
1 tablespoon fresh lime juice, plus more to taste
Chopped fresh cilantro

In a large saucepan, heat the oil over medium-high heat. Add the onion and cook, stirring, until softened and well browned, about 10 minutes. Add the garlic and ginger and cook for about 1 minute, until aromatic. Add the cumin, turmeric, cayenne (if using), and curry powder and cook, stirring, for about 1 minute, until aromatic, adding a tiny bit of water if the mixture starts to stick to the bottom of the pan. Add the carrots, sweet potato, broth, coconut milk, and salt, increase the heat to high, and bring to a simmer. Reduce the heat to medium-low, cover, and cook until the carrots and sweet potato are softened, about 30 minutes. Add the orange zest, orange juice, lime zest, and lime juice.

Working in batches, transfer the soup to a blender and blend until smooth (be careful when blending hot liquids). Return the soup to the saucepan, taste, and add more salt and/or lime juice if needed. Spoon into bowls and serve with a drizzle of oil and a sprinkle of cilantro on top.

Swap It Out

- Use all carrots or all sweet potato.
- Use hot curry powder if you'd like more heat.

Next Level, Please!

Add a little Secret White Sauce (page 263) to the soup.

(page 263)

TURMERIC: THE GOLDEN-COLORED SUPER SPICE

It gives mustard its bright yellow color, it's a backbone ingredient in Indian curry powder, and it's one of the strongest natural anti-inflammatories around. Turmeric outperforms pharmaceuticals in many studies on inflammation thanks to curcumin, the pigment responsible for its color. Curcumin shows potential to relieve arthritis, keep away various cancers, and prevent Alzheimer's disease. In India, where turmeric is an everyday ingredient in curries, the rate of Alzheimer's is among the world's lowest. How to get more turmeric into your diet? Enjoy it in curries, like the one on page 111, or add a little to your scrambles, meat dishes, soups, stews, bone broth, smoothies, tea, or even dessert (see page 299). Turmeric has a mild flavor, so a little will enhance the color but won't change the flavor of your food. I put it in just about everything I can to make sure I get it into my system daily!

FOOD *for* LIFE

TOMATO AND ROASTED GARLIC CREAM SOUP

Tomatoes are a summer treat, but I always find myself craving a hot bowl of tomato soup when the weather cools down, just as tomato season ends. Of course preserving tomatoes is an option, but the process is too involved for my busy lifestyle. This is why I have made good-quality canned tomatoes my friend! Canned tomatoes have a whole lot of their anti-cancer antioxidant lycopene intact, and I make sure the brand I choose comes in a BPA-free can (see sidebar on page 53). Coconut milk and an ample amount of roasted garlic give creamy body and flavor to this dairy-free soup. *Serves 4 to 6*

1 tablespoon extra-virgin olive oil
1 medium yellow onion, chopped
2 sprigs fresh thyme
1½ teaspoons dried oregano
¼ teaspoon red pepper flakes
1 tablespoon sherry vinegar, plus more to taste
1 (28-ounce) can diced tomatoes with juices
1½ cups Very Veggie Broth (page 248), Basic
   Bone Broth (page 245), or good-quality
   store-bought broth
1½ teaspoons sea salt, plus more to taste
Cloves from 1 head Toaster Oven Roasted
   Garlic (page 47)
1 (14-ounce) can unsweetened coconut milk
1 tablespoon pure maple syrup, or to taste
1 tablespoon minced fresh flat-leaf parsley

In a medium saucepan, heat the oil over medium heat. Add the onion and thyme and cook, stirring occasionally, until the onion is softened and lightly colored, about 10 minutes. Add the oregano and red pepper flakes and cook for about 2 minutes, until aromatic. Add the vinegar and cook for 1 minute, stirring to release any browned bits from the bottom of the pan.

Add the tomatoes and their juices to the pan, then add the broth and salt, increase the heat to high, and bring to a simmer. Reduce the heat to medium-low, cover, and simmer for 30 minutes to blend the flavors. Turn off the heat.

Remove and discard the thyme sprigs. Transfer the soup to a blender, add the roasted garlic, and blend until smooth. Return the soup to the pan and add the coconut milk and maple syrup. Bring to a simmer over medium heat and cook for 5 minutes. Taste and add more salt and/ or vinegar if needed. Spoon into bowls, top with the parsley, and serve.

Swap It Out

- Add 1 cup cooked cannellini beans to pack your soup with protein.
- Use rosemary instead of parsley.

Next Level, Please!

Add a little Secret White Sauce (page 263) to the soup.

PASS ON THE BPA, PLEASE!

I urge you to choose tomatoes from a can that's free of the synthetic estrogen BPA (bisphenol A). And do the same when you're buying canned beans, other canned foods, and foods or drinks packaged in plastic. Many studies show that BPA causes or is linked to a host of health problems, including fertility issues, increased risk for cancer, and impaired brain development, in particular for developing fetuses and infants. The term *synthetic estrogen* alone tells me that it's probably something I want my family to avoid! BPA is most commonly used in plastic bottles and canned foods, with about 75 percent of cans being lined with it (even organic food can be put into BPA-lined cans). The good news is that more and more companies are opting out of BPA; go to the Environmental Working Group's website (ewg.org) to find out which ones and show your support for them at the supermarket.

MUSHROOM BARLEY SOUP WITH MINI MEATBALLS

Mini meatballs speckled with dill make this thick, stewlike mushroom barley soup a hearty starter or meal in a bowl. Serve it with a salad accompaniment such as my Simple Red Cabbage Salad (page 59).

The meatballs can be made in advance and kept in the refrigerator until you're ready to add them to the soup. And why not double the meatballs and freeze them for future batches of mushroom barley soup? Or you could pop a few of them into some simmering bone broth (page 245), add a whole grain and greens, and an impromptu dinner is ready to put on the table. To freeze the meatballs, place them on a baking sheet with some space between each and freeze for 1 to 2 hours, until solid, then transfer them to a freezer bag and freeze until ready to use. *Serves 4 to 6 (makes about 8 cups)*

2 tablespoons extra-virgin olive oil
2 large shallots, finely chopped
1 medium carrot, finely chopped
1 large celery stalk, finely chopped
4 garlic cloves, finely chopped
1 pound cremini mushrooms, sliced
Sea salt
¼ cup sherry (optional)
6 cups Basic Bone Broth (page 245), Very Veggie Broth (page 248), or good-quality store-bought broth
1 tablespoon tamari or soy sauce
½ cup pearl barley
½ teaspoon freshly ground black pepper

MEATBALLS
8 ounces ground beef
1 large egg, beaten
½ cup Sprouted Wheat Bread Crumbs (page 57) or store-bought whole-grain bread crumbs

½ teaspoon dill seeds
1 teaspoon garlic powder
1 teaspoon onion powder
½ teaspoon sea salt
¼ teaspoon red pepper flakes (optional)
3 tablespoons minced fresh dill
3 ounces green beans, thinly sliced (about 1 cup)
2 teaspoons fresh lemon juice, or to taste
Sea salt and freshly ground black pepper
2 tablespoons chopped fresh dill
Sour cream or plain Greek yogurt (optional)

In a large saucepan, heat the oil over medium heat. Add the shallots, carrot, and celery and cook until starting to soften, about 5 minutes. Add the garlic and cook for about 2 minutes, until fragrant. Add the mushrooms and a pinch of salt, cover, and cook, opening the lid to stir a couple of times, until the mushrooms soften and release their liquid, about 10 minutes (covering the pan keeps the mushrooms from sticking and avoids the need for additional oil). Uncover, increase the heat to medium-high, and cook for 5 minutes more, or until the liquid released by the mushrooms has mostly evaporated. Add the sherry (if using) and cook until it has evaporated, about 2 minutes. Add the broth, tamari, barley, 2 teaspoons salt, and the pepper and bring to a boil. Reduce the heat to low, cover, and cook until the barley is nearly tender, about 30 minutes.

Meanwhile, to make the meatballs: In a medium bowl, combine the beef, egg, bread crumbs, dill seeds, garlic powder, onion powder, salt, red pepper flakes (if using), and fresh dill. Mix well with your hands to thoroughly incorporate the ingredients. Rinse your hands to remove any stickiness from the meat, then form the mixture into about 1-inch rounds (to make about 18 meatballs).

Add the meatballs to the soup in a circular fashion around the pan, pushing them down a little to submerge them. Return the soup to a simmer, then cover, reduce the heat to low, and simmer until the meatballs are just about cooked through, about 5 minutes. Uncover, add the green beans, and cook until the meatballs are fully cooked through, the barley is tender, and the green beans are crisp-tender, about 3 minutes.

Stir in the lemon juice, taste, and adjust the seasonings with more salt, pepper, and/or lemon juice if needed. Stir in the fresh dill, spoon into bowls, and serve, topped with a spoonful of sour cream if you like. The soup may thicken as it sits; add more bone broth or water to thin it out.

Swap It Out

- Substitute white button mushrooms or portobellos for the creminis.
- Add caraway seeds to the meatballs in place of the dill seeds.
- Serve with my Fennel and Jicama Salad (page 65) and swap in fennel fronds for the fresh dill, getting two recipes out of one ingredient!
- Use another meat such as ground turkey, chicken, or lamb instead of the beef. Or for a simplified, any-night version of mushroom barley soup, skip the meatballs and add shredded cooked meat at the end.
- To make the soup a vegan one, use Very Veggie Broth (page 248) and swap in chickpeas or tofu for the meatballs.

Next Level, Please!

- While barley contains gluten, it has less gluten than wheat, making mushroom barley soup an option for those of us limiting but not eliminating gluten. If further limiting or eliminating the gluten, see the following options.
- Try spelt or einkorn instead of the barley. Both are wheat varieties, but ancient ones that haven't been subject to the hybridization of modern wheat. Some people with wheat sensitivities do better with these. Add up to 10 minutes additional cooking time.
- To make this recipe completely gluten-free, substitute short-grain brown rice for the barley and use gluten-free bread crumbs.

Sprouted Wheat Bread Crumbs

A sprouted grain is one that is soaked until it begins to sprout. Sprouting helps break down the proteins and carbohydrates in grains and makes the grain easier to digest, which is why I like to buy sprouted-grain bread and make bread crumbs out of it. If sprouted-grain bread is unavailable or gluten is an issue, use another type of whole-grain bread or gluten-free bread. Sprinkle coarse bread crumbs over pasta, greens, or soup, or grind them finely to coat chicken or other proteins. *Makes about 3 cups coarse bread crumbs or about 2 cups fine bread crumbs*

5 slices sprouted-wheat bread, defrosted if frozen
1 tablespoon extra-virgin olive oil
2 teaspoons Italian seasoning (optional)
¾ teaspoon garlic powder
¾ teaspoon sea salt

Preheat the oven to 350°F.

Tear the bread into small pieces. Place in a food processor and process into coarse crumbs. Use the crumbs fresh for meatballs or to top a casserole or to add a crisp topping to anything that's going under the broiler.

Spread the bread crumbs in an even layer on a rimmed baking sheet. Bake, stirring occasionally, until browned and dry. Immediately transfer the bread crumbs to a large bowl (while they are still hot, they will better absorb the oil), drizzle with the oil, add the Italian seasoning (if using), garlic powder, and salt, and toss to coat. If you'd like fine bread crumbs to use as a breading, return the bread crumbs to the food processor and process until finely ground. The bread crumbs will keep in an airtight container in the refrigerator for up to 1 month or frozen for up to 3 months.

SIMPLE RED CABBAGE SALAD

This salad is a staple in my house because it is so easy to make. I prepare a big batch of it at the beginning of the week so it's ready to serve with my meals for several days. It's quicker than a typical salad and goes well alongside fish, chicken, beef, and vegetarian mains and is adaptable to whatever other vegetables you want to add. This is my bare-bones, get-dinner-to-the-table-in-a-flash version of cabbage salad. I've also shared some suggestions for when you have time to fancy it up!

Because cabbage is firm, it keeps for days without getting soggy, which makes it easy to get some raw veggies into your meals regardless of what else is on the menu. Sometimes I'll massage the cabbage for a few seconds with a pinch of salt to start to soften it before dressing and serving. *Serves 4 to 6*

1 small red cabbage (about 2 pounds), cored and shredded
2 tablespoons fresh lemon juice, plus more to taste
1 tablespoon honey or pure maple syrup
¾ teaspoon garlic powder
¾ teaspoon onion powder
1 teaspoon sea salt, plus more to taste
½ teaspoon freshly ground black pepper
1½ tablespoons extra-virgin olive oil

Place the cabbage in a large bowl. In a small bowl, whisk together the lemon juice, honey, garlic powder, onion powder, salt, and pepper. Add the oil and whisk until emulsified. Add the dressing to the cabbage and toss to coat. Taste and add more salt and/or lemon juice if needed.

Swap It Out

When I have a little more time, I like to supplement my salad by adding ½ jalapeño, chopped; a grated carrot or parsnip; 2 tablespoons finely chopped fresh flat-leaf parsley, mint, or cilantro; and 2 scallions, white and light green parts thinly sliced.

Next Level, Please!

- Add some sauerkraut to your salad for a mixed raw and fermented cabbage salad. See page 259 for how to make your own, or check the refrigerator section of the supermarket and look for the words *live, raw, unpasteurized,* or *contains live and active cultures* on the label. Pickles on the shelf are pasteurized and contain no live cultures. Or take it a step further and make your own pickles; learn how on page 257.
- Add a drizzle of flax oil just before serving.

CANCER-FIGHTING CRUCIFERS

One of the most powerful anti-cancer upgrades you can make to your diet is to eat more cruciferous veggies. You've got quite a few to choose from: arugula, bok choy, broccoli, Brussels sprouts, cabbage (red and green), cauliflower, collard greens, horseradish, kale, mustard greens, radishes, rutabaga, turnips, and watercress are all cruciferous vegetables. Cruciferous vegetables are high in vitamins, minerals, and fiber, and a diet rich in crucifers has been correlated with a lower risk for a variety of cancers. Glucosinolates, a group of sulfur-containing compounds that give crucifers their pungent bite, may be responsible for their anti-cancer effects. And these effects may be multiplied when you eat your crucifers raw. That's why I like to add a raw element, often my favorite crucifer—red cabbage—to many of my meals. Red cabbage contains a bonus plant-based chemical called anthocyanin polyphenols, which account for its red color, work as an antioxidant, and protect the body against free radicals and cancer and other diseases. These are the same polyphenols that are famously found in berries, red and purple grapes, and red wine. Note that large amounts of raw crucifers may interfere with the incorporation of iodine into the thyroid hormone, so those with thyroid conditions might consider enjoying their crucifers cooked more often than raw.

HEIRLOOM TOMATOES WITH GOAT CHEESE, CAPERS, AND FRESH HERBS

As soon as I set this salad down on the table, it steals the show! It has a beautiful, bright presentation, and the aroma from the fresh herbs is hard to resist.

With their often whimsical names—Early Girl, Green Zebra, Hillbilly, Moneymaker, Tiny Tim, and Yellow Pear, to name a few—heirloom tomatoes are fun to shop for and a highlight of summer. Heirlooms are non-hybrid tomatoes, which means they aren't uniform in color, size, shape, or flavor the way a typical supermarket tomato is, and they offer a totally new tasting experience with every type. Look for local varieties at your neighborhood farmers' market or greengrocer. A good tomato speaks for itself—a light drizzle of olive oil, flaky sea salt, and a scattering of fresh herbs are all you need to showcase nature's perfection. *Serves 4*

2 large heirloom tomatoes (or a mixture of sizes), cut into wedges
1 teaspoon capers in brine, drained
½ ounce soft goat cheese, at room temperature
1 to 2 teaspoons caper brine, to taste
Extra-virgin olive oil
Handful of small mixed fresh herb leaves, such as mint, cilantro, parsley, basil, Thai basil, and/or thyme, or a single herb
Flaky sea salt
Coarsely cracked black pepper

Arrange the tomato wedges decoratively on a platter. Scatter the capers around the tomatoes, then do the same with the goat cheese. Carefully drizzle the caper brine over the tomatoes to lightly season them. Drizzle some oil all over, then arrange the herbs over the platter. Sprinkle with salt and finish with a generous grinding of pepper. Serve immediately.

Swap It Out

- Skip the goat cheese to make the salad dairy-free.
- Drizzle a little truffle oil over the tomatoes for a special treat. Or swap in truffle salt for the sea salt.
- Use mozzarella slices in place of the goat cheese.

Next Level, Please!

- Grow your own windowsill or porch herb garden. Most recipes call for a small amount of herbs; a snip from a pot guarantees freshness and saves on grocery bills. If you live in an apartment, you can set up a small garden next to a sunny window.
- Swap in pickle juice (page 257) for the caper juice for a dash of live and active cultures.

SALT MATTERS

Our bodies need salt to survive, and if you want your food to have flavor, you've got to add some salt to it! Salt doesn't just make food salty; it brings out the natural flavors in the food as well. My choice for salt is 100 percent unrefined sea salt, as it contains a host of trace minerals that are essential to our well-being, making it well worth its salt! You won't find those minerals in table salt, as they are stripped away through processing; table salt is also fortified with unnatural additives. A "pure" white color typically indicates a refined salt—even if it is sea salt—so you'll be safe to pick a salt that is off-white to gray or pink. Flaky sea salt makes a lovely finish to salads. By choosing unprocessed foods and seasoning with unprocessed sea salt, you've instantly upgraded your diet!

FENNEL AND JICAMA SALAD WITH LEMON AND PINK PEPPERCORN DRESSING

This salad is all about the crunch! Fennel, cucumber, and jicama, a root veggie best enjoyed raw to make the most of its crispy texture, join forces in this lemony, light salad. Pink peppercorns add a pretty burst of color and delicate fruity flavor, but if they aren't available, feel free to swap in extra cracked black pepper. *Serves 4*

¼ cup sun-dried tomatoes (not packed in oil)
3 tablespoons extra-virgin olive oil
¼ cup fresh lemon juice
¾ teaspoon flaky sea salt, or to taste
1 teaspoon pink peppercorns, lightly crushed with your fingers, plus more for garnish
1 large fennel bulb, halved, cored, and thinly sliced, fronds reserved
1 small jicama (about 1¼ pounds), peeled, halved, and cut into thin matchsticks
1 small cucumber, peeled and chopped
⅓ cup black olives, pitted and sliced
1 ounce feta cheese, crumbled
Coarsely cracked black pepper

Place the sun-dried tomatoes in a small bowl and add hot water to cover. Set aside for about 20 minutes, then drain and thinly slice them.

Meanwhile, in a small lidded jar, combine the oil, lemon juice, salt, and pink peppercorns. Cover and shake until emulsified.

Finely chop the fennel fronds to make ¼ cup and set aside.

In a large bowl, combine the fennel, jicama, cucumber, olives, and sun-dried tomatoes. Add the dressing and toss to coat. Stir in the fennel fronds and cheese, finish with a little salt, a couple of grinds of pepper, and a sprinkling of pink peppercorns lightly crushed between your fingers. Spoon into bowls and serve.

Swap It Out

- Serve on a bed of arugula or mixed field greens.
- Add ½ cup cooked white beans for protein.

AVOCADO, ASPARAGUS, AND ARTICHOKE SALAD

Oh, how I love all the ingredients in this salad! I just had to bring them together on one plate. Artichoke hearts preserved in olive oil are a treat, and with every jar there's ample flavorful oil just waiting to be transformed into dressing! Add a little lemon juice, adjust the seasonings, partner the hearts with crisp and creamy veggies, and a scrumptious salad is yours to bring to the table. This goes nicely with my Seared Steak and Spinach (page 99).

It's easiest to cook asparagus in a wide skillet or sauté pan (there are special asparagus steamers, and if you got one as a wedding present, now's the time to pull it out; otherwise, there's no need to go out and buy one), where it will fit without bending, and you can pick out thinner spears with tongs earlier so they don't get overcooked.

Serves 4

1 (6-ounce) jar artichoke hearts in extra-virgin olive oil
Sea salt
1 bunch thin asparagus, woody ends snapped off
1 avocado, pitted, peeled, and sliced
Fresh lemon juice
1 tablespoon finely chopped fresh flat-leaf parsley
2 tablespoons pine nuts, toasted

Remove the artichoke hearts from the oil and slice them. Place them in a bowl and add the oil from the jar.

Fill a bowl with water and ice. Fill a wide skillet or sauté pan with water and bring to a boil over high heat. Salt the water, then add the asparagus and return to a simmer. Reduce the heat to medium and cook for 3 to 5 minutes, until the asparagus is crisp-tender when pierced with the tip of a paring knife. Using tongs, remove the asparagus from the water and place it in the ice water for about 20 seconds, until fully cooled. Drain and place on a paper towel–lined plate to absorb excess water.

Chop the asparagus and add it to the bowl with the artichoke hearts. Add the avocado and add lemon juice and additional salt if needed. Top with the parsley and pine nuts, spoon onto plates or bowls, and serve.

Next Level, Please!

Blanch your asparagus in Basic Bone Broth (page 245); after you remove the asparagus, add the woody stems, cook for about 20 minutes, then strain to make a light asparagus sipping broth or base for another soup. Or freeze the stems and cook them with your next batch of broth with the other vegetables.

ARTICHOKES: THE HEART OF THE MATTER

Early spring is artichoke season, with annual festivals celebrating the vegetable around the world. We have a huge one right here in my home state of California, in the city of Castroville, "The Artichoke Center of the World." I love artichokes, from the leaves to the heart. And speaking of heart, did you know that artichokes are a heart-healthy food? They are known to regulate cholesterol and triglycerides, and their potassium content can help lower blood pressure. Artichokes contain a good amount of folic acid, crucial for women who are pregnant or looking to get pregnant. We all know about the antioxidant properties of dark chocolate, blueberries, and red wine, but did you know that artichokes also score high in the antioxidant department? And thanks to their high fiber content, artichokes help with digestion to keep you regular, and their natural diuretic properties combat bloating and water retention so you can look your best!

SHAVED BEET, ENDIVE, AND CHICKPEA SALAD WITH TAHINI GARLIC DRESSING

I never had the pleasure of tasting a beet until I was in my mid-twenties. Before then, beets were a veggie I would pass right by at the salad bar. But once I tasted fresh beets marinated in a citrus vinaigrette, I fell all the way in love with them.

Beets can take a long time to roast, steam, or boil; eating them in the raw is a quick-to-the-table alternative way to enjoy this hearty root. All you need to do to eat your beets uncooked is to slice them super-thin using either a vegetable peeler or a mandoline slicer, if you happen to have one. Red, yellow, or candy-stripe beets all make a striking presentation in this salad; yellow provides the most contrast, and red may lend a light pink hue to the entire salad. Sturdy endive joins forces with the beets, chickpeas add protein, and a thick tahini-based dressing with bold lemony flavors brings it all together. Add a grain such as black rice (page 220) to upgrade your side salad to supper. *Serves 4*

DRESSING

3 tablespoons fresh lemon juice
¼ cup tahini
¼ cup extra-virgin olive oil
¼ cup water
3 garlic cloves, cut in half
½ teaspoon sea salt
¼ teaspoon freshly ground black pepper
1 teaspoon chopped fresh flat-leaf parsley or
    cilantro

SALAD

2 small beets, peeled and sliced paper-thin
    using a vegetable peeler or mandoline
2 medium Belgian endives, leaves separated
    and coarsely chopped
1 cup cooked chickpeas (see page 107)
4 cups arugula leaves
1 scallion, cut into thin slices on an angle
1 tablespoon tan or black sesame seeds

To make the dressing: Combine all the dressing ingredients except the parsley in a blender and blend until smooth. Add the parsley and blend for a couple of seconds just to combine.

To make the salad: Combine the beets, endive, and chickpeas in a salad bowl. Add about half the dressing and toss to coat. Add the arugula and toss to coat again. Add more dressing if needed. Divide the salad into bowls, sprinkle with scallion slices and sesame seeds, and serve.

Next Level, Please!

Finish the salad with a drizzle of flax oil.

EDAMAME SUCCOTASH SALAD

I've never been a fan of lima beans, but I love a good succotash. So I found a way to make succotash to my liking—by swapping in fresh soybeans, known as edamame, for the lima beans that typically join up with corn and peppers to make this dish. If you see fresh edamame in the pod at your farmers' market, now's your chance to try it! Edamame in the pod looks a little like green beans, and the pods are sometimes still attached to the stem when you find them at the market. Frozen edamame—either in the pod or shelled—is an easy alternative; you'll find it in the frozen vegetable aisle. The corn can be added to the salad bowl in the raw, freshly cut off the cob, or cooked briefly to bring out its natural sweetness. *Serves 4*

DRESSING

1 tablespoon apple cider vinegar
1½ teaspoons grated lemon zest
2 tablespoons fresh lemon juice, or to taste
2 teaspoons Dijon-style mustard
1½ tablespoons honey
1 teaspoon sea salt, or to taste
½ teaspoon freshly ground black pepper
¼ cup extra-virgin olive oil

2 tablespoons minced fresh tarragon
2 tablespoons minced fresh mint
A sprinkling of feta cheese (optional)

SALAD
Sea salt
1 pound fresh or frozen edamame in the pod, or
    2 cups (10 ounces) shelled frozen edamame
1½ cups corn kernels (from 2 ears of corn) or
    thawed frozen corn kernels
½ small red onion, chopped
1 roasted or fresh red bell pepper, finely chopped
1 or 2 jalapeños, finely chopped (seeded for
    milder tastes)
1 cup cherry tomatoes, quartered

To make the salad: Bring a large saucepan of water to a boil and salt the water. Add the edamame and cook for 3 to 5 minutes, until the beans are bright green. Scoop the edamame out of the water and drain. If using edamame in the shell, pop the beans out of their shells (if you've got kids, get them to join in on the fun!). If you'd like to cook your corn (leaving it raw is an equally good option), return the water to a boil, add the corn, and cook until crisp-tender, about 2 minutes. Drain and let cool.

In a salad bowl, combine the edamame, corn, onion, bell pepper, jalapeños, and tomatoes and toss to combine.

To make the dressing: In a small bowl, whisk together the vinegar, lemon zest, lemon juice, mustard, honey, salt,

and pepper. Add the oil and whisk until emulsified.

Add the dressing, tarragon, and mint to the salad and toss to coat. Taste and add more lemon juice and/or salt if needed. Spoon into bowls and serve, topped with a sprinkling of cheese, if you like.

Swap It Out

Use sliced (½-inch-thick) green beans or chopped and seeded cucumber in place of the edamame, or go traditional and use lima beans.

TUNA AND PICKLE SALAD

Who knew that tuna salad could be a source of live and active cultures! Pickles add an addictively delicious tang to this American classic. Go ahead and try this salad on a bed of lettuce leaves or kale, or serve it classic sandwich-style on whole-grain bread. *Makes about 1 cup*

1 (5-ounce) can chunk white tuna in olive oil
1½ tablespoons minced celery
1½ tablespoons minced carrot
3 tablespoons minced "live" pickles, homemade (page 257) or store-bought
2 teaspoons finely chopped fresh flat-leaf parsley or celery leaves
2 tablespoons olive oil mayonnaise, plus more if needed
½ teaspoon grated lime zest
2 teaspoons fresh lime juice, plus more to taste
Splash of pickle juice from the jar, plus more if needed
½ teaspoon chili powder
Sea salt and freshly ground black pepper

Place the tuna in a large bowl. Add the celery, carrot, pickles, parsley, mayonnaise, lime zest, lime juice, pickle juice, and chili powder. Season with salt and pepper and stir with a fork to combine, breaking up any large chunks of tuna. Taste and adjust the consistency and seasonings, adding more mayonnaise, lime juice, pickle juice, or salt as needed.

Swap It Out

- Use Avocado Caesar (page 75) dressing in place of the mayonnaise.
- Use sauerkraut (see page 259 for my recipe) or another pickled vegetable in place of the pickles.
- Use Greek yogurt instead of mayo.
- Use canned salmon instead of tuna.

Next Level, Please!

- Choose a pickle from the refrigerated section of the supermarket and look for the words *live, raw, unpasteurized,* or *contains live and active cultures* on the label. Pickles on the shelf are pasteurized and contain no live cultures. Or take it a step further and make your own pickles; learn how on page 257.

- If you're looking to reduce your calories, use tuna packed in water rather than oil.
- Choose a mayonnaise based on an unrefined oil such as extra-virgin olive oil. Or try one of the tasty new avocado-based mayos on the market or a vegan mayonnaise.

DON'T LEAVE OUT THE CELERY LEAVES

We all know what to do with the stalks, but did you know you can use the leaves, too? They taste a lot like parsley, and you can use them in much the same way, chopped and added to salads, soups, and more. And whatever you don't use, save to flavor your next pot of Very Veggie Broth (page 248) or Basic Bone Broth (page 245).

KALE CAESAR SALAD

The popularity of the classic Caesar inspired me to create a salad of my own to enjoy at home. This version calls for kale and romaine and substitutes avocado for the egg yolk for its creamy dressing base. Anchovy paste gives salty, umami flavor (it is available in the supermarket packaged in tubes), but to make this salad vegan, you can use miso instead. Add sliced hard-boiled egg or some leftover shredded chicken, shrimp, or quinoa, and you've made your Caesar a meal. And dulse, a type of seaweed, takes this salad to the next level. Read more about this superfood that even kids will love on page 76. You'll have a little dressing left over; you can use it to make my Tuna and Pickle Salad (page 73) or to toss with a simple bowl of sturdy greens. Shake or whisk the dressing well before using. *Serves 4 to 6 (makes about ¾ cup dressing)*

DRESSING

½ small ripe avocado, peeled and chopped
2 tablespoons water
1 garlic clove, chopped
1 teaspoon anchovy paste or miso
1 tablespoon apple cider vinegar
1 tablespoon fresh lemon juice
2 teaspoons Dijon mustard
½ teaspoon sea salt, or to taste
½ teaspoon freshly ground black pepper
½ cup extra-virgin olive oil

SALAD

1 bunch kale, stemmed, leaves torn or chopped
    into bite-size pieces
Sea salt
1 romaine lettuce heart, torn or chopped into
    bite-size pieces
1 cup cherry tomatoes, halved or quartered if
    large (optional)
¼ cup sliced almonds, toasted, or coarse
    Sprouted Wheat Bread Crumbs (page 57)

1 teaspoon dulse flakes (optional)
Freshly ground black pepper

To make the dressing: In a blender or mini food processor, combine all the dressing ingredients and blend until emulsified, adding a little more water if the dressing is too thick.

To make the salad: Place the kale in a salad bowl, add a pinch of salt, and massage the kale for 1 to 2 minutes to start to soften it. Add the lettuce and toss to combine. Whisk the dressing and add some (there will be some left over) to the greens. Toss to coat. Add the cherry tomatoes (if using), almonds, and dulse and lightly toss. Taste and add more salt and/or pepper if needed. Spoon into bowls and serve.

DULSE: THE BAR FOOD TURNED SUPERFOOD

Dulse is a form of seaweed that's incredibly good for you. Now, I know the word *seaweed* isn't exactly sexy, but if I were to tell you that dulse provides more minerals and trace elements than plants grown on land, you just might join me in calling dulse a superfood!

Dulse is extremely rich in vitamins, minerals (in particular iodine and potassium), antioxidants, fiber, and protein. Fresh dulse tastes like the ocean, but when it's toasted, it's a combination of salty and smoky, a little like bacon, which is okay by me because it got my daughter, Sydney, to become a fan of seaweed! Taking advantage of its abundant availability, pubs in Ireland traditionally would set out bowls of dulse leaves for snacking on between sips of beer.

Dulse granules are available in convenient shaker containers from Maine Coast Sea Vegetables (see Resources, page 305). They can be added to any number of dishes, from meatballs (page 191) to chili (page 105) to salad (you'll love it in my Caesar salad on page 75), quietly giving everyday foods a nutritional boost. Dulse granules are also delicious sprinkled over popcorn or scrambled eggs or whisked into salad dressing. I keep a shaker of it handy for all these uses and more! Whole-leaf dulse can be panfried for a couple of minutes in a little oil, until it darkens in color and crisps up, and munched on as a snack or added to a sandwich to make a DLT!

SMOKY SHRIMP COBB SALAD WITH CITRUS DRESSING

Give me some sunshine, good music, and a flavorful salad, and I am a happy girl. My husband is a fan of Cobb salad, and I created this recipe with him in mind. I prefer my Cobb casual-style, with everything tossed together and finished with a light citrus dressing to play off the smoky, slightly sweet shrimp and allow the ingredients to really shine. *Serves 4*

SHRIMP
2 teaspoons unrefined coconut oil, melted
1 teaspoon honey
1 teaspoon smoked paprika
¼ teaspoon sea salt
16 large shrimp (about 12 ounces), peeled and deveined

DRESSING
1 tablespoon apple cider vinegar
1 medium shallot, minced
1 teaspoons grated orange zest
2 tablespoons fresh orange juice
1 teaspoon grated lime zest
1 tablespoon fresh lime juice
1 teaspoon Dijon mustard
1 teaspoon honey
½ teaspoon sea salt
¼ teaspoon freshly ground black pepper
2 tablespoons extra-virgin olive oil

SALAD
1 head romaine lettuce, chopped
1 ripe avocado, pitted, peeled, and chopped
1 large tomato, seeded and chopped
4 turkey bacon slices, cooked and crumbled
2 tablespoons chopped fresh chives
½ cup crumbled blue cheese (optional)
2 hard-boiled eggs, quartered

To marinate the shrimp: In a large bowl, whisk together the coconut oil, honey, paprika, and salt with a fork to combine. Add to the shrimp and stir to coat. Set aside for up to 20 minutes while you prepare the salad. (You can marinate the shrimp up to a day ahead; cover and refrigerate until ready to cook.)

To make the dressing: In a small bowl or jar, whisk together the vinegar, shallot, orange zest, orange juice, lime zest, lime juice, mustard, honey, salt, and pepper. Whisk in the oil until emulsified.

To cook the shrimp: Heat a grill pan or cast-iron skillet over medium-high heat. Place the shrimp on the pan in one layer and cook until pink, about 3 minutes on each side. Transfer to a plate and set aside while you assemble the salad.

To assemble the salad: In a salad bowl, toss the lettuce with the avocado and tomato. Add the dressing and toss to coat. Top with the bacon, sprinkle on the chives and blue cheese, and arrange the hard-boiled eggs and shrimp over the salad. Serve immediately.

Swap It Out

- For shrimp that's both smoky and spicy, use hot smoked paprika or swap in chipotle powder.
- For a more traditional Cobb, use poached chicken instead of the shrimp. Turkey breast is another tasty option.

Make It Snappy

QUICK, LUSCIOUS 30-MINUTE MEALS

North African–Inspired Chickpea Bowl   83

Shrimp with Stir-Fried Broccoli and Carrots   84

Seared Tuna and Soba Noodle Salad with Wasabi Pea Crunch   87

Simple Seared Salmon with Sweet-and-Sassy Barbecue Sauce
and Wilted Arugula   89

Chicken-and-Egg "Fried" Brown Rice with Shiitakes,
Carrots, and Peas   93

Poached Chicken   95

Ginger and Black Peppercorn Beef with Napa Cabbage   97

Seared Steak and Spinach   99

The Greatest of All Time Burger   100

Everyone's in a hurry these days, and we moms and dads always have a million things to do before the day is done. While I love to spend time in the kitchen, there are many days when half an hour is all I've got. When I can make a great meal in thirty minutes or less, I have that much more time to spend kicking back with my husband and kids. Popular cooking shows and a growing awareness of what's good for us have raised the bar of what we expect in our everyday meals. We want food that's fast, easy, and realistic, but we also want knockout flavor, and we want it to please every member of the family. That's a tall order! That's why I've shared some of my favorite fast, super-flavorful recipes in this chapter, dishes I've been making for years, like a chicken-and-egg fried rice that skips the frying (page 93), a peppery, gingery cabbage-and-beef stir-fry (page 97), and a shrimp and broccoli (page 84) that can't be beat. Also included is salmon served with a tangy barbecue sauce (page 89) and a simple method for searing steak (page 99). The chapter concludes with a recipe inspired by one of my father's favorite meals, The Greatest of All Time Burger (page 100).

NORTH AFRICAN–INSPIRED CHICKPEA BOWL

This is a hearty vegetarian meal with international flavor. When I want to excite my palate, I make this for dinner! Although the ingredients list is a little longer than some of my other recipes, when you have a few choice pantry ingredients on hand, it becomes fast and easy to put together. The flavorings in this dish are based on a blend called harissa that's used in North African cooking. It's the spices and seasonings that transform simple dishes like this one into something really special.

1 tablespoon extra-virgin olive oil
1 large yellow onion, finely chopped
1 medium red bell pepper, finely chopped
3 garlic cloves, pressed through a garlic press
1 (1-inch) piece fresh ginger, peeled and grated
1 (2-inch) cinnamon stick (optional)
1½ teaspoons ground coriander
1½ teaspoons ground cumin
¼ teaspoon cayenne pepper, or to taste
1 tablespoon tomato paste
2 medium tomatoes, chopped
2 cups cooked chickpeas (see page 107)
1½ teaspoons sea salt, plus more to taste
8 ounces green beans, ends trimmed, cut into ½-inch pieces
1 tablespoon fresh lemon juice, plus more to taste
¼ cup green olives, pitted and sliced
¼ cup chopped fresh mint
Cooked brown rice or other grain, for serving

In a large saucepan, heat the oil over medium heat. Add the onion and bell pepper and cook until starting to soften, about 5 minutes. Add the garlic and ginger and cook until fragrant, about 1 minute.

Add the cinnamon, coriander, cumin, and cayenne and cook, stirring, for 30 seconds, or until aromatic, adding a tiny bit of water if the mixture starts to stick to the bottom of the pan. Add the tomato paste and cook for 1 minute. Add the chopped tomatoes, chickpeas, and salt, bring to a simmer, then reduce the heat, cover, and simmer for about 15 minutes, adding a little water if the mixture starts to get dry (depending on how juicy your tomatoes are).

While the stew is cooking, bring a medium saucepan of water to a boil and salt it. Add the green beans and blanch until crisp-tender and bright green, 4 to 5 minutes. Drain, then add to the stew and cook for about 1 minute for the flavors to come together. Stir in the lemon juice, then the olives, and finally the mint. Taste and add more salt and/or lemon juice if needed. Remove the cinnamon stick if you used one. Spoon into bowls and serve, over brown rice or another grain if you like.

SHRIMP WITH STIR-FRIED BROCCOLI AND CARROTS

I love a good stir-fry, and a successful one is all about prep and planning. Once you get your pan good and hot, things move fast, so having your ingredients measured, chopped, and ready ensures that each is cooked to perfection and the finished dish puts a smile on your face. Pay special attention to the shrimp, adding them one by one around the pan to evenly sear them before adding the veggies. This technique takes an extra four minutes, but you'll still get dinner to the table in under half an hour, and you won't be stuck with rubbery, overcooked shrimp! Chili-garlic sauce can be found in Asian markets or in the Asian aisle of some supermarkets. If it's unavailable, substitute sriracha sauce. *Serves 4*

3 tablespoons tamari or soy sauce
2 tablespoons rice vinegar
1 tablespoon toasted sesame oil
1 tablespoon water
1 tablespoon honey
1 tablespoon chili-garlic sauce
3 garlic cloves, pressed through a garlic press
¼ teaspoon freshly ground white pepper
1 tablespoon cornstarch or arrowroot powder
1½ pounds large or extra-large shrimp, peeled and deveined
Sea salt
2 tablespoons untoasted sesame oil
1 large head broccoli, cut into small florets
1 small white onion, thinly sliced into half-moons
1 medium carrot, cut into ¼ by 1-inch matchsticks
½ cup chopped fresh cilantro leaves (optional)
¼ cup chopped unsalted roasted peanuts
Cooked brown rice, quinoa, or rice noodles, for serving

In a small bowl, whisk together the tamari sauce, vinegar, toasted sesame oil, water, honey, chili-garlic sauce, garlic, and white pepper. Whisk in the cornstarch to dissolve and set aside.

Rinse the shrimp and pat dry with paper towels. Season with salt.

In large skillet, heat 1 tablespoon of the untoasted sesame oil over medium-high heat. Looking at the skillet as the face of a clock, add the shrimp one by one in clockwise order without touching and cook without stirring until the shrimp start to turn pink, about 2 minutes. Using tongs, turn the shrimp in the order you placed them in the pan and cook until the second side starts to turn pink and the shrimp are almost cooked through, another 2 minutes or so. If your shrimp don't all fit in the pan at once, cook them in two batches, using half the oil with each batch. Transfer the shrimp to a medium bowl along with any juices from the pan.

In the same pan, heat the remaining 1 tablespoon untoasted sesame oil over medium-high heat. Add the broccoli, onion, and carrot and cook, stirring almost continuously, until the vegetables are crisp-tender, 3 to 5 minutes. Return the shrimp and any accumulated juices to the pan. Quickly whisk the soy sauce mixture to make sure the cornstarch has fully dissolved, add it to the pan, and cook, stirring continuously, until the vegetables and shrimp are cooked through and the sauce is thickened, about 1 minute. Spoon into bowls and serve over rice, quinoa, or rice noodles.

Next Level, Please!

If your shrimp come unpeeled, make Almost-Instant Shrimp Broth (page 131) with them, and it will be ready as soon as dinner is. Or use it as a base for miso soup (page 37) or your next pot of gumbo (page 129).

Swap It Out

- Use mint or basil instead of cilantro.
- Instead of the peanuts, try sesame seeds, chopped cashews, or hemp seeds.

SEARED TUNA AND SOBA NOODLE SALAD WITH WASABI PEA CRUNCH

Though fresh tuna can be a bit of a splurge, its simple deliciousness rewards the busiest of moms and dads with an outstanding meal when there's little time to dedicate to dinner. Although there are three components to this recipe, I promise it will be on the table in thirty minutes or less! To prep in advance, marinate the snow peas and bell pepper ahead of time.

Soba is a whole-grain Japanese noodle made from buckwheat. It typically contains a small amount of wheat; if you are eating gluten-free, look for 100 percent buckwheat soba noodles. Wasabi peas give the salad a lively crunch and pop of flavor, and a dollop of zesty sour cream adds a cooling, creamy finish to the dish. *Serves 4*

12 ounces soba noodles

VEGETABLES
2 tablespoons fish sauce
2 tablespoons rice vinegar
1 tablespoon fresh lime juice
½ teaspoon freshly ground black pepper
2 tablespoons toasted sesame oil
1 cup snow peas, ends trimmed and cut into thin strips
½ medium yellow, orange, or red bell pepper, minced

TUNA
1 pound fresh sushi-grade tuna
½ teaspoon sea salt, plus a pinch
1 teaspoon coarsely ground black pepper
1½ tablespoons tan or black sesame seeds, or a mixture
1 tablespoon untoasted sesame oil

ZESTY SOUR CREAM
1 teaspoon grated lime zest
Pinch of sea salt
¼ cup sour cream

GARNISHES
½ cup wasabi peas, coarsely crushed with a knife or pulsed in a food processor
2 large scallions, thinly sliced on an angle
Lime wedges

Bring a large pot of water to a boil (do not salt it). Add the noodles and stir to submerge them. Cook according to the package directions until fully cooked (not al dente), 5 to 8 minutes. Meanwhile, fill a large bowl with cold water. Drain the noodles, then add them to the bowl of cold water. Rub the noodles with your hands, rinsing off extra starch (this keeps the noodles from getting gummy or mushy). Drain again and set aside in a bowl.

To marinate the vegetables: In a large bowl, whisk together the fish sauce, vinegar, lime juice, and black pepper. Whisk in the toasted sesame oil until emulsified. Add the snow peas and bell pepper and toss to coat. Set aside to marinate, stirring a couple of times, while you finish the dish.

To cook the tuna: Sprinkle the tuna on both sides with the salt. On a large flat plate, combine the black pepper and sesame seeds and gently press the fish into the mixture to coat.

In a large skillet, heat the untoasted sesame oil over medium-high heat. Add the fish and sear on both sides, about 1 minute per side for rare, or a little more if you like yours cooked through. Transfer to a cutting board and thinly slice across the grain.

To make the zesty sour cream: In a small bowl, whisk the lime zest and salt into the sour cream.

To serve: Add the soba noodles to the bowl with the snow peas and bell pepper and their dressing and toss to coat. Divide the noodles among bowls and arrange the sliced tuna on top. Finish with a dollop of zesty sour cream and a scattering of wasabi peas and scallions. Serve with lime wedges alongside.

Swap It Out

- Substitute crispy chickpeas for the wasabi peas. This crunchy snack food can be found in packages of various flavors in the snack food aisle. Choose a brand that's roasted, not fried. Crispy chickpeas also are great for high-protein snacking!
- Use plain Greek yogurt in place of the sour cream.

Next Level, Please!

- Find an all-natural brand of wasabi peas in the natural food store—they won't have that bright neon pea color many of us are accustomed to, but they will be equally tasty and 100 percent guilt-free.
- Use organic bell peppers whenever possible, as this veggie consistently makes the Environmental Working Group's Dirty Dozen, an annual list of the twelve most heavily pesticide-sprayed fruits and veggies. Find the current Dirty Dozen list at ewg.org.

SIMPLE SEARED SALMON WITH SWEET-AND-SASSY BARBECUE SAUCE AND WILTED ARUGULA

Salmon is a favorite in my house, so I serve it up regularly in a variety of ways. And when I slather salmon in my homemade barbecue sauce, I always get requests for seconds! The barbecue sauce keeps for up to two weeks and easily doubles, so you can enjoy it with my Pulled Barbecue Beef (page 119), too. *Serves 4 (makes about 1 cup sauce)*

SWEET-AND-SASSY BARBECUE SAUCE

1 tablespoon extra-virgin olive oil
1 small onion, finely chopped
1 small red bell pepper, finely chopped
2 garlic cloves, minced
¼ cup apple cider vinegar
¼ cup soy sauce
¼ cup Dijon mustard
⅓ cup ketchup
½ cup fresh orange juice
3 tablespoons pure maple syrup
2 tablespoons molasses
½ teaspoon smoked paprika
¼ teaspoon cayenne pepper
¾ teaspoon sea salt

SALMON AND ARUGULA

4 (6-ounce) skin-on salmon fillets
Sea salt and freshly ground black pepper
1 tablespoon extra-virgin olive oil
4 large handfuls of arugula
Fresh lemon juice
Flaky sea salt

WILD FOR SALMON

When I shop for fish, I look for the "wild" label, because wild fish is typically more nutritious than farmed fish, with a better balance of fatty acids, and an overall more sustainable choice. And when it comes to salmon, going wild is nonnegotiable at my house. That's because farmed salmon is often injected with pink dye to make it look like it has the healthy pigments of wild salmon. Recently the FDA has approved GMO salmon (learn more about GMOs on page 98), the first genetically modified fish, designed to grow twice as fast as natural salmon. GMO salmon requires no special label, so the only way I know my salmon is GMO- and dye-free is to purchase wild. The cost is often higher, but my family's health is too precious to take chances in these untested waters.

To make the barbecue sauce: In a medium saucepan, heat the oil over medium heat. Add the onion and cook until softened and starting to brown, about 7 minutes. Add the bell pepper and cook until softened, about 5 minutes. Add the garlic and cook until softened, about 2 minutes. Add the vinegar, soy sauce, mustard, ketchup, orange juice, maple syrup, molasses, paprika, cayenne, and salt. Increase the heat to medium-high, bring to a simmer, and cook for about 20 minutes, until the mixture starts to thicken. Transfer to a blender and blend until smooth (be careful when blending hot liquids). Use immediately, or let cool, transfer to an airtight container, and refrigerate until ready to use. It will keep for up to 2 weeks.

To make the salmon and arugula: Season the salmon with salt and black pepper. Heat a large skillet over medium-high heat. Swirl in the oil. Add the salmon fillets, skin-side down, and cook without moving them until the sides are cooked halfway up the fillets. Flip, brush the tops of the fillets with barbecue sauce, and cook until the sides are fully cooked for medium-rare, a minute or so more for medium. Transfer the salmon to plates and add the arugula to the pan. Cook, stirring continuously with tongs, until it is just wilted. Add the arugula to the plates with the salmon and finish the greens with a squeeze of lemon, a sprinkle of flaky salt, and a little black pepper.

CHICKEN-AND-EGG "FRIED" BROWN RICE WITH SHIITAKES, CARROTS, AND PEAS

Isn't it exciting when you find ways to make "bad" foods good for you? Well, chicken fried rice is one of my all-time favorites, and here it's converted into a dish that fits into a healthy lifestyle on all days of the week, not just cheat days. To make it healthy, I skip the frying, use whole-grain brown rice as a base, and add shiitake mushrooms, which have strong detoxifying powers. This dish is a great way to bring new life to leftovers: leftover chicken, leftover rice, even leftover vegetables can go into the pan. Note that cooled or cold rice is a must for this dish (rice will keep for up to five days in the refrigerator, so you can make it well in advance); if you start with hot rice, the grains may clump together, making mush out of your fried rice. *Serves 4*

4 large eggs
1 teaspoon sea salt
Pinch of ground turmeric
2 tablespoons untoasted sesame oil
1 small yellow onion, finely chopped
1 large carrot, cut into thin matchsticks
12 medium shiitake mushrooms, stemmed and
    thinly sliced
2 garlic cloves, thinly sliced
3 cups cooked brown rice (see page 219),
    cooled
1 cup shredded or chopped leftover chicken
    (see page 94)
½ cup fresh or thawed frozen peas
1½ tablespoons tamari or soy sauce, or to taste
2 teaspoons rice vinegar, or to taste
1 teaspoon toasted sesame oil
½ teaspoon freshly ground white pepper
2 scallions, white and light green parts only,
    thinly sliced
1½ tablespoons sesame seeds (optional)
Sriracha sauce (optional)

Beat the eggs in a large bowl, then beat in the salt and turmeric.

In a large skillet or a wok if you've got one, heat the untoasted sesame oil over medium-high heat. Add the onion and carrot and cook until slightly softened, about 2 minutes. Add the mushrooms and garlic and cook for 2 minutes, or until slightly softened and the garlic and onions are lightly browned. Add the eggs and cook, stirring with a rubber spatula, until almost set. Stir in the rice, chicken, and peas and stir-fry, breaking up the eggs and letting the rice rest a few seconds between stirs, until everything is hot, about 2 minutes. Add the tamari, vinegar, toasted sesame oil, and white pepper and cook for 1 minute. Remove from the heat, spoon into bowls, and serve, topped with the scallions, sesame seeds (if using), and a hit of sriracha, if you like.

Swap It Out

- Try corn instead of peas.
- Choose a different grain, such as quinoa or millet or even riced cauliflower, for a portion of the rice—you can find prepared riced cauliflower in the produce aisle of some grocery stores or make your own by pulsing small cauliflower florets in a food processor until they're about the size of rice.

Next Level, Please!

Save the stems from the shiitakes to add to Basic Bone Broth (page 245) or Very Veggie Broth (page 248). Keep a bag or container in the freezer that you can add vegetable scraps to and make soup when it's full.

POACHED CHICKEN

When you're scrambling to put dinner together, having leftover chicken in the fridge is a lifesaver. Chicken from last night's roast is perfect, but when that's not an option, I open the freezer to find my handy packets of poached chicken. When cooked just right, poached chicken is tender and juicy, and it can transform a soup or salad into a meal. You can include poached chicken in my Cheddar Chicken Enchilada Skillet (page 135), and you can even add it to breakfast dishes such as my Chicken and Egg Breakfast Tacos (page 33). This recipe can easily double. *Makes 2 chicken breasts or legs*

2 skinless chicken breasts or legs (boneless or bone-in)
½ teaspoon sea salt

Place the chicken in a large saucepan. Add the salt, any flavoring ingredients you choose, and cold water to cover by about 1 inch. Place over medium-high heat and bring to a boil, skimming off any foam that rises to the top. Reduce the heat to low, cover, and cook for 10 to 15 minutes, until the chicken is cooked through and registers 160°F on an instant-read thermometer. Let the chicken cool completely in the poaching liquid. Remove the chicken from the poaching liquid and place it on a cutting board. Use as directed in your recipe—whole, sliced, or shredded—or slice or shred it and freeze in freezer bags.

Next Level, Please!

- Poach your chicken in Basic Bone Broth (page 245) for added flavor and nutrition, then drink the supercharged broth.
- If you use bone-in chicken, save the bones for your next batch of bone broth. Or return the bones to the poaching liquid and cook until the liquid has reduced by about half for a quick, light bone broth.
- Add flavoring ingredients such as a couple of smashed garlic cloves, a bay leaf, chopped onion or shallot, turmeric, black peppercorns, and/or fresh herbs.
- Use the flavorful chicken poaching broth instead of water to cook brown rice, quinoa, or another grain.

GINGER AND BLACK PEPPERCORN BEEF WITH NAPA CABBAGE

This super-simple stir-fry is packed with peppery, limey flavor and contains a healthy dose of crucifers (see page 60 to learn why they are an important part of a healthy diet) in the form of napa cabbage. I like my stir-fries clean- and fresh-tasting, so instead of bottled sauces I make a quick homemade sauce out of soy sauce, mirin, garlic, ginger, and pepper and thicken it with just a little cornstarch or arrowroot to bring the sauce together. *Serves 4*

1½ tablespoons tamari or soy sauce
1 tablespoon mirin (Japanese rice wine) or white wine
1½ tablespoons fresh lime juice
1 teaspoon coarsely ground black pepper
3 garlic cloves, pressed through a garlic press
1 tablespoon grated fresh ginger
2 teaspoons cornstarch or arrowroot powder
2 tablespoons untoasted sesame oil
1 pound flank steak, patted dry, halved lengthwise, and cut crosswise into ¼-inch-thick strips
½ teaspoon sea salt
1 small orange or red bell pepper, finely chopped
1 pound napa cabbage, leaves and stems separated and cut into 1-inch pieces
¼ cup slivered almonds, toasted

In a small bowl, whisk together the tamari, mirin, lime juice, black pepper, garlic, ginger, and cornstarch and set aside.

In large skillet or wok, if you've got one, heat 1½ teaspoons of the oil over medium-high heat. Toss the beef with the salt and quickly add half the beef to the pan in one layer. Cook, undisturbed, for 1 minute, then cook, stirring, until the meat is almost completely cooked through, another 30 seconds or so. Transfer to a bowl with any juices from the pan. Repeat with another 1½ teaspoons oil and the remaining beef.

Wipe the pan clean with a paper towel, then add the remaining 1 tablespoon oil and the bell pepper and cabbage stems. Cook, stirring often, until crisp-tender, about 2 minutes. Add the cabbage leaves and beef with its juices, then quickly whisk the soy sauce mixture, add it to the pan, and cook, stirring continuously, until the beef is cooked through and the sauce is slightly thickened, 1 to 2 minutes. Sprinkle in the almonds, spoon into bowls, and serve.

Swap It Out

- Try bok choy or snow peas instead of the napa cabbage.
- Up the black pepper by ½ teaspoon if you'd like your stir-fry extra peppery.

WHAT ARE GMOS?

Genetically modified organisms, or GMOs, are foods that have had their DNA altered or modified in some way, typically from a bacteria, plant, virus, or animal. For example, tomatoes developed to resist frost take on the genes from flounder, a cold-water fish. GMO salmon, a breed of fish that grows twice as fast as natural salmon, has been FDA-approved recently, as have apples resistant to browning and potatoes that won't bruise. Crops are not only sprayed, but genetic modification means they now can contain pesticides right inside them! More than 80 percent of corn, including cornstarch used for cooking and baking, and 90 percent of soybeans grown in the United States are GMO, and canola oil is a genetically modified oil.

While there are no long-term studies on the health concerns of GMOs, recently the World Health Organization has classified glyphosate, a weed killer used on genetically modified crops, as a possible carcinogen. I personally believe that food should not be tampered with by genetic modification, as nature created it perfectly to begin with! Since GMO foods are not labeled as such, the only way to avoid them is to favor organic food (by law, organic food cannot contain GMOs) or products with the "Non-GMO Project Verified" seal on them, and to shop at local farms and farmers' markets when you can.

GRASS-FED BEEF AND BUTTER

If you love beef and butter, I've got good news for you! What animals are fed dramatically affects the nutritional content of their products. So if you choose grass-fed beef (ideally 100 percent grass-fed and grass-finished rather than grain-finished), you'll be bypassing the hormones and pesticide-containing feed that get passed on to you from conventional beef. If you're watching your waistline, more good news! Grass-fed beef is lower in calories and fat than conventional beef (comparable to skinless chicken) and higher in omega-3 fatty acids. It also contains more vitamin E, adding to its heart-protective and cancer-defensive benefits. Grass-fed beef is higher in conjugated linoleic acid (CLA), which helps create lean muscle and might even assist in weight loss.

Grass-fed butter partners with grass-fed beef in its heart-healthy profile: it's rich in vitamins A, D, and E and is another great source of CLA. It also contains the antioxidant beta-carotene, which is better absorbed when paired with fats. And grass-fed butter is one of our best sources of vitamin K_2, a little-known nutrient with great importance: getting enough of it can reduce your risk for both heart disease and osteoporosis. It pays to be choosy with your ingredients, and nowhere is that more apparent than with beef and butter!

SEARED STEAK AND SPINACH

I love a good steak that's been seasoned just right and cooked in butter! Grass-fed beef and grass-fed butter, both high in omega-3 fatty acids and heart-supportive foods when eaten as part of a balanced diet, make this dish stand out.

Resist the urge to touch your steak until a crust forms on the bottom, then flip it and sear the second side in the same way; that way, it will come out perfectly seared and juicy inside. Two bunches of spinach may seem more than a family could eat at a sitting, but after it's cooked, it reduces down to just about a cup and a half—what an easy way of getting lots of greens into your meal! *Serves 4*

2 (8- to 10-ounce) sirloin, New York strip, or Porterhouse steaks (1 to 1½ inches thick)
Sea salt and freshly ground black pepper
1 teaspoon onion powder
Unrefined coconut oil
2 tablespoons unsalted butter, cut into ½-tablespoon pieces
3 garlic cloves, pressed through a garlic press
2 bunches spinach (about 12 ounces)
4 teaspoons fresh lemon juice, or to taste

Season the steaks with salt and pepper and the onion powder. Heat a large skillet over medium-high heat until very hot. Add just enough oil to thinly coat the bottom of the pan. Add the steaks and cook, undisturbed, for 4 minutes, then flip them and add 1 tablespoon of the butter to the pan. Using a spoon, baste the steaks with the melting butter. Cook, again without touching the steaks, for 3 to 4 minutes for medium-rare (add an extra minute on either side for medium), then place the steaks on a cutting board. Let rest while you cook the spinach.

Add the garlic to the juices in the pan and leave for a few seconds to sizzle, then add the spinach, in batches as needed, tossing it with tongs to wilt it. Using tongs, remove the spinach from the pan, squeezing out as much liquid as you can. Stir in 2 teaspoons of the lemon juice and season with salt and pepper. Add the remaining 1 tablespoon butter to the juices in the pan and cook until melted and reduced to a sauce consistency, 3 to 4 minutes. Stir in the remaining 2 teaspoons lemon juice.

Cut the steaks in half lengthwise, then cut them into thin pieces across the grain. Divide the steak among four plates, drizzle with the sauce, add the spinach, and serve.

Swap It Out

Instead of finishing with the pan sauce, top your steaks with chimichurri (page 155).

THE GREATEST OF ALL TIME BURGER

Some of my best memories from summers spent with my dad in the small town of Berrien Springs, Michigan, where he was living when I was a teenager, are of going out for a burger together. My stepmother always encouraged him to eat a healthy diet, and for the most part he would. But he had a way of convincing us—"Don't you just want a burger and an ice-cold Coke?" he'd slyly ask—and we'd be off to the local burger joint, where they knew his order without having to ask. A burger with mustard, onion, and American cheese was his all-time greatest. I know they have the grill going in heaven on a regular basis for the G.O.A.T.! *Serves 4*

1½ pounds ground beef

1½ tablespoons Worcestershire sauce

1 teaspoon onion powder

1½ teaspoons sea salt

Freshly ground black pepper

4 good hamburger buns, such as Ezekiel brand, split and toasted

Toppings: mustard, onion rounds, and cheese slices

If you have the time, take the beef out of the refrigerator 10 to 20 minutes before you are ready to cook it.

Heat a large, heavy-bottomed skillet over medium-high heat until very hot, or preheat a grill to high.

Place the beef in a large bowl, add the Worcestershire sauce and onion powder, and mix with your hands until the ingredients are just combined (do not compact the meat or it may result in a dense burger).

Lightly dampen your hands. Divide the beef into 4 equal portions. Gently form each into a loose ball, then pat the balls into ¾-inch-thick patties. Press down in the center of each patty with your thumb to make a ¼-inch-deep or so indentation (this keeps your burgers from puffing up in the center when they cook). Season the patties well on both sides with the salt and pepper to taste. Place on the pan or grill indented-side up and cook on each side for about 3 minutes for rare, 3½ minutes for medium-rare, 4 minutes for medium, and 5 minutes for well-done.

Transfer to a plate and let sit for about 5 minutes for the burgers to finish cooking and so the juices can redistribute throughout the patties, then put the burgers on buns and add your choice of toppings.

Next Level, Please!

These days I know that a good burger is only as good as the meat that goes into it, so for me the greatest burgers are made with grass-fed beef (see page 98), with the bun upgraded from white to whole grain. And I often go "protein style" and wrap my burger in lettuce instead of a bun.

Been There, Done That

DELICIOUS MAKE-AHEAD MAIN DISHES

Most days I pick the kids up from school around half past three, we're home by four, and by five I'm in the kitchen with the goal of having dinner ready at six. The timeline is tight, and the days when I make dinner in advance, I'm able to drop the multitasking and fully focus on my kids, help with their homework, and get in some playtime with them (my son, Curtis Jr., loves his LEGOs, and we're currently at work on a thousand-piece set). Coming home to a clean kitchen and knowing that dinner only needs to be warmed gives me a major sense of accomplishment. And when it comes to entertaining, you can enjoy the evening so much more when dinner's done before the company comes. In this chapter, I'll share with you the stewed chicken I've been making since I was a kid (page 115), a vegetarian chili based on beans and mushrooms (page 105), gorgeous stuffed peppers (page 109), and an authentic South Indian curry (page 111). Some dishes take minutes to put together, while others spend some time simmering or roasting, but none are difficult to make, and all will be ready when you are!

CREMINI MUSHROOM, BLACK BEAN, AND CORN CHILI

One thing many of the most long-lived people in the world have in common is a diet rich in beans. It's no wonder: beans have more protein by weight than beef (at a fraction of the price), and they're filled with vitamins, minerals, and heart-healthy fiber. Chili is one of my favorite dishes to showcase my love of beans, and I like to add finely chopped mushrooms to give body and meaty texture to the dish. Fresh corn adds a sweet lightness, and coffee and cocoa—two ingredients you wouldn't expect to see in chili—add a depth that really makes this chili stand out.

Chili gets better the longer you cook it, so plan ahead to allow for the full hour and a half it takes to get to chili perfection. To further thicken your chili, you can blend a portion of it and then return it to the pan. *Serves 8*

2 tablespoons extra-virgin olive oil
2 teaspoons cumin seeds
1 large yellow onion, chopped
1 large red bell pepper, chopped
4 garlic cloves, minced
1 pound cremini mushrooms, finely chopped or pulsed in the food processor (in batches, if necessary)
2 tablespoons tomato paste
2½ tablespoons chili powder
¾ teaspoon ground chipotle chile
1 tablespoon balsamic vinegar, plus more to taste
½ cup brewed coffee, cooled
2 tablespoons unsweetened cocoa powder
2 (15-ounce) cans black beans, drained, or 3 cups cooked black beans (see page 107)
1 (28-ounce) can whole tomatoes with juices
2½ teaspoons sea salt, plus more to taste

1½ cups Very Veggie Broth (page 248) or good-quality store-bought broth, plus more if needed
1½ cups fresh or thawed frozen corn kernels
½ cup chopped fresh cilantro

OPTIONAL GARNISHES
Sour cream or plain Greek yogurt
Guacamole or avocado chunks
Shredded Jack cheese
Sliced scallions
Pickled jalapeños
Chopped red onion
Lime wedges

In a large saucepan, heat the oil over medium heat. Add the cumin seeds and cook until fragrant, about 30 seconds. Add the onion and bell pepper and cook, stirring occasionally, until softened, about 10 minutes. Add the garlic and cook for about 1 minute, until aromatic. Add the mushrooms, cover, and cook until the mushrooms release their liquid, about 5 minutes, lifting the lid to stir a couple of times, then cook until the liquid released by the mushrooms has been absorbed, about 5 minutes more. Add the tomato paste and cook for 1 minute. Stir in the chili powder and chipotle and cook, stirring often, until aromatic, adding a tiny bit of water if the mixture starts to stick. Add the vinegar and stir to release any bits stuck to the bottom of the pan. Add the coffee and cook until it has been almost completely absorbed, about 5 minutes. Add the cocoa powder, beans, whole tomatoes (crushing them in with your hands) and their juices, the salt, and broth. Bring to a simmer, then partially cover, reduce the heat to low, and cook for about 1½ hours, until the chili is a bit thickened but still a little soupy. Add the corn and cook until just cooked through, about 5 minutes. Turn off the heat and stir in the cilantro. If you've got a half hour to spare, let the chili sit to further develop the flavors and thicken. Taste and add more salt and/or an additional splash of vinegar and serve with your choice of garnishes.

Swap It Out

- Use white button or portobello mushrooms instead of creminis.
- Use pinto or red kidney beans in place of black beans, or try a mix of beans.

Next Level, Please!

- Add 2 teaspoons dulse seaweed granules for added nutrients. Read about dulse on page 76.
- Cook your beans from scratch (see sidebar, opposite page).

HOW TO COOK BEANS AND CHICKPEAS

Cooking beans from scratch takes a little advance planning, but it's simple, costs less than opening a can, and ensures that there are no chemicals in your beans (see page 53). Beans freeze well, so you might cook up a big pot of beans on a Sunday and freeze some to have them on hand for whenever you get an urge for chili or another bean dish (see page 105 or 123 for ideas).

Soak the beans for a few hours in salted water, drain, then cook them in salted water. This method results in evenly cooked beans and softer skins with fewer bursted beans. Try it out! Cooking time depends on the variety, size, and age of the bean (older beans can take longer to soften). *Makes 3 to 4 cups beans*

8 ounces dried beans or chickpeas (about 1¼ cups)

1 tablespoon plus ½ teaspoon sea salt

1 piece kombu seaweed (about 3 by 4 inches; optional, see page 76)

Place the beans in a large bowl and add 1 tablespoon of the salt and 2 quarts water. Cover with a kitchen towel and soak the beans at room temperature for 8 to 24 hours. Drain and rinse well. Place the beans in a large saucepan and add the remaining ½ teaspoon salt, the kombu (if using), and water to cover by a couple of inches. Bring to a boil over medium-high heat and cook for 15 minutes. Reduce the heat to low and simmer until the beans are softened, 30 minutes to 2 hours, depending on the bean variety and age, adding more water if the water level drops below the top of the beans. Drain.

LAMB AND MILLET–STUFFED PEPPERS

I like my stuffed peppers simple—a grain, meat, and veggies, and a little cheese to hold everything together. Rice is the base of many stuffed pepper recipes, and quinoa recently has become a popular choice. This recipe changes things up by using millet, a tiny grain that becomes creamy when cooked, perfect for stuffing into a pepper. Millet can be found in natural foods stores and some supermarkets. Blanching the peppers first to soften them a little before stuffing ensures that your peppers are evenly cooked when they come out of the oven. While it's an extra step, you can use that same water to cook the millet, maximizing your kitchen efficiency.

You can stuff the peppers up to a day ahead. Cover and refrigerate them, then take them out of the fridge to bring them to room temperature while you preheat the oven. Add ten minutes to the baking time. Serve with a salad, such as my Simple Red Cabbage Salad (page 59), to complete your meal. You can use any ground meat you like for this recipe. *Serves 2 to 4*

4 medium red, orange, or yellow bell peppers, or a combination
Sea salt
⅓ cup millet
8 ounces ground lamb
1 large leek, white and light green parts only, cleaned well and chopped
2 garlic cloves, minced
2 cups loosely packed baby spinach leaves
1 (14-ounce) can diced tomatoes, drained
1 cup shredded cheddar or Monterey Jack cheese
3 teaspoons finely chopped fresh thyme
½ teaspoon freshly ground black pepper

Cut off the stem and a bit of the top of the bell peppers and remove and discard the cores. Chop the flesh from the tops and save it to add to the filling.

Bring a large pot of water to a boil over high heat and salt it well. Add the bell peppers and push them down with tongs or a slotted spoon to fill the cavities with water and submerge them (if all four don't fit at once, cook two at a time). Cook until they just start to soften, about 4 minutes. Using tongs or a slotted spoon, remove the bell peppers from the pot, turning them upside down to drain all the water. Place them on a paper towel–lined plate cut-side down and leave for 2 minutes to drain, then stand them up again so they don't continue to steam.

Return the water to a boil, add the millet, then reduce the heat to medium-high and boil for 20 to 25 minutes, until softened but not mushy. Drain and transfer to a large bowl.

Preheat the oven to 350°F.

While the millet is cooking, heat a large skillet over medium-high heat. Add the lamb and cook, breaking it up with a wooden spoon, for 3 to 4 minutes, until the fat starts to render. Add the leek, chopped bell pepper tops, and 1 teaspoon salt and cook, stirring with a wooden spoon to break up the meat, until the meat is cooked through and lightly browned and the vegetables are softened, another 5 minutes or so, adding a tiny bit of water if the mixture starts to stick to the bottom of the pan. Add the garlic and cook for 1 minute. Add the spinach and cook, stirring continuously, until wilted, about 1½ minutes (add the spinach in batches if the pan starts getting full, stirring until each batch starts to wilt). Transfer the mixture to the bowl with the millet and add the tomatoes, ¾ cup of the cheese, 2 teaspoons of the thyme, and the black pepper. Stir well to combine.

Place the bell peppers cut-side up in a 9-inch square baking dish. Divide the filling among the peppers, packing it in if the filling is ample (and if there's any leftover filling, enjoy it as a cook's treat), sprinkle with the remaining cheese, and top with the remaining 1 teaspoon thyme. Place in the oven and bake until the cheese is lightly browned and bubbling and the filling is heated through, about 30 minutes. Arrange the bell peppers on plates and serve.

Swap It Out

If you have a leftover whole grain such as brown rice or quinoa in the fridge, you can use it in place of the millet. You'll need 1 cup cooked grain.

SOUTH INDIAN COCONUT CHICKEN CURRY

My cowriter, Leda Scheintaub, and her husband, Nash Patel, run Dosa Kitchen, a food truck based in southern Vermont. There they serve South Indian favorites using the farm-fresh ingredients of the Green Mountain State. So naturally I enlisted them to create this recipe for my book! I asked for a simple, everyday chicken curry made with spices easily found at the supermarket, and the result is the authentic flavors of South India. Making your curry at home allows you to use the best ingredients, including free-range chicken, a heart-healthy oil, and lots of veggies, something you wouldn't typically expect when you order takeout. The spice blend yields enough to make this recipe 4 times. *Serves 6*

2 tablespoons unrefined coconut oil
1 large red onion, chopped
3 tablespoons South Indian Curry Spice Mix (recipe follows)
2 pounds boneless dark meat chicken, cut into 1-inch pieces
1½ teaspoons sea salt, plus more to taste
1 cup small cauliflower florets
¼ cup diced (½-inch cubes) carrots
1 cup unsweetened coconut milk
½ cup Basic Bone Broth (page 245), good-quality store-bought broth, or water
1 cup packed chopped fresh spinach or baby spinach leaves (about 2 ounces)
Cooked brown rice (see page 219), for serving

In a large saucepan, heat the oil over medium-high heat. Add the onion and cook, stirring often, until softened and well browned, about 7 minutes. Add the spice mix and cook, stirring often, for 2 minutes. Add the chicken and salt and stir well to coat the chicken in the spice mix. It's okay if some of the spice mix sticks to the bottom of the pan; it will release when you add the coconut milk. Cook for 5 minutes so the spices can begin to work their way into the chicken. Add the cauliflower, carrots, coconut milk, and broth and bring to a simmer.

Cover, reduce the heat to low, and simmer until the chicken is cooked through and the vegetables are tender, about 15 minutes. Add the spinach and stir until wilted, about 20 seconds. Taste, add more salt if needed, and serve over rice.

South Indian Curry Spice Mix

Makes ¾ cup (enough for 4 chicken curries)
½ cup ground coriander
4½ teaspoons ground cumin
4 teaspoons cayenne pepper
2 teaspoons ground turmeric
½ teaspoon ground cardamom
¼ teaspoon ground cinnamon
¼ teaspoon ground allspice
¼ teaspoon freshly grated nutmeg
¼ teaspoon ground cloves

In a small bowl, whisk together all the ingredients. Transfer to a jar, cover with the lid, and store in the pantry for up to 6 months.

THREE-PEPPER BASIL CHICKEN BOWL

This aromatic basil-and-bell-pepper chicken is cooked in a thin, light sauce, perfect for serving over rice to soak up all the delicious juices. For a thicker sauce, seed the tomatoes before chopping them. Since it's so easy to put together, I've made it a big-batch recipe, enough for company or for leftovers to pack into lunchboxes. *Serves 8*

2 teaspoons extra-virgin olive oil
1½ pounds boneless, skinless chicken thighs, cut into 1-inch pieces
1 medium onion, chopped
1 medium red bell pepper, chopped
1 medium orange or yellow bell pepper, chopped
1 jalapeño, seeded if you like it less spicy and chopped
2 garlic cloves, minced
1 large tomato, chopped
1 teaspoon sea salt, or to taste
½ cup chopped fresh basil
Cooked brown rice (see page 219), for serving

In a large sauté pan, heat the oil over medium-high heat. Add the chicken and cook, without stirring, for about 3 minutes (so the chicken can start to release its fat

and avoid sticking to the pan), then cook, stirring often, until the chicken starts to brown, about 10 minutes. Add the onion, bell peppers, jalapeño, and garlic and cook, stirring often, for about 10 minutes, until the vegetables are softened. Add the tomato and salt, then reduce the heat to medium and cook for about 10 minutes more, until the chicken and vegetables are very tender and the sauce has thickened slightly. Stir in the basil and serve over rice.

STEWED CHICKEN AND GRAVY

This recipe has a special place in my heart, as I've been making it since I was a teen. I can remember the first time I set out to make stewed chicken and gravy, blindly figuring it out along the way. I have since prepared this dish for friends and family countless times, and it has evolved along the way just as I have! I can't tell you how many text messages and phone calls I've gotten from girlfriends asking "How do you make that stewed chicken dish?" What sets my chicken and gravy apart is that I skip the traditional gravy made with oil and flour to lighten it up and cut down on cooking time, but don't worry, it's so well seasoned you won't be sacrificing a single bit of deliciousness! Serve over brown rice to sop up the flavorful gravy. Note that you can use either skin-on or skinless chicken, but skin-on will get you the best sear. *Serves 6*

SPICE RUB
2 tablespoons onion powder
1 tablespoon garlic powder
2 teaspoons paprika
2 teaspoons sea salt
1 teaspoon ground turmeric
¼ teaspoon freshly ground white pepper

CHICKEN AND GRAVY
6 bone-in chicken thighs
6 bone-in chicken legs
2 teaspoons fresh lemon juice
¼ cup unrefined coconut oil
1 medium yellow onion, chopped
1 bunch scallions, finely chopped
1 tablespoon minced garlic
2 teaspoons chopped fresh thyme leaves, or
   1 teaspoon dried thyme
1 tablespoon Super-Sassy Seasoning (page 117)
2 bay leaves
2 cups water

1 tablespoon cornstarch or arrowroot powder
Sea salt
2 tablespoons chopped fresh flat-leaf parsley

To make the spice rub: In a small bowl, whisk together all the spice rub ingredients.

To make the chicken and gravy: Place the chicken in a large bowl and toss with the lemon juice. Sprinkle the spice rub over the chicken and mix well to massage the spices into the chicken. (You can do this a day ahead for added flavor; cover and refrigerate until ready to cook.)

In a large saucepan, heat 2 tablespoons of the oil over medium-high heat. Add the chicken thighs and cook until browned on both sides, about 5 minutes per side. Transfer the chicken thighs to a large bowl. Add the remaining 2 tablespoons of oil to the pan,

then add the chicken legs and cook until browned on both sides, about 5 minutes per side. Add the chicken legs to the plate with the thighs. Add the onion, scallions, and garlic to the pan, reduce the heat to medium, and cook until they start to color, about 5 minutes. Add the thyme, Super-Sassy Seasoning, and bay leaves and cook for 1 minute.

Pour in 1 cup of the water and stir to scrape up any browned bits from the bottom of the pan. Return the chicken and any accumulated juices from the plate to the pan and add the remaining 1 cup water. Bring to a simmer, then reduce the heat to medium-low and simmer, uncovered, for about 40 minutes, turning the chicken occasionally to make sure it cooks evenly and adding more water if the level comes down too low, until it is cooked through.

Transfer ½ cup of the broth to a bowl, let it cool, then whisk in the cornstarch. Stir the cornstarch mixture back into the pot and cook, stirring often, for about 10 minutes, until the sauce is thick enough to coat a spoon. Season with salt. Transfer to serving dishes, sprinkle with the parsley, and serve.

Next Level, Please!

Use Basic Bone Broth (page 245) instead of water for the gravy.

Super-Sassy Seasoning

Like most home cooks, I have go-to seasonings, the ones I use most often. My custom blend incorporates my favorite spices and eliminates the need to pull out multiple spice jars every time I cook. It is salt-free, so you can use it generously and season with salt separately. This blend perks up veggie dishes, grains, soups, chicken, beef, and fish dishes, and even scrambled eggs or omelets. Whisk it into a little olive oil, season with salt and fresh lemon juice, and it becomes a marinade or salad dressing. *Makes a scant ½ cup*

2 tablespoons onion powder
2 tablespoons garlic powder
2 teaspoons celery seeds
2 teaspoons dried ground thyme
2 teaspoons dried ground parsley
1 teaspoon dried ground marjoram
1 teaspoon freshly ground black pepper

In a small bowl, combine all the ingredients. Transfer to a jar, cover, and store in a cool, dark place for up to 6 months. Stir before using.

PULLED BARBECUE BEEF

Anytime I have a barbecue at my house, this dish is sure to be on the menu. Slow-cooked, exceptionally tender beef finished with homemade barbecue sauce gets them every time! Serve on buns or as is with your choice of sides. Some of my favorites are Simple Cabbage Salad (page 59), Skinny Fries (page 181), Cheesy Quinoa and Rice Bake (page 222), and Green Beans with Turkey Bacon (page 215). *Serves 6 to 8*

1 (3-pound) chuck roast
2 teaspoons sea salt
1 tablespoon Super-Sassy Seasoning (page 117)
2 tablespoons unrefined coconut oil or extra-virgin olive oil
About 3 cups Basic Bone Broth (page 245)
Sweet-and-Sassy Barbecue Sauce (page 89)
Whole-grain buns (optional)

Preheat the oven to 300°F.

Season the chuck roast evenly with the salt, then rub the Super-Sassy Seasoning all over it.

In a large Dutch oven or ovenproof pan, heat the oil over medium-high heat. Place the meat in the pot and sear it for about 2 minutes on each side, until deeply browned and crusty, taking care not to let the spices burn and lowering the heat if they threaten to scorch. Transfer the beef to a plate, add 1 cup of the broth, and stir to release any browned bits from the bottom of the pan. Return the beef to the pan, add enough broth to cover the meat halfway, and bring to a simmer. Turn off the heat, cover the pan, place in the oven, and roast for 2½ to 3 hours, until the meat is fall-apart tender. Remove from the oven, place the beef on a plate or cutting board to cool, then shred it. Transfer the beef to a bowl and add as much barbecue sauce as you like, as well as some of the pan liquid as needed to keep it moist. Serve on buns or directly on the plate with your choice of sides.

Next Level, Please!

For even more flavor and nutrition, add a halved onion and a couple of carrots to the pot; brown them all over before adding the beef, then remove them and return them to the pot just before putting it in the oven.

Cut to the Chase

COMFORTING ONE-POT SUPPERS

I love to throw everything into one pot and come out with a masterpiece! These recipes deliver comfort from a single pot, pan, or skillet while keeping the kitchen tidy and clean. The chapter includes a classic roast chicken seasoned with my sassy spice blend (page 143), kid-friendly turkey tacos (page 139) and an enchilada skillet (page 135), a classic lamb chop (page 141), and a vegetarian ratatouille. Also here are two Louisiana family favorites, jambalaya (page 125) and gumbo (page 129)—recipes that have been passed down and that I've changed up to make them my own. I'm especially proud to share this part of my heritage with you!

STOVETOP RATATOUILLE

I try to make it to my local farmers' market as often as possible to see what organic goodies I can find. This light vegetable stew featuring tomatoes, eggplant, zucchini, and bell peppers screams summer, making it a choice farmers' market meal (though living in California means I have the luxury of extending the season). Ratatouille is usually a side, so I added beans to mine to make it a balanced meal. Salting the eggplant before cooking it and cutting it into fairly small pieces makes it easy to cook it evenly on the stovetop without any undercooked spots, and adding the zucchini at the end ensures that it's nice and tender but not overcooked. *Serves 4 (makes 8 cups)*

1 medium eggplant (about 1 pound), peeled or unpeeled—your choice

Sea salt

2 tablespoons extra-virgin olive oil, plus more for drizzling

1 large yellow onion, chopped

2 medium red or yellow bell peppers, or a combination, chopped

1 bay leaf

3 garlic cloves, minced

½ teaspoon fennel seeds

½ teaspoon dried oregano

½ teaspoon dried thyme, crumbled

½ teaspoon freshly ground black pepper, plus more to taste

¼ teaspoon red pepper flakes

4 medium tomatoes (about 1¾ pounds), chopped

2 tablespoons tomato paste

1 tablespoon red wine vinegar, plus more to taste

2 medium zucchini (about 1 pound), cut into ½-inch pieces

1 cup cooked adzuki beans, black beans, cannellini beans, or lentils

¼ cup sliced pitted Kalamata olives

½ cup chopped fresh basil

2 tablespoons finely chopped fresh flat-leaf parsley

Cut the eggplant into ¾-inch pieces. Place them in a colander, add ½ teaspoon salt, toss, and set aside for about 30 minutes while you prep your ingredients. Pat the eggplant dry with a paper towel.

In a large saucepan, heat the oil over medium heat. Add the onion and cook, stirring often, until starting to soften, about 5 minutes. Add the bell pepper and cook for 2 minutes, or until just starting to soften. Add the bay leaf and garlic and cook for about 1 minute, until aromatic. Add the fennel, oregano, thyme, black pepper, and red pepper flakes and cook for 1 minute, adding a tiny bit of water if the mixture starts to stick to the pan. Add the eggplant and ½ teaspoon salt and cook, stirring, for 1 minute. Cover, reduce the heat to medium-low, and cook for 5 minutes, or until the eggplant is starting to soften. Add the tomatoes, tomato paste, and vinegar. Increase the heat to medium-high, bring to a simmer, then reduce the heat to medium-low and cook, uncovered, for 10 to 15 minutes, until the eggplant and tomatoes are almost completely softened and the tomatoes start to thicken into a light sauce. Add the zucchini and cook for 5 to 10 minutes, until the eggplant and zucchini are softened, taking care not to overcook the zucchini. Add the beans and stir until heated through. Turn off the heat and stir in the olives, basil, and parsley, then taste and add more salt, black pepper, and/or vinegar if needed. Remove the bay leaf, spoon into bowls, and serve, drizzled with a little oil.

FROM DINNER TO PARTY DIP

To turn your ratatouille into a dip or spread, add a little olive oil and pulse it in a food processor until mostly smooth with chunks of veggies still visible. Next time you're entertaining, serve it with crackers, chips, or To Live for Flatbread (page 153) alongside dips like hummus (page 228) or ranch dip (page 152). You could also spread it over flatbread, pizza-style, with or without a sprinkling of feta cheese or some yogurt.

Next Level, Please!

Save a little of your ratatouille to blend into Secret Red Sauce (page 265) so the kids (and parents, too!) get a bonus hit of veggies with any dish that calls for tomato sauce.

LOUISIANA-STYLE JAMBALAYA

One thing I know about people from Louisiana is that they can cook. And every one of them thinks that nobody else can throw down in the kitchen as good as they can! My mother's side of the family is from Lake Charles, Louisiana, so I've tasted many jambalayas over the years. Whenever I have a question about this or any other Creole dish, I rely on my aunt Diane and grandma Ethel to give me some tips. There are so many ways to make jambalaya—with or without chicken, with different types of sausage, spicy or mild, with crab or shrimp. I've prepared it with a variety of ingredients depending on what I have on hand and it's always good! Making jambalaya might seem a little involved, but most of the work is in prepping the ingredients and having them ready. And it's a perfect make-ahead meal that everyone loves. This Creole favorite is a very hearty dish, so I like to serve a nice big green salad to help with digestion—and also to keep me from eating too much! *Serves 4 to 6*

1 pound boneless, skinless chicken thighs, cut into 1-inch pieces
2 teaspoons sea salt
½ teaspoon freshly ground black pepper
¾ teaspoon smoked paprika
2 tablespoons extra-virgin olive oil
1 medium onion, chopped
2 medium shallots, chopped
2 celery stalks, chopped
1 medium green bell pepper, chopped
1½ teaspoons garlic powder
Cayenne pepper (optional)
½ cup Basic Bone Broth (page 245), good-quality store-bought broth, or water, plus more if needed
⅓ cup canned tomato puree
8 ounces smoked andouille sausage, cut crosswise into ½-inch-thick slices
1 pound large shrimp, peeled and deveined

3 cups cooked brown rice (see page 219)
¼ cup chopped fresh flat-leaf parsley, plus more for garnish

Place the chicken in a large bowl and season with ½ teaspoon of the salt, the pepper, and paprika. Set aside for up to 30 minutes while you prep the rest of the ingredients.

In large heavy saucepan or Dutch oven, heat 1 tablespoon of the oil over medium heat. Add the chicken and cook, undisturbed, for 5 minutes (this allows the fat to render to keep the chicken from sticking to the pan), then stir and cook until lightly browned on the second side, about 5 minutes more. Transfer the chicken to a bowl.

Add the remaining 1 tablespoon of oil to the pan. Add the onion, shallots, celery, and bell pepper and cook, stirring, until softened and starting to brown, about 10 minutes. Stir in the garlic powder and a pinch or two of cayenne, if you like, and cook for 1 minute, scraping the bottom of the pan if the spices start to stick. Add the broth, raise the heat a little, and stir to scrape up any browned bits stuck to the bottom of the pan.

Return the chicken and its juices to the pan and add the tomato puree and 1 teaspoon of the remaining salt. Bring to a simmer, then cover, reduce the heat to low, and cook for 15 minutes, lifting the lid and stirring once or twice. Add the sausage, shrimp, and the remaining ½ teaspoon salt. Raise the heat to medium-high and bring the mixture to a simmer, then reduce the heat to medium-low, cover, and cook for about 5 minutes, lifting the lid and stirring once or twice, until the shrimp are nearly cooked through and the sausage is warmed through.

Slowly stir in the rice, and if the mixture is slightly dry, add a little broth to moisten it (you're looking for saucy, not soupy). Cover and let sit for 10 minutes. Stir in the parsley and serve, with a little extra parsley sprinkled on top for garnish.

THE SMART CHOICE FOR SHRIMP

Shrimp is the most popular seafood in the country. It's convenient, easy to prepare, and a great source of protein. But did you know that most of our shrimp is imported from industrial shrimp farms, often far away from our shores? The pesticides and other chemicals that are used in their processing are passed on to us when we eat them. Wild is the smartest, most sustainable choice when it comes to shrimp, so whenever the fish counter has fresh or frozen wild domestic shrimp, grab a bag or two and keep them handy in your freezer.

SEAFOOD GUMBO

Of all the dishes that originated from Louisiana, gumbo is the most famous. Growing up, I remember my grandmother waking up early in the morning and chopping ingredients to go into her large pot of gumbo. Seafood is expensive, so it wasn't a dish she made often. I guess that's why whenever gumbo was cooking, a group of people would inevitably appear to feast on it. Some of my family members would even show up carrying their own large soup bowl!

In 2002, when I was living in Las Vegas, I decided to make my first pot of gumbo. I had just fought and won a World Championship belt and had lots of friends in town. I wanted to prepare a great meal for them, so I called my grandma Ethel, and she gave me directions over the phone. My mother was standing over my pot chuckling because she said my roux was too light in color. Looking back on the first pot I made a decade and a half ago, I'm proud of how my personal recipe has evolved . . . and I've learned how to be patient and take the time to get my roux just the right color. Honestly, though, I usually don't even cook with a recipe; I season as I go and am always pleased with the results. Feel free to add your own touches to make this gumbo your own! *Serves 8*

1½ teaspoons sea salt, plus more to taste
1 tablespoon Super-Sassy Seasoning (page 117)
1½ teaspoons Old Bay Seasoning
½ teaspoon paprika
6 boneless, skinless chicken thighs (about 1½ pounds)
½ cup plus 1 tablespoon extra-virgin olive oil
⅔ cup white whole wheat flour
1 medium yellow onion, finely chopped
3 scallions, finely chopped
3 celery stalks, finely chopped
3 tablespoons minced garlic
4 cups Basic Bone Broth (page 245), Almost-Instant Shrimp Broth (see page 131), or good-quality store-bought broth, heated to lukewarm

1 (8-ounce) bottle clam juice
6 ounces andouille sausage or another firm smoked sausage, sliced ⅓-inch thick
½ teaspoon freshly ground black pepper
1 pound small shrimp, peeled and deveined
1 (8-ounce) container lump crabmeat, drained if necessary
2 teaspoons fresh lemon juice, plus more to taste
¼ cup chopped fresh flat-leaf parsley
Cooked brown rice (see page 219), for serving

In a small bowl, mix together ½ teaspoon of the salt, the Super-Sassy Seasoning, Old Bay Seasoning, and paprika.

Put the chicken in a large bowl and toss with the seasoning mix to coat it all over.

In a large, heavy saucepan, heat 1 tablespoon of the oil over medium-high heat. Place the chicken in the pan (in two batches if it doesn't all fit at once) and cook for about 5 minutes on each side, until lightly browned all over. Transfer to a plate and wipe out the pan. (If any bits are stuck to the bottom of the pan, add a small amount of the broth, stir to release them, and pour the flavorful liquid onto the chicken, then wipe out the pan.)

In the same pan, heat the remaining ½ cup oil over medium-high heat for about 2 minutes to get it good and hot. Reduce the heat to medium and add the flour, gradually stirring it in with a wooden spoon to smooth out any lumps and form a paste. Cook, stirring continuously, until a deep reddish-brown (somewhere between milk chocolate and dark chocolate in color) roux is formed, 20 to 25 minutes, reducing the heat a little if the roux starts coloring too quickly and scraping the bottom of the pan to prevent burning.

Add the onion, scallions, celery, and garlic and cook, stirring often, until the vegetables soften, about 5 minutes. Add the broth in a slow, steady stream, stirring well. Add the clam juice, increase the heat to high, and bring to a boil. Chop the chicken into bite-size pieces and add it to the pan along with the sausage. Add the remaining 1 teaspoon of salt and the pepper. Bring to a simmer, then reduce the heat to medium-low and simmer for 30 minutes, stirring occasionally as the gumbo thickens. Stir in the shrimp and crab and cook for about 3 minutes, until the shrimp are cooked through and the crab is heated through. Stir in the lemon juice and parsley; taste and add more lemon juice and/or salt if needed. Serve over rice.

Almost-Instant Shrimp Broth

If your shrimp come unpeeled, don't throw out those shells! Make a quick shrimp broth from the shells that's tasty, full of calcium, and packed with flavor. Use it as the base of your gumbo, to make miso soup (page 37), or in place of water when you cook a grain. The shells also can be frozen in a freezer bag and saved for another time. *Makes 1 quart*

Shells from 1 to 1½ pounds shrimp
Sea salt
Fresh lime or lemon juice (optional)

Put the shells in a small saucepan and add 1 quart water and a couple of pinches of salt. Bring to a simmer over medium-high heat, then reduce the heat to low and simmer for 20 to 30 minutes. Strain and let cool completely. Store in an airtight container in the refrigerator for up to 4 days or in the freezer for up to 4 months.

MAKING BROTH FOR GUMBO

If you purchase unpeeled shrimp for your gumbo, I recommend making Almost-Instant Shrimp Broth with the shells, as shrimp broth will give your gumbo the most authentic flavor. But any good broth will work: Basic Bone Broth (page 245), Very Veggie Broth (page 248), or a good store-bought broth. Many fish stores or counters sell prepared shrimp broth that you can use. I like to supplement my broth with some dried shrimp or ground shrimp shells while it simmers for that extra seafood flavor. Dried shrimp can be found in a package (not refrigerated) in Asian and Latin American markets, and shrimp shells can be found at some fish counters. Note that the broth needs to be heated to lukewarm before it's added to the roux; if it's too hot or too cold, it could cause the sauce to break.

ZESTY LIME AND OREGANO SEARED CHICKEN BREAST

This is a fresh and clean-tasting dish that goes perfectly over pasta or rice (I love it with Coconut Black Rice, page 220) and served with salad or any number of my side dishes. One of the most common complaints about chicken breast is that it cooks up too tough. Marinating your chicken breast in citrus tenderizes it, with reliably moist and juicy results. You can marinate for as little as one hour but not much longer than four hours, as it can start to break down and become mealy. Remove the chicken tenders from the breasts, reserve them for another use, or marinate them along with the breasts. Tenders will cook much quicker than the breasts, in about half the time. Use coconut cream or coconut milk instead of cream to make this dish dairy-free. *Serves 4*

2 large boneless, skinless chicken breasts, (about 1½ pounds), cut in half horizontally
Sea salt and freshly ground black pepper
1 medium red onion, sliced into half-moons
½ teaspoon grated lime zest
¼ cup fresh lime juice
1 tablespoon chopped fresh oregano leaves, or 1 teaspoon dried oregano
3 tablespoons extra-virgin olive oil, plus more for the pan
½ cup heavy cream

Season the chicken liberally with salt and pepper and place it in a large zip-top bag with the onion. Add the lime zest, lime juice, oregano, and oil, seal the bag, and massage the chicken to fully coat it in the marinade. Refrigerate for 1 to 4 hours, massaging the chicken whenever you have a moment to evenly marinate it.

Just before you're ready to serve, heat a large skillet over medium-high heat. Lightly oil the pan. Massage the chicken in the marinade a final time, then remove the chicken from the marinade, letting the excess marinade drip off (leaving the onions in the bag), and place it in the pan (if the chicken doesn't all fit in the pan, cook it in two batches). Cook for about 3 minutes, until nicely browned on the bottom, then flip and cook on the second side for 2 to 3 minutes, until just cooked through. Transfer the chicken to a plate and tent with aluminum foil to keep it warm. Add the onions and the remaining marinade to the pan and cook until the onions are crisp-tender and the marinade juices have thickened, about 5 minutes. Reduce the heat to medium-low, stir in the cream, and cook until heated through and thickened, about 3 minutes. Place the chicken breasts on plates, top with the onions and sauce, and serve.

CHEDDAR CHICKEN ENCHILADA SKILLET

If you've got leftover chicken and salsa on hand, this recipe is one of my quickest to put together. It's sure to become a family favorite because it delivers flavorful, crispy, cheesy satisfaction with barely any dishes to wash after dinner. For an extra-crispy topping, finish the dish under the broiler rather than on the stovetop. Shredded turkey or beef could easily be substituted for the chicken, and for added fiber, add black beans in place of a portion of the chicken. *Serves 4*

1 tablespoon extra-virgin olive oil
1 medium red onion, chopped
3 cups shredded or chopped cooked chicken (see page 94)
2 cups Green Salsa (page 28), Roasted Tomato Salsa (page 34), or good-quality store-bought salsa
Sea salt and freshly ground black pepper
1 cup crumbled tortilla chips
¾ cup shredded cheddar cheese

OPTIONAL GARNISHES
Chopped avocado
Sliced scallions or chopped fresh cilantro
Chopped red onion
Chopped fresh tomato
Hot sauce

Heat the oil in a large skillet over medium heat. Add the onion and cook until softened, about 5 minutes. Add the chicken and salsa, season with salt and pepper, and cook until heated through. Top with the tortilla chips, then the cheese, cover, and cook until the cheese has melted. Garnish as desired and serve.

Next Level, Please!

- Turn the dish into a chicken and rice or quinoa skillet by swapping out the chips for rice or quinoa (stir it in rather than adding it at the end). Or swap in riced cauliflower for a grain-free skillet dish.
- Add leftover veggies to the mix or stir in a handful of leafy greens along with the chicken.

CHOOSING CORN, STAYING CLEAR OF CORN SYRUP

Corn is big business in America. More than a quarter of supermarket items, from kernels to candy, soda, ketchup, chicken, and even some non-food choices, contain corn products. A lot of that corn goes into making our food sweet: almost half of our sweeteners appear in the form of high-fructose corn syrup, a cheap sugar substitute that some health experts claim contributes to insulin resistance, a precursor of type 2 diabetes.

Shopping for corn products isn't complicated if you remember a few key tips: read ingredients lists and steer clear of high-fructose corn syrup in favor of more wholesome sweeteners, and in order to keep your kitchen GMO-free, choose organic whenever you can. Nearly all corn grown in the United States—more than 90 percent—is genetically modified (organic corn cannot contain GMOs). And because corn is a staple of animal feed, organic, grass-fed beef is an attractive choice. When picking out corn tortillas, look for not much more than corn on the ingredients list—no stabilizers, gums, or artificial ingredients. And when it comes to chips, choose a brand made with unrefined oils that's baked rather than fried. Better-quality products cost a little more, but your health is worth it!

LOADED GROUND TURKEY TACOS

I know that I'm biased, but in my opinion, my turkey tacos are the best! Not only do they taste damn good, they get extra points because they contain a generous amount of veggies and are actually good for you. I skip the store-bought taco seasoning and take the extra five minutes to put together my own nutritious spice blend, then use it generously to load my tacos with flavor. The veggies can barely be detected, making these tacos a balanced meal that the whole family can get excited about. Make sure to pulse the zucchini or cauliflower into tiny pieces with no chunks remaining and peel the zucchini for kids who haven't discovered their love for veggies yet. This recipe easily doubles—change up the toppings and you'll have a different dinner the second night! Or double just the spice mix and you'll have it set to go for your next taco night. You could also sprinkle some on chicken thighs or breasts and sear them in a skillet for a quick meal. The mix will keep for up to six months in a tightly covered jar. *Makes 12 tacos*

1 large zucchini (about 1 pound), or ½ small head cauliflower, or a combination
1 tablespoon extra-virgin olive oil or unrefined coconut oil, plus more for cooking the tortillas
1 large yellow onion, chopped
3 garlic cloves, minced
1 pound ground turkey

TACO SEASONING MIX
1½ teaspoons chili powder
¾ teaspoon paprika
1½ teaspoons ground cumin
½ teaspoon onion powder
½ teaspoon garlic powder
¼ teaspoon ground turmeric
Pinch of cayenne pepper (optional)
1¼ teaspoons sea salt, or to taste
¼ teaspoon freshly ground black pepper

3 scallions, sliced
Unrefined coconut oil cooking spray
12 soft corn tortillas

OPTIONAL TOPPINGS
Grated Jack or cheddar cheese
Shredded romaine lettuce
Chopped seeded tomatoes
Roasted Tomato Salsa (page 34)
Green Salsa (page 28)
Simple Cabbage Salad (page 59) or shredded cabbage
Gochujang Guacamole (page 227)
Chopped fresh cilantro
Lime wedges
Hot sauce

Coarsely chop the zucchini or cut the cauliflower into small florets, transfer half to a food processor, and pulse until finely chopped (for cauliflower, the goal is the size of grains of rice). Transfer to a bowl and repeat with the remaining zucchini or cauliflower.

In a large skillet, heat the oil over medium-high heat. Add the onion and cook until softened and starting to brown, about 10 minutes. Add the garlic and cook until aromatic, about 1 minute. Add the turkey and cook, stirring with a wooden spoon to break up the meat, until lightly browned and no longer pink, 7 to 10 minutes.

Meanwhile, make the taco seasoning mix: In a small bowl, combine all the seasoning mix ingredients.

Add the taco seasoning mix to the skillet with the meat and cook, stirring often, for 5 minutes, reducing the heat and/or adding a tiny bit of water or oil if the mixture starts to stick. Stir in the zucchini or cauliflower and cook until it has softened, about 5 minutes, again adding a tiny bit of water or oil if the mixture starts to stick. Stir in the scallions.

Heat a separate medium skillet over medium-high heat and spray it with cooking spray. Add a tortilla and heat, pressing down on it with a spatula to keep it flat, until malleable, about 30 seconds on each side, or a little longer if you'd like your tortilla slightly crispy. I like to keep my tortillas flat, but feel free to fold them if you like. Transfer to a plate and repeat with the remaining tortillas, adding cooking spray to the pan as needed. To keep your tortillas warm while you are cooking the rest, place them on a baking sheet in a preheated 200°F oven as each is heated.

Fill the tortillas with the ground turkey mixture and finish with any toppings you wish to use.

Swap It Out

- As a time-saver, use store-bought organic taco shells.
- Serve the filling over rice, quinoa, or millet instead of stuffing it into tacos.

Next Level, Please!

- Skip the oil and heat your tortillas directly over a burner (watching all the time) on both sides until pliable and slightly charred in spots.
- The vegetables will release a good amount of water when processed, potentially making for a juicy filling. If you'd prefer a thicker taco filling, squeeze the veggies in a clean kitchen towel to remove the liquid. Pour the liquid into a little cup, add a pinch of salt, and drink the slightly sweet vegetable water, or add it to your next soup or stew.

GARLIC AND ROSEMARY SEARED LAMB RIB CHOPS

My family goes crazy for lamb chops, but in most homes, lamb doesn't get the attention that beef, pork, and poultry do. All I can say is that they're missing out! Chops are a fairly expensive cut of lamb, so you might break this one out for a special family dinner or celebratory meal. Whether you're searing a chop, skewering chunks of lamb onto kebabs (page 155), or cooking up a pan of ground lamb and veggies (page 147), lamb can be juicy, tender, and full of flavor with few added seasonings needed when done right. The key to perfectly cooked chops is in the timing, with a goal of getting a good sear on the outside without overcooking them inside. When you've got that simple method down, the results are nothing short of high-end, restaurant-quality food in the comfort of your home! *Serves 4*

3 tablespoons extra-virgin olive oil

2 tablespoons minced garlic

2 tablespoons finely chopped fresh rosemary

1 teaspoon sea salt, plus more to taste

½ teaspoon coarsely ground black pepper, plus more to taste

12 lamb rib chops

½ cup Basic Bone Broth (page 245), plus more if needed

12 ounces green beans, trimmed and cut into ½-inch pieces

2 teaspoons fresh lemon juice, or to taste

¼ cup chopped toasted and skinned hazelnuts or another nut (optional)

In a small bowl, whisk together 2 tablespoons of the oil, the garlic, rosemary, salt, and pepper.

Place the chops on a baking sheet and rub them all over with the seasoned oil, massaging it into the meat with your fingers. Set aside to marinate for 15 to 30 minutes. (To marinate the ribs in advance, place the marinade into a zip-top bag, add the ribs, and massage the marinade into the ribs. Seal and refrigerate for up to 1 day.)

In a large skillet with a lid, heat 1½ teaspoons of the oil over medium-high heat. Add half the chops and sear on each side for 2 to 3 minutes for medium-rare, another minute on each side for medium. Transfer the chops to a large plate and scrape out the pan drippings onto the chops. (If any bits are stuck to the bottom of the pan, add a very small amount of broth and stir to break them up, then pour the broth over the ribs and wipe out the pan.) Tent the chops with aluminum foil. Add the remaining 1½ teaspoons of oil to the pan and cook the remaining chops in the same way. Add the second batch to the plate with the first and let rest for 5 minutes.

Pour the broth into the pan and stir to scrape up any browned bits from the bottom of the pan. Bring to a simmer, then stir in the green beans, reduce the heat to medium, cover the pan, and steam until crisp-tender, lifting the lid to stir a couple of times and adding a little more broth if the pan starts to dry out before the green beans are done, about 5 minutes. Season with salt and pepper, add the lemon juice, and stir in the hazelnuts (if using).

Divide the chops among four plates and drizzle the juices from the plate on top. Serve with the green beans alongside.

SUPER-SASSY ROAST CHICKEN AND POTATOES

This cookbook wouldn't be complete without a classic roast chicken dish. My personal spin on the classic is to spice the chicken with my Super-Sassy Seasoning. The secret to moist and crispy roast chicken is to start out at high heat to crisp up the skin, then baste, reduce the heat, and roast until the chicken is juicy and tender inside. The breast cooks faster than the dark meat, so I start with the breast side down to keep it from overcooking by the time the legs and thighs are done. Potatoes cook right into the pan juices to complete this comforting, satisfying family meal. Serve with a nice big salad, such as my Fennel and Jicama Salad (page 65). *Serves 4*

1 (3½- to 4-pound) whole chicken
1½ tablespoons extra-virgin olive oil
2 teaspoons Super-Sassy Seasoning
  (page 117)
1 teaspoon sea salt, plus more to taste
½ cup white wine, Basic Bone Broth (page
  245), or good-quality store-bought broth
1½ pounds new potatoes
Lemon wedges

Preheat the oven to 450°F. Take the chicken out of the refrigerator to come to room temperature while you're preheating the oven.

In a small bowl, whisk together 1 tablespoon of the oil, the Super-Sassy Seasoning, and salt and set aside.

Pat the chicken dry with paper towels. Season the chicken all over, including the cavity, with the seasoned oil and tie the legs together with kitchen twine.

Pour the wine into the prepared pan and place the chicken breast-side down in the pan. Roast for 20 minutes to start to crisp up the skin. Meanwhile, scrub the potatoes, cut them in half, and toss with the remaining ½ tablespoon oil and a sprinkle of salt.

Transfer the chicken to a plate (use heavy-duty tongs or a wooden spoon to grab it through the cavity and lift), flipping it breast-side up. Arrange the potatoes cut-side down in the pan to create a platform for the chicken and place the chicken on top of the potatoes. Return to the oven to roast for about 5 minutes, until starting to brown. Reduce the oven temperature to 325°F and roast for about 45 minutes, basting occasionally, until an instant-read thermometer inserted into the thickest part of the thigh registers 165°F and the potatoes are cooked through.

Remove the chicken from the oven and tilt the chicken so the juices from the cavity drip into the pan, then place the chicken on a carving board to rest for 5 to 10 minutes.

Transfer the potatoes to a serving bowl and pour any drippings into a sauceboat. Carve the chicken and serve, with the pan drippings and potatoes and some lemon wedges and salt for sprinkling alongside.

Next Level, Please!

- **Nonorganic potatoes are on the Environmental Working Group's "Dirty Dozen" list of most heavily pesticide-sprayed produce, so favor organic potatoes and leave the skins on, as there's plenty of nutrition found there.**
- **Add fresh herbs such as thyme, rosemary, and sage and a halved lemon, lime, or orange to the cavity of the chicken for added flavor.**
- **Toss a head's worth of unpeeled garlic cloves in with the potatoes. Once the dish is done, pop them out of their skins and whisk them into the pan juices for a creamy, garlicky pan sauce.**

SEVEN SIMPLE SANDWICH SUGGESTIONS

Whatever you had for dinner last night, chances are, it will make an amazing sandwich today! Here are seven of my favorites. I encourage you to peek into the fridge, get creative, and come up with your own signature sandwich combos!

1. Shredded Super-Sassy Roast Chicken (page 143) sandwich with roasted garlic mayo (page 163) and arugula

2. Citrus grilled vegetables (page 156) and melted cheese

3. Turkey Patty (page 190) sliders with marinara sauce or ranch dip (page 152)

4. English muffin pizza with Secret Red Sauce (page 265) and broken-up meatballs (page 191)

5. Pancake (page 171), sausage, and maple syrup roll-up sandwich

6. Ratatouille (page 123) or North African–Inspired Chickpea (page 83) wrap

7. Hummus (page 228) and pickle (page 257) or sauerkraut (page 259) wrap

LAMB AND ROOT VEGGIE SKILLET

Lamb releases a lot of fat when it's cooked, but this dish is far from fatty. That's because the veggies cook right into the lamb—no need to brown them in oil first, saving both calories and steps and speeding up the time it takes to get dinner to the table. The recipe calls for a couple of cups of root vegetables, which equals one medium carrot, parsnip, and beet, but you don't have to be exact—this simple, comforting skillet dish welcomes changing up according to the season and what your crisper drawer reveals on any given day. *Serves 4*

1 pound ground lamb
1 medium onion, chopped
2 garlic cloves, finely chopped
1 jalapeño, seeded (optional)
2 cups chopped (½-inch pieces) mixed root vegetables, such as carrots, parsnips, and beets
¾ teaspoon sea salt, plus more to taste
¼ teaspoon freshly ground black pepper
2 kale leaves, stemmed and chopped or torn into pieces
1 teaspoon fresh lime or lemon juice, plus more to taste
2 tablespoons finely chopped fresh herbs, such as flat-leaf parsley, cilantro, and mint, or 2 teaspoons finely chopped more potent herbs, such as rosemary, oregano, and thyme

In a large skillet, combine the lamb, onion, garlic, and jalapeño (if using) and cook over medium heat, stirring to break up the meat, for 10 minutes, or until the fat starts rendering from the lamb and the onion starts to soften. Add the root vegetables, salt, and pepper and cook, stirring often, until the vegetables are softened, about 20 minutes. Add the kale and cook, stirring continuously, until wilted, 3 to 5 minutes. Add the lime juice and herbs, taste, and adjust the seasonings with salt and/or lime juice if you like.

Swap It Out

- Try other seasonal roots, such as turnip, rutabaga, sunchokes, or winter squash for an aboveground swap.
- Add a splash of coconut milk and/or some grated fresh coconut to your skillet.
- Reduce the salt and season your skillet with tamari, soy sauce, or fish sauce.
- Use beef instead of lamb.

Talk of the Town

TANTALIZING CROWD-PLEASERS

I don't know about you, but when I take the time to cook for company, I want to see a smile on people's faces and empty plates all around. These are some of my favorite recipes for entertaining, and they're all quite easy to put together. There's my famous oven-"fried" chicken (page 164) that gets an upgrade by skipping the deep-fryer, a gluten-free flatbread you can be proud of (page 153), a cheese spread made with just one ingredient (page 151), and a dairy-free ranch dip based on cashews (page 152). A choice of veggie or lamb kebabs (pages 156 and 155) can be made either on the grill or under the broiler. And a talk-of-the-town chocolate truffle (page 166) without a grain of refined sugar will please any sweet tooth. When I entertain, I like to bring out foods that people are used to eating, but healthier versions, and nobody guesses how healthy they are! It takes a little more thought, but at the end of the night, no one leaves the house feeling weighed down; in fact, they feel even better than when they arrived!

FRESH HERB CHEESE SPREAD

This spread takes the concept of Greek yogurt—yogurt that's been strained to concentrate it—a step further, and turns it into a creamy cheese spread that makes a fantastic presentation. The flavor is sophisticated, but it couldn't be simpler to make. Just strain the yogurt overnight, season with your favorite herbs, and scoop it up with a vegetable stick, cracker, or flatbread (page 153). If you don't have cheesecloth, a layer of unbleached paper towel will do in a pinch. *Makes about 2 cups*

1 quart plain yogurt
Extra-virgin olive oil
Flaky sea salt
Herbs and spices such as thyme leaves, coarsely ground black pepper, and red pepper flakes or paprika

Line a strainer with a double layer of cheesecloth (leaving enough overhang to cover the yogurt) and set it on top of a bowl tall enough to catch the liquid that drips out (a couple of cups will be released) without touching the strainer. Put the yogurt in the strainer, cover with the cheesecloth overhang, and refrigerate for 12 to 24 hours.

Lift the cheesecloth from the strainer and invert the yogurt onto a medium plate.

Discard the liquid in the bowl. Take the back of a spoon or spatula and move it around the plate over the yogurt to make large circular swirls on the plate. Liberally drizzle oil over the yogurt, then sprinkle with salt and your choice of herbs and spices.

Swap It Out

Add a small amount of turmeric or beet juice to give your dip an eye-catching color.

RICH RANCH DIP

Nutrient rich, that is! This dip features all the familiar flavors of ranch but with a freshness you just can't get from tearing open a packet. My ranch is dairy-free, with cashews providing the dip's signature creamy consistency, and a light fermentation giving it a tangy taste and a bonus blast of gut-healthy probiotics. If you're new to fermentation, this dip is a great first recipe, as all that's needed is a bottle of probiotic capsules to get you started: open them up, whisk them into blended cashews, and let sit overnight while the friendly bacteria do their magic, turning nuts into silky-smooth sour cream. For a second step into fermentation, turn to the Next Level, Please! chapter (page 242), where we learn to make kefir and transform cucumbers into pickles and cabbage into kraut. Serve the ranch with your choice of crudités or dip chicken fingers (page 192) into it. *Makes about 2 cups*

2 cups raw cashew pieces (about 8 ounces)
3 probiotic capsules
½ teaspoon garlic powder
½ teaspoon onion powder
½ teaspoon dried dill
¼ teaspoon ground celery seed
1 teaspoon sea salt
½ teaspoon freshly ground black pepper
1 teaspoon fresh lemon juice, plus more to taste
1 teaspoon apple cider vinegar, plus more to taste
1 teaspoon minced fresh chives, plus more for sprinkling

Place the cashews in a large bowl, add cold water to cover by a few inches, cover with a clean kitchen towel, and set aside on the counter away from direct sunlight for at least 3 hours or up to overnight. Drain, then transfer the cashews to a blender, add 1¼ cups fresh cold water, and blend until smooth, adding a little more water to get the blade moving if needed. Transfer to a bowl. Open the probiotic capsules and whisk the contents into the cashews, then cover with the kitchen towel and set aside for at least 8 hours or up to 24 hours (go for a shorter time if it's particularly warm out), until it tastes nice and tangy.

Vigorously whisk the mixture for about 30 seconds, adding a little more water if needed to reach a dip consistency. Add the garlic powder, onion powder, dill, celery seed, salt, pepper, lemon juice, and vinegar and whisk to fully incorporate the ingredients. Whisk in the chives. Taste and add more lemon juice or vinegar if needed to reach your desired level of tanginess. Spoon into a bowl and serve, sprinkled with chives, or store in an airtight container in the refrigerator for up to 2 weeks.

TO LIVE FOR FLATBREAD

If you are like me and love bread but don't love what happens when you eat too much wheat, this recipe is for you! Easy to make and versatile, this gluten-free flatbread is enriched with almond flour and almond milk, making it high in protein and low in carbohydrates and sugar. My favorite way to finish my flatbread is with garlic and rosemary, but depending on what you're serving or topping it with, you may omit them or swap them out for other seasonings. Scoop up hummus (page 228), ratatouille dip (page 123), or another favorite party spread with a piece, or think of it as your own personal pizza, flatbread-style, with endless topping possibilities. Steamed veggies, thinly sliced shiitake mushrooms, or raw spinach leaves would be welcome here, as would dots of soft goat cheese or slices of fresh mozzarella. Add leftover chicken for protein, or lay out thin slices of winter squash before baking. Go for just about anything in your refrigerator that catches your attention! *Makes one 9-inch flatbread*

½ cup cup-for-cup replacement gluten-free flour blend, such as Steve's GF Cake Flour
½ cup almond flour
½ teaspoon sea salt, plus more for sprinkling
4 tablespoons (½ stick) unsalted butter
½ cup almond milk
1 large egg, beaten
Extra-virgin olive oil
2 teaspoons finely chopped garlic (optional)
1 teaspoon finely chopped fresh rosemary (optional)

Place a 9- or 10-inch cast-iron skillet or heavy-bottomed pizza pan in the oven and preheat the oven to 450°F.

In a medium bowl, whisk together the gluten-free flour, almond flour, and salt and set aside.

In a small saucepan, melt the butter over low heat and whisk in the almond milk. Remove from the heat, add the beaten egg, and whisk to combine.

Pour the egg mixture into the flour mixture and, using a wooden spoon, stir until the ingredients are well combined and the dough has the consistency of a thick batter (not runny), about 1 minute. If the batter appears to have lumps, that's okay.

Carefully remove the hot skillet from the oven and brush or spray it lightly with oil. Scrape the dough into the skillet and, using a metal spatula (quickly dip the spatula in water first), quickly spread the dough flat out to the edges of the pan. Sprinkle the top with the garlic and rosemary (if using) and a little salt and press down on the toppings lightly with your fingers so they adhere to the dough. Bake for 12 to 15 minutes, until the flatbread is lightly browned. Remove the pan from the oven and use a spatula to immediately slip the flatbread out of the skillet and onto a serving plate or board. Finish the flatbread with a light drizzle of oil. The flatbread will keep, well wrapped in plastic wrap, at room temperature for up to 3 days or frozen for up to 1 month.

Swap It Out

- **Try coconut flour in place of the almond flour and coconut oil or olive oil in place of the butter to make your flatbread dairy-free.**
- **Swap the almond milk for coconut milk or another nut milk.**

A FESTIVE HOLIDAY SPREAD

Come the holidays, at my home you'll find a spread with favorites such as these:

- Fresh Herb Cheese Spread (page 151)
- To Live for Flatbread (page 153)
- Cornbread/Cornbread Dressing (page 200)
- A+ Mac and Cheese (page 189)
- Roasted Root Veggies (page 221)
- Black-Eyed Peas and Sausage (page 217)
- Light-and-Creamy Spinach (page 207)
- Oven-"Fried" Chicken Wings (page 164)
- Cheesy Quinoa and Rice Bake (page 222)
- Coconut Black Rice (page 220)
- Stovetop Ratatouille (page 123)
- Garlic and Herb Lamb Kebabs (page 155)
- Citrus Veggie Skewers (page 156)
- Simple Seared Salmon with Super-Sassy Barbecue Sauce and Wilted Arugula (page 89)
- Garlic and Rosemary Seared Lamb Rib Chops (page 141)

GARLIC AND HERB LAMB KEBABS

I have always been a big fan of Mediterranean cuisine, and the cooking of that region inspired me to create this simple but flavorful recipe. Juicy chunks of lamb are grilled to tenderness and slathered with chimichurri, a pungent herb marinade that does double duty as a sauce for the finished kebabs. Serve the kebabs with basmati rice and slices of the juiciest tomatoes you can find. These kebabs are especially designed for entertaining: they won't take you away from the fun of the party, as the sauce is made ahead of time and the lamb marinates overnight. Then all that's left to do is fire up the grill and mingle with your guests as your kebabs cook away. The recipe scales up to as many guests as you anticipate. The kebabs can be made on either an outdoor grill or under your oven's broiler. *Makes about 6 skewers (with about 1 cup sauce)*

CHIMICHURRI
1 cup packed fresh flat-leaf parsley leaves
1 cup packed fresh cilantro leaves
1 cup packed fresh mint leaves
1 large shallot, finely chopped
4 garlic cloves, finely chopped
1 jalapeño, seeded and finely chopped
¾ cup extra-virgin olive oil
3 tablespoons red wine vinegar
¾ teaspoon sea salt, or to taste

2 pounds boneless leg of lamb, trimmed of
    excess fat and cut into 1¼-inch cubes
1 large red onion, quartered and separated into
    individual pieces
Flaky sea salt
2 medium tomatoes, sliced
Brown rice (page 219)

To make the chimichurri: In a food processor, combine the parsley, cilantro, mint, shallot, garlic, and jalapeño and process until finely chopped but not pureed, stopping and scraping down the sides of the processor bowl once or twice, about 1 minute total. Transfer the mixture to a medium bowl, stir in the oil and vinegar, and add the salt.

Transfer ½ cup of the chimichurri to a small bowl or container, cover, and refrigerate. Remove from the refrigerator 30 minutes before serving to use as a sauce.

Put the remaining chimichurri in a large bowl or heavy-duty zip-top bag. Add the lamb and toss or massage the marinade into the meat. Cover or seal and refrigerate for at least 3 hours or up to 2 days. Remove the meat from the marinade and lightly pat with paper towels.

Preheat a grill to medium-high or preheat the broiler.

Starting and ending with a red onion

slice, loosely thread the onion and lamb onto skewers, alternating the two. Place on a baking sheet and sprinkle with flaky salt. Place the skewers on the grill or in a broiler pan and grill or broil, turning once or twice, for about 10 minutes for medium-rare, a couple more minutes for medium, or to the desired doneness.

Arrange the kebabs on a serving platter and drizzle with the reserved chimichurri. Add the tomato slices and some basmati rice, sprinkle with salt, and serve.

CITRUS VEGGIE SKEWERS

When it's summertime, I like to break out the skewers! Especially when I'm looking for a beautiful presentation to entertain guests. Setting up your skewers with compatible veggies— ones that cook for the same amount of time—ensures that you reach that sweet spot of juicy, crisp, and tender for each ingredient. Here I share two of my favorite combinations: corn plus cherry tomatoes and bell peppers, mushrooms, and zucchini. The skewers are sprinkled with herbs and anchored with citrus wedges that you then squeeze over the veggies to flavor them. Serve with my Garlic and Herb Lamb Kebabs (page 155), or for an impromptu summer meal, season steaks or chicken breasts with my Super-Sassy Seasoning (page 117) and throw them on the grill with your skewers. The skewers can also be cooked under the broiler. Note that you'll need metal rather than wooden skewers to spear through the sturdy corncobs, and if you wind up with any vegetables remaining, spear them in any order you like. *Makes about 12 skewers*

CORN AND TOMATO SKEWERS

1 large orange, cut into 12 small wedges

3 ears corn, shucked and cut crosswise into 1½-inch chunks

12 large cherry tomatoes

Extra-virgin olive oil

Sea salt

Sprinkling of fresh orange zest

Minced fresh rosemary

Red pepper flakes

BELL PEPPER, MUSHROOM, AND ZUCCHINI SKEWERS

3 lemons, cut into 4 wedges

2 red, orange, or yellow bell peppers, cut into 1-inch pieces

12 ounces cremini mushrooms

1 large zucchini, cut into 1-inch wedges

Extra-virgin olive oil

Sea salt

Sprinkling of fresh lemon zest

Lots of cracked black pepper

Preheat a grill to medium-high or preheat the broiler.

To make the corn and tomato skewers: Spear an orange wedge onto a metal skewer. Follow it with a chunk of corn, then a cherry tomato. Add another chunk of corn, followed by a second cherry tomato and a final corn chunk. Finish with an orange wedge anchor. Brush all over with oil, sprinkle with salt, and rub some orange zest, rosemary, and red pepper flakes onto the vegetables. Repeat to make 6 skewers total.

To make the bell pepper, mushroom, and zucchini skewers: Spear a lemon wedge onto a metal skewer. Follow it with a bell pepper wedge, a mushroom, then a zucchini wedge. Repeat to fill up the skewer, ending with a lemon wedge. Brush all over with oil, sprinkle with salt, and rub some lemon zest and black pepper over the vegetables. Repeat to make 6 skewers total.

Place all the skewers on the grill or on a broiler pan and grill or broil, turning once or twice, for about 10 minutes, until the vegetables are juicy and charred in spots. Transfer the skewers to a platter. For each skewer, squeeze the juice from the citrus anchor over the veggies, then dig in.

CRAB AND SPINACH–STUFFED PORTOBELLO MUSHROOMS

I cohost a show called *We Need to Talk*, which was the first national all-female sports talk show to appear on television. This recipe comes from a Super Bowl cooking segment where I served up a few of my favorite healthy tailgating recipes. I wanted to offer folks options beyond the typical fried wings, pasta salad, and pizza. While this recipe isn't exactly the lightest one in the book, the mushrooms are packed with protein-rich crab and I've skipped the typical bread crumb binder to make them gluten-free. The filling can be stuffed into smaller cremini mushrooms and served as a passed appetizer (after you remove the stems of smaller mushrooms, use a small spoon to scoop out a little of the flesh to make the indentations a little bigger). *Makes 6 stuffed mushrooms*

⅔ cup sun-dried tomatoes
Boiling water
6 large portobello mushrooms (4 to 5 inches)
4 tablespoons extra-virgin olive oil
3 garlic cloves, pressed through a garlic press
Sea salt and freshly ground black pepper
1 medium onion, finely chopped
½ teaspoon paprika
6 ounces chopped fresh spinach or baby
    spinach leaves
2 teaspoons minced fresh thyme
1 tablespoon capers in brine, drained
1 tablespoon fresh lemon juice
⅔ cup grated Parmesan cheese
1 cup sour cream
3 cups fresh or canned premium crabmeat,
    drained and lightly pressed to remove excess
    liquid if necessary
1½ cups grated mozzarella cheese or Pepper
    Jack cheese, or a combination (4½ ounces)
1 tablespoon finely chopped fresh flat-leaf
    parsley

Preheat the oven to 375°F.

Put the sun-dried tomatoes in a medium bowl and add boiling water to cover. Soak for about 30 minutes, until completely softened and pliable. Drain and mince the tomatoes.

Meanwhile, brush off any dirt from the mushroom caps with a lightly dampened paper towel or mushroom brush. Carefully cut off the stems and brush off any dirt. Mince the stems and set aside. Using a spoon (a grapefruit spoon with serrated edges would be perfect), scrape out the dark gills from the underside of the caps.

In a small bowl, combine 2 tablespoons of the oil with one-third of the garlic and brush the garlic oil on the rounded side of the mushrooms. Sprinkle with salt and pepper and place the mushroom caps on a

baking sheet with their cavities facing up. Sprinkle the cavities with salt and pepper.

In a large skillet, heat the remaining 2 tablespoons oil over medium heat. Add the onion and cook for 2 minutes, or until softened. Add the sun-dried tomatoes and minced mushroom stems and cook for 2 minutes, or until softened. Add the remaining garlic and cook for 20 seconds. Stir in the paprika and ¾ teaspoon salt, then add the spinach and stir until the spinach is wilted, about 30 seconds. Turn off the heat and add the thyme, capers, and lemon juice. Stir in the Parmesan and sour cream, then stir in the crab.

Divide the filling evenly among the mushroom caps. Bake for 15 minutes. Open the oven door, sprinkle the mozzarella evenly over the mushrooms, and bake for 5 minutes more, or until the cheese has melted and the mushrooms are juicy and tender. Remove from the oven and transfer the mushrooms to a second baking sheet lined with paper towels to sop up any juices released by the mushrooms. Transfer to a serving platter, sprinkle with the parsley, and serve.

Next Level, Please!

Don't discard the mushroom gills. Save them to cook with your bone broth (page 245) or vegetable broth (page 248) to add a rich mushroom flavor.

QUINOA AND PARMESAN–DUSTED SHRIMP WITH ROASTED GARLIC MAYO

Crispy shrimp are always a delicious choice for an appetizer menu. These oven-baked shrimp take just a few minutes to put together and easily double or triple so you can keep them coming as your guests ask for more. To coat the shrimp, I use whole-grain quinoa flour, and panko and Parmesan cheese to provide a crispy finish. Change up the flavor of your shrimp or mayo by adding seasonings such as curry powder, cayenne, oregano, or thyme. *Serves 4*

ROASTED GARLIC MAYO
4 cloves Toaster Oven Roasted Garlic (page 47)
½ cup olive oil mayonnaise

SHRIMP
Extra-virgin olive oil or unrefined coconut oil cooking spray
3 large egg whites
½ cup quinoa flour (see Note)
1 teaspoon garlic powder
1 teaspoon sea salt
½ teaspoon freshly ground black pepper
¾ cup whole-grain or gluten-free panko bread crumbs
1 pound large tail-on shrimp, peeled and deveined
¼ cup finely grated Parmesan cheese

To make the roasted garlic mayo: In a small bowl, whisk the roasted garlic into the mayonnaise, mashing it up and blending it in. Refrigerate until ready to use.

To make the shrimp: Preheat the oven to 400°F. Coat a baking sheet with cooking spray.

In a medium bowl, beat the egg whites until foamy. In a second bowl, whisk together the quinoa flour, garlic powder, salt, and pepper. Place the panko in a third bowl.

One by one, dredge the shrimp in the seasoned quinoa flour, then dip them into the egg whites, allowing the excess to drip off, then toss in the panko to coat, shaking off any excess. Arrange the breaded shrimp in a single layer on the prepared baking sheet and coat them with cooking spray. Bake for about 8 minutes, until the coating is starting to color. Flip the shrimp, sprinkle the cheese on top, and bake for 7 minutes more, or until lightly browned with a crispy cheese coating. Place on a platter and serve immediately, with the roasted garlic mayo alongside.

NOTE: If your grocery store doesn't carry quinoa flour, make your own by grinding whole dry quinoa in a spice grinder.

OVEN-"FRIED" CHICKEN WINGS

These wings are everything you want and need in good fried chicken, minus the deep fryer! They go into the oven, where they bake to crispy, falling-off-the-bone perfection. Go ahead and give both the chicken and the pan a generous spray with the oil before you pop it into the oven; getting a crispy texture and flavor depends on it. Don't worry—I've swapped out refined vegetable oil for heart-healthy extra-virgin olive oil or coconut oil, so you can trade out your guilt for pure delight with each juicy, crunchy bite.

The dish is quick to put together—just season, give your wings a shake in some flour, spray, and bake until they're nicely browned all over. Wings are my favorite part of the chicken, but there's no reason you couldn't "fry" drumsticks, thighs, breasts, or tenders in the same way. And once you make these wings a time or two, you may be inspired to season your "fried" chicken using your own signature spice mix! *Serves 4*

1¼ teaspoons sea salt
1 teaspoon freshly ground black pepper
1 teaspoon onion powder
1 teaspoon garlic powder
1 teaspoon paprika
¾ teaspoon ground thyme
12 chicken wings (about 2½ pounds), wing tips trimmed, cut in half at the joint (or left whole if you like)
¾ cup whole wheat flour
Extra-virgin olive oil or unrefined coconut oil cooking spray
Lemon wedges and/or sriracha or another hot sauce, for dipping

Preheat the oven to 425°F. Line a baking sheet with parchment paper.

In a small bowl, combine ¾ teaspoon of the salt, ½ teaspoon of the pepper, the onion powder, garlic powder, paprika, and thyme.

Place the wings in a large bowl, put on a pair of disposable gloves (or wash your hands really well), and massage the rub into the chicken. Make sure you coat them well so every bite will be bursting with flavor.

Place the flour in a large zip-top bag or paper bag and shake in the remaining ½ teaspoon salt and ½ teaspoon pepper. Seal and shake to work the salt and pepper into the flour. Open the bag, add the seasoned wings to the flour, seal the bag again, and shake to coat the wings evenly.

Generously coat the prepared pan with cooking spray—the equivalent of about 1½ tablespoons. Put the wings on the pan in a single layer with a little space between each. Generously coat the tops of the wings with cooking spray, the equivalent of 1½ tablespoons or so.

Bake until nicely browned and crisp (note

that you do not need to flip the wings), 45 to 55 minutes. Serve with lemon wedges on the side for squeezing and sriracha, if you like.

Swap It Out Variations

- **She Be Stinging "Fried" Chicken:** Add ½ to 1 teaspoon cayenne pepper to the spice mix.
- **Smoking "Fried" Chicken:** Substitute smoked paprika for the plain paprika.

- **Gluten-Free "Fried" Chicken:** Substitute gluten-free oat flour, quinoa flour, or cassava flour for the wheat flour.

Next Level, Please!

- Substitute ground flaxseed for up to 2 tablespoons of the flour. Use golden flax to keep the color light.
- If you've started a broth-making habit, save the wing tips to add to your next batch of Basic Bone Broth (page 245).

COCOA-DUSTED
CHOCOLATE TRUFFLES

Yep, they are as good as they sound, and five minutes is all it takes to whip up these little beauties. With no refined sugar added, the rewards are naturally sweet! My sweetener of choice is dates, as they come with bonus minerals—magnesium, potassium, and iron—along with lots of fiber so you don't get a sugar shock when you pop one into your mouth. Roll your truffles in cocoa, coconut, or both, with or without a sprinkling of crushed pink peppercorns to add a burst of color. If your office has a freezer, store a few there, then when you've got a craving for something sweet, you can bypass the vending machine and enjoy a treat that won't make you crash an hour later.

Makes about 24

8 ounces pitted dried dates
½ cup almonds
2 tablespoons maple syrup
1 tablespoon unrefined coconut oil
¼ cup unsweetened cocoa powder, plus more
   for rolling
½ teaspoon pure almond extract
½ teaspoon ground cinnamon
½ teaspoon grated lemon zest
¼ teaspoon sea salt
Unsweetened grated coconut (optional)
Crushed pink peppercorns (optional)

In a food processor, combine the dates, almonds, maple syrup, oil, cocoa powder, almond extract, cinnamon, lemon zest, and salt and process until the dates and almonds break down with some almond pieces still visible and the mixture starts to form a ball. Remove from the machine. Spread a little cocoa powder and/or grated coconut over a plate. Form the mixture into roughly 1½-inch balls and roll them in the cocoa powder (or coconut), pressing it in with your hands and adding a sprinkle of pink peppercorns to the mix, if you like. Place on a decorative plate and serve, or cover and store in the refrigerator for up to 2 weeks or in the freezer for up to 3 months.

Swap It Out

- Add 2 tablespoons currants or dried blueberries, or try goji berries for their superfood nutrients and pretty pink color.
- Add a small handful of mini chocolate chips for an extra sweet treat.

Picky . . . Not Tricky!

EASY KID-PLEASING FOODS

When the kids aren't thrilled with what's on their plate, we parents are just as unhappy. I know this all too well, as on a scale of one to ten, my kids are a full ten in the picky eating department. That's why I've gone through hours and hours of experimentation in the kitchen to come up with foods that my kids and I can agree on. The recipes in this chapter are tried, tested, and true and are adaptable to wherever your kids fall on the picky eating scale. In the very first chapter I mentioned that when you start the day with a healthy breakfast, you're much more likely to keep it up for the rest of the day. Well, that goes for kids, too, so I've started this chapter with the most nutritious, delicious pancakes (page 171) possible that the whole family can join in on. Spaghetti for breakfast (page 177) is another compelling choice, and from there the fun keeps coming, with cauliflower pizza (page 185), mac and cheese (page 189), and turkey patties (page 190). When you bring your kids into the kitchen, they have more of a stake in what they eat: simple things like adding the blueberries to their blueberry muffins (page 173), choosing colors for their confetti egg and cheese muffins (page 175), and breading their chicken fingers (page 192) really engage younger kids with their food. Once you get in the groove of making homemade "fast foods" for and with your children, you will never go back to the processed stuff!

GOLDEN FLAX AND HONEY PANCAKES WITH STRAWBERRY SYRUP

I love eating a healthy breakfast—but I also love eating pancakes with my kids. These hotcakes steer clear of the refined flour found in most supermarket pancake mixes while sneaking in a little golden flax for its subtle nutty flavor and a boost of omega-3 fatty acids. Alkalizing millet flour and slightly sweet oat flour add whole-grain goodness, and a cup-for-cup gluten-free flour base completes the gluten-free profile of the pancake mix. Sometimes I'll add a little sweetener to my pancake batter to keep my kids from going too heavy with the syrup.

   The mix is so simple to put together—now any morning can be a pancake morning! With a luscious strawberry syrup to pour over your pancakes, your kids won't think to miss the fake stuff. Along with the syrup, I love to add a dollop of plain Greek yogurt and a sprinkling of toasted nuts to finish my pancakes. Note that the batter will be a little thicker and stiffer than traditional pancake batter, making it more of a scooping batter than a pouring batter. *Makes 10 to 12 pancakes and about 1½ cups syrup*

STRAWBERRY SYRUP
2 cups fresh or thawed frozen strawberries
½ cup water
1 teaspoon fresh lemon juice
½ cup pure maple syrup
PANCAKES
1 cup Any-Morning Pancake Mix (recipe
   follows)
1 large egg
1 teaspoon pure vanilla extract
1¼ cups buttermilk, plus more if needed
1 tablespoon unsalted butter or unrefined
   coconut oil, melted, plus more for the pan
1 tablespoon honey
Cup-for-cup replacement gluten-free flour
   blend, such as Steve's GF Cake Flour, if
   needed

To make the strawberry syrup: Combine the strawberries, water, and lemon juice in a blender and blend until smooth. Pour into a small saucepan and stir in the maple syrup. Bring to a boil over high heat, then reduce the heat to medium and cook for 3 to 5 minutes, until the mixture thickens slightly and coats the back of a spoon. Remove from the heat and serve the syrup hot, warm, or cold. (Leftovers are great over plain yogurt or ice cream.)

   To make the pancakes: Place the pancake mix in a medium bowl. In a large bowl, whisk together the egg, vanilla, and buttermilk. In a separate small bowl, whisk together the melted butter and honey, then add to the buttermilk mixture and whisk to incorporate. Add the pancake mix to the wet ingredients and whisk to combine. You're looking for a batter that's medium-thick in consistency and not runny. Adjust the consistency as needed by adding more buttermilk to thin the batter or more gluten-free flour to thicken the batter. (Note that the batter will thicken as it sits.)

Heat a large griddle over medium heat and lightly grease the surface with a bit of butter. When the butter begins to sizzle, spoon (rather than pour) ¼ cup of the batter onto the pan and spread it with the spoon or the bottom of a flat dry-measuring cup into a round. Repeat to fill the pan, but do not overcrowd the pancakes. Cook for 3 to 4 minutes, until bubbles begin to form on top of the pancakes, then flip them using a metal spatula. Cook for 2 to 3 minutes more, until the edges appear dry. Reduce the heat if the pancakes are cooking too fast. Transfer finished pancakes to a heatproof plate and keep warm in a low oven until ready to serve. Repeat with the remaining batter.

Serve with the strawberry syrup alongside.

Any-Morning Pancake Mix

Makes enough for 4 batches of pancakes

2 cups cup-for-cup replacement gluten-free flour blend, such as Steve's GF Cake Flour
1 cup millet flour

1 cup oat flour
¾ teaspoon sea salt
1 tablespoon baking powder
2 teaspoons baking soda
2 teaspoons golden flax meal

Place the gluten-free flour, millet flour, oat flour, and salt in a large bowl and whisk to combine. Sift in the baking powder and baking soda and whisk to distribute them evenly. Add the flax meal and whisk again, making sure the ingredients are well blended. The mix can be stored in a glass jar in the refrigerator for up to 1 month or put in a freezer bag and frozen for up to 3 months (use it straight from the freezer).

Swap It Out

- Double the millet flour and omit the oat flour, or double the oat flour and omit the millet flour.
- Add chopped nuts or seeds to the pancake batter.
- Swap ground chia seeds for the flax meal.
- Add banana slices or berries to your pancakes (set them on the pancakes just after pouring the batter into the pan).
- Simplify by skipping the strawberry syrup and finishing with a simple drizzle of pure maple syrup (*not* pancake syrup).

BLUEBERRY AND CINNAMON MUFFINS

My son, Curtis Jr., loves blueberries, but my daughter, Sydney, picks them out even if it means she's only left with a few crumbs of a muffin. But they both can agree on cinnamon and vanilla, so I'll add blueberries to half the batch of these muffins and leave the rest berryless (doing so decreases the yield by one muffin). If your kids prefer raspberries or blackberries or that's what's in season, by all means toss them in. The crumble topping pretties up the muffins but could easily be omitted to keep them simple and super fast to make. *Makes 9 muffins*

CINNAMON CRUMBLE TOPPING
4 tablespoons (½ stick) unsalted butter, at room temperature
¼ cup raw sugar
¼ cup almond meal
¼ cup cup-for-cup replacement gluten-free flour blend, such as Steve's GF Cake Flour
½ teaspoon ground cinnamon

MUFFINS
Unrefined coconut oil cooking spray (if not using paper liners)
1¼ cups cup-for-cup replacement gluten-free flour blend, such as Steve's GF Cake Flour
1 teaspoon ground cinnamon
1 teaspoon baking powder
½ teaspoon baking soda
½ teaspoon sea salt
1 tablespoon golden flax meal
⅓ cup raw sugar
½ cup honey
⅓ cup plus 1 tablespoon unrefined coconut oil, melted
2 large eggs, at room temperature
½ cup plain yogurt
1 teaspoon pure vanilla extract

½ teaspoon grated lemon zest (optional)
1 cup fresh blueberries

To make the crumble topping: In a small bowl, beat the butter with the sugar using a wooden spoon until combined. Add the almond meal, gluten-free flour, and cinnamon and rub the ingredients together using your hands until they barely clump together when pressed with your fingers. Set aside while you make the muffins.

To make the muffins: Preheat the oven to 350°F. Line 9 cups of a muffin pan with paper liners or grease them with cooking spray.

Sift the gluten-free flour, cinnamon, baking powder, baking soda, and salt into a medium bowl. Whisk in the flax meal and set aside.

In the bowl of a stand mixer fitted with the paddle attachment, beat the sugar, honey, and oil on medium-high speed until smooth and slightly thickened, about 2 minutes. The raw sugar will remain somewhat grainy; this is okay. Beat in the eggs until well blended, about 1 minute. Turn the mixer off, add the yogurt, vanilla, and lemon zest (if using), and beat on medium speed until the ingredients are combined, about 30 seconds. Turn the mixer off, add the dry ingredients, then turn the mixer to low speed and beat for about 30 seconds, until the ingredients look well moistened. Turn the mixer off, remove the bowl, and use a rubber spatula to fold the blueberries into the batter, then give the batter a final thorough mixing by hand.

Scoop the batter into the prepared muffin cups, filling them three-quarters full. Generously sprinkle the tops with the cinnamon crumble and bake for 20 to 25 minutes, until the tops are golden brown and just firm to the touch and a cake tester inserted into the center of a muffin comes out clean. Remove the muffin pan from the oven and place it on a wire rack. If you didn't use paper liners, release the muffins by running a small knife along the inside edge of each cup and removing them from the pan. The muffins will keep, wrapped in plastic wrap, at room temperature for up to 3 days or in the freezer for up to 2 months.

BLUEBERRIES: A FRUIT WITH BENEFITS

Low in calories and sugar and high on the superfood list, blueberries are a fruit with many impressive benefits. They are high in fiber, vitamins C and K, and manganese, and their antioxidant content is greater than any other fruit. Blueberries may help to regulate blood pressure and protect against heart disease, keep cholesterol in the body from being damaged, improve brain function, protect against cancer, and, like their cranberry cousins, fight urinary tract infections. Blueberries even may help revert aging and improve vision and memory. And, of course, the little blueberry is an absolute treat added to muffins, sprinkled onto yogurt, or eaten out of hand. Now *that's* a food for those who want it all!

CONFETTI EGG AND CHEESE MINI MUFFINS

When kids get involved in the kitchen, they tend to make healthier food choices. These adorable little muffins are a great place to start. Have your kids pick vegetables in their favorite colors and arrange them in muffin cups, then pour in some egg, bake, and watch them enjoy the confetti colors that appear when they bite into their creation. I know lots of kids—mine included—get thrown off by colors, so if they don't like a particular color, try another until they find one they like. And if color is completely out at this point, go for veggies that will blend right in, such as peeled zucchini or cauliflower. I've provided a recipe for convenience, but you barely need one if you remember this muffin-making formula: half an egg, a couple tablespoons of veggies (fresh or frozen), and a tablespoon of cheese equals one muffin. These muffins reheat easily, making them a handy make-ahead breakfast option for kids of all ages. *Makes 12 mini muffins*

Extra-virgin olive oil or unrefined coconut oil cooking spray

1½ cups mixed confetti vegetables (see Note)

6 large eggs

⅛ teaspoon ground turmeric

½ teaspoon sea salt

¼ cup ricotta cheese (optional)

About ¾ cup shredded Jack, cheddar, or other melting cheese

Preheat the oven to 375°F. Spray a 12-cup muffin pan well with cooking spray, making sure you get the sides.

Sprinkle 2 tablespoons of the vegetables—a mix or a single veggie—into each muffin cup. Crack the eggs into a liquid measuring cup (for easy pouring) and beat in the turmeric and salt.

Pour an even amount of the egg in each veggie-filled muffin cup, filling them about halfway full (if you overfill them, they will shoot up from the pan like a soufflé and possibly overflow). If using ricotta, spoon 1 teaspoon into the center of each muffin. Top each with 1 tablespoon of the shredded cheese. Bake until set, about 15 minutes. The muffins will puff a little, then sink as they cool. Let cool in the pan on a wire rack for a couple of minutes, then run a butter knife around the inside edges to dislodge and remove the muffins. The muffins will keep in an airtight container in the refrigerator for up to 1 week. Reheat in the toaster oven or serve cold.

NOTE: To make confetti out of your veggies, chop them really small, about the size of confetti, but leave corn and peas whole. Place each in a separate bowl for your kids to pick from. Here are some choices:

YELLOW: yellow bell pepper, yellow squash, or corn

ORANGE: orange bell pepper, carrots

RED: red bell pepper

GREEN: scallions, peas, or green bell pepper

NEUTRAL: peeled zucchini or cauliflower

Swap It Out

- Top your muffins with Green Salsa (page 28) or Roasted Tomato Salsa (page 34).
- Add a little crumbled cooked turkey bacon or sausage to your muffins.
- Omit the cheese for dairy-free kids.
- Add seasonings such as garlic powder, onion powder, Super-Sassy Seasoning (page 117), or whatever spices you know your kids will like.

SPAGHETTI FOR BREAKFAST

Like many kids, my two little munchkins love pasta at all times of the day! So I created a breakfast pasta recipe for them to enjoy. When you think of it, it's not much different from eggs and toast, so why not let your kids "indulge" in spaghetti for breakfast? Just make sure your pasta is a wholesome, whole-grain one and both parents and kids will be happy. If you have spaghetti left over from dinner, you can put it to good use here, and feel free to use any type of pasta, from fettuccine to elbows or spirals. A small amount of turmeric adds to the bright-eyed "sunny" effect of this breakfast dish. Make extra for the adults in the family: I know they'll love it as much as the kids do! *Serves 2 (or 4 littler kids)*

4 large eggs, beaten
½ teaspoon sea salt, plus more to taste
⅛ teaspoon ground turmeric
2 tablespoons unsalted butter or extra-virgin olive oil
1 or 2 garlic cloves, pressed through a garlic press (optional)
4 ounces cooked whole wheat or gluten-free spaghetti noodles
Freshly ground white pepper
Freshly grated Parmesan cheese (optional)

In a large bowl, beat the eggs. Beat in the salt and turmeric. Melt the butter in a large skillet over medium heat. Add the garlic (if using) and stir until fragrant, about 30 seconds. Add the eggs and noodles and stir continuously until the eggs are set and they coat the noodles nicely, about 3 minutes. Season with salt and pepper and serve with a sprinkle of cheese, if you like.

Swap It Out

- For dairy-free kids, cook the eggs in olive oil and omit the cheese.
- Add any healthy toppings you think your kids will like: halved cherry tomatoes, chopped parsley or basil, turkey bacon, or sausage, for starters.

Next Level, Please!

- Swap in soba noodles, made from buckwheat (and often a little wheat), to change up your spaghetti options. Choose 100 percent buckwheat soba if you want it to be gluten-free.
- Stir in a handful of spinach or another tender green such as Swiss chard once your kids are up for adding a little green to their plate.
- Swap in a whole grain such as brown rice or quinoa for the spaghetti.

FLAX OIL TO THE FINISH

Flax oil is a rich source of omega-3 fatty acids; it is great for the heart, brain, and gut, making it a healthy finish to any number of dishes. But only when you add it at the end or whisk it into dressings or other cold preparations, as heat destroys flax's omega-3s by destroying its health-supportive properties. Choose cold-pressed flax oil from the refrigerated section and keep it refrigerated after opening (flax oil can go rancid quickly, and once it's rancid, it goes from healthy to toxic).

SKINNY FRIES

I kicked the fryer to the curb and opted to make these fries a healthy carb companion to a burger (page 100), turkey patty (page 190), or steak (page 99). These skinny fries are wholesome enough to serve as a snack with a little bowlful of marinara sauce (page 203), ketchup, or roasted garlic mayo (page 163) for adults and more adventurous young ones. Try sprinkling on a little Super-Sassy Seasoning or swap the salt for garlic salt. To prep the potatoes in advance, slice them, put them in a bowl of cold water, and refrigerate them for up to eight hours. Drain and pat well to dry just before baking them. Take care to slice the potatoes into equal-size shapes to ensure even browning. This recipe easily doubles to fill up two baking sheets. *Serves 4*

4 medium russet potatoes (about 2 pounds), peeled
2 tablespoons extra-virgin olive oil or melted unrefined coconut oil
Sea salt

Position a rack in the center of the oven and preheat the oven to 450°F.

Cut the potatoes lengthwise into ¼-inch-thick slices (if you have a mandoline, pull it out for this recipe), then cut the slices lengthwise into ¼-inch skinny fry shapes. Pat them dry with paper towels. Place the potatoes in a large bowl, drizzle on the oil, and toss to coat well. Arrange the potatoes on two large baking sheets with a small amount of space between each. Bake until the potatoes are well browned and crisp, tossing them a few times, 35 to 40 minutes. Transfer the fries to a bowl, immediately toss with salt, and serve.

PASS THE KETCHUP, BUT SKIP THE CORN SYRUP

It's America's favorite sweet and savory condiment, and we love to slather it over just about everything. Ketchup has some good things going for it: it's low in calories and high in lycopene, the cancer-combatting, heart-healthy antioxidant found in cooked tomatoes, and it contains a good amount of vitamins A, C, and E. But typical supermarket ketchup is filled with sugar, often in the form of high-fructose corn syrup, and many brands contain chemicals such as MSG in the guise of so-called natural flavorings. Now that you've upgraded your burger (pages 100 and 190), fries (pages 181 and 203), and chicken fingers (page 192), why not do the same for your ketchup? Just choose an organic, low-sugar brand, bring it to the table, and your fast-food makeover will be complete!

SPAGHETTI AND MEATBALLS

This meatball packs in nutrition while leaving out the usual bread crumbs and cheese, making it perfect for gluten- and dairy-free kids and adults. Flax adds fiber and dulse, a form of seaweed, is a concentrated source of minerals. My daughter, Sydney, loves dulse (some say it tastes a little like bacon, so what's not to love?), but you don't have to be a fan of seaweed to flip for these meatballs; even the pickiest of eaters wouldn't know it's in them. If your kids absolutely veto "green stuff" in their food, omit the parsley, but the zucchini that goes into the sauce gets blended in and won't be detected. Serve over your choice of whole wheat or gluten-free spaghetti with or without a little Parm sprinkled on top. *Serves 6 to 8 (makes about 24 meatballs)*

2 pounds ground beef, turkey, or lamb, or a
  combination of beef and lamb
2 tablespoons dried dulse flakes
2 tablespoons golden flax meal
1 tablespoon minced fresh flat-leaf parsley
  (optional)
1 teaspoon Italian seasoning
2 teaspoons garlic powder
2 teaspoons onion powder
1½ teaspoons sea salt
¼ teaspoon freshly ground black pepper
6 cups Secret Red Sauce (page 265)
Cooked whole-grain or gluten-free spaghetti
Grated Parmesan cheese (optional)
Red pepper flakes (optional, for spice-loving
  kids and adults)

In a large bowl, combine the beef, dulse, flax meal, parsley (if using), Italian seasoning, garlic powder, onion powder, salt, and black pepper; wearing disposable gloves or using clean hands, mix very well to incorporate all the ingredients. Form the mixture into about 24 equal-size balls measuring about 1½ inches each. Place them on a plate as they are formed. Set aside.

In a large wide sauté pan (10 to 12 inches wide) rather than a saucepan (so the meatballs will easily fit without crowding), bring the sauce to a simmer over medium heat. Using a slotted spoon, gently add the meatballs to the sauce and lightly stir so the meatballs get coated in the sauce. Return to a simmer, then reduce the heat to low, cover, and simmer for 25 minutes, or until the meatballs are cooked through. Serve the meatballs and sauce over spaghetti, with or without cheese and red pepper flakes sprinkled on top.

GLAZED CARROT COINS

These are no ordinary glazed carrots! You will be surprised at just how delicious a simple carrot dish can be. Not to mention that these carrots are supercharged with bone broth for a boost of flavor that will have the kids coming back for seconds and bonus nutrition to satisfy the health-conscious parent. Serve with turkey patties (page 190) or chicken fingers (page 192) or make them a part of your holiday spread. Don't be tempted to rush as you slice the carrots; take the time to cut them into a uniform size so the coins cook at the same rate and finish with an even coating of glaze. *Serves 4*

1½ tablespoons unsalted butter or unrefined coconut oil
¼ teaspoon ground turmeric
¼ teaspoon ground cinnamon
1½ pounds carrots, cut into ¼-inch rounds
1 cup Basic Bone Broth (page 245), Very Veggie Broth (page 248), or good-quality store-bought broth
3 tablespoons honey or maple syrup
¾ teaspoon sea salt
Splash of fresh lemon juice (optional)

In a large skillet or sauté pan, melt the butter over medium heat. Add the turmeric and cinnamon and stir to dissolve the spices into the butter. Add the carrots and cook, stirring occasionally, until the carrots are well coated in the spices and start to soften, about 5 minutes. Add the broth, honey, and salt, increase the heat to medium-high, and bring to a high simmer. Cook, stirring occasionally and a little more frequently toward the end, until the carrots are soft and the liquid has reduced to a glaze that nicely coats the carrots, 25 to 30 minutes. Add the lemon juice, if desired, and serve.

CHEESY CAULIFLOWER PIZZA

Let's be honest—it's hard to top a real New York–style cheese pizza! But I think we can all agree that pizza is notoriously on top of the "cheat meal" list. That's what makes cauliflower cheese pizza so appealing to me—it's a great fill-in for the real thing that you can enjoy much more often, even regularly if you go easy on the cheese. Note that you'll want to brown this crust really well; the extra baking time is what firms it up. Any toppings you'll find on a traditional pizza will be at home on your cauliflower pizza; just go lightly with them, as this crust is more delicate than a flour-based pizza crust. My kids love spaghetti for breakfast (page 177) and they flip for pizza, so when it's cauliflower pizza night I'll often roll out an extra crust to bake for them in the morning. A breakfast of champions! *Makes one 12-inch pizza*

PIZZA CRUST
1 large head cauliflower (about 2¼ pounds), broken into florets and stems chopped
1 large egg
½ cup shredded mozzarella cheese (about 2 ounces)
¼ cup grated Parmesan cheese
1 teaspoon garlic powder
¼ teaspoon sea salt

TWO OF MY FAVORITE TOPPINGS
Secret Red Sauce (page 265), mozzarella, and basil
Green Salsa (page 28), turkey bacon, and Jack cheese

Preheat the oven to 350°F.

To make the pizza crust: Pulse half the cauliflower in a food processor until broken down into pieces about the size of grains of rice. Spread the cauliflower out over a baking sheet in an even layer. Pulse the remaining cauliflower and spread it out over a second baking sheet in an even layer. Bake, stirring a few times, until the cauliflower is completely dried and lightly browned in some places, about 30 minutes. Remove from the oven and let cool completely.

Increase the oven temperature to 450°F and place a baking sheet turned upside down (so the pizza slides off easily after it comes out of the oven) in it to heat it up like you would a pizza stone (or use a pizza stone if you happen to have one).

Return the cauliflower to the food processor and pulse for about 10 seconds to further break it down. Add the egg, mozzarella, Parmesan, garlic powder, and salt and process for about 20 seconds, scraping down the sides of the processor bowl once or twice, until a dough is formed.

Place the dough on a sheet of parchment

paper. Form the dough into a round about 12 inches in diameter and ¼ inch thick with a rim around the sides to contain the toppings.

Slide the parchment paper onto the preheated baking sheet and bake for 10 to 12 minutes, until well browned. Remove from the oven, add your choice of sauce and toppings, and bake until the toppings are heated through and the sauce is bubbling, about 5 minutes. Remove from the oven, cut into slices, and serve.

Swap It Out

To save time on cauliflower prep, use 2 pounds of store-bought riced cauliflower (you'll find it in the produce aisle of some supermarkets); roast and blend as directed above.

MIX-AND-MATCH SCHOOL LUNCHBOX IDEAS

I hate to admit it, but packing my kids' lunchboxes has always given me anxiety. The two are pretty hard to please when it comes to their take-to-school meals. They generally don't care for sandwiches, and I refuse to give them junk, so I have to be creative if I want them to actually eat what I pack. My solution: make dinners that with a few tweaks can easily be transformed into a lunchbox meal the next day. These are some of my favorite mix-and-match ideas.

THE STAR

Turkey Patties (page 190) with Rich Ranch Dip (page 152)

Roast Chicken (page 143) wrap with mayo

Crispy Baked Chicken Fingers (page 192)

Tuna and Pickle Salad (page 73) sandwich

Chicken and Egg "Fried" Brown Rice (page 93)

Hummus (page 228) and roasted vegetable (page 221) wrap

Confetti Egg and Cheese Mini Muffins (page 175)

PBJ and banana whole wheat tortilla pinwheels

THE EXTRAS

Glazed Carrot Coins (page 183)

Sweet-and-Salty Sweet Potato Salad (page 208)

Cucumber slices with Rich Ranch Dip (page 152)

Celery sticks with nut butter

Cherry or grape tomatoes

Hummus (page 228)

Nut mixes (pages 233 to 235)

Guacamole (page 227)

Pickle (page 257)

THE FINISH

Berries, grapes, an orange, or a banana

Dried apples

Mini fruit kebabs

Cinnamon-Swirl Greek Yogurt (page 231)

Any Berry Fruit Leather (page 239)

Chunky Chocolate Chip Cookies (page 285)

Cocoa Maca-Roons (page 283)

A+ MAC AND CHEESE

Mac and cheese is an all-time kids' favorite. But unfortunately it's usually served up in the form of white flour pasta and processed cheese that's full of toxic chemicals. My kids like their mac and cheese light and scoopable, but you could add a second egg for a firmer casserole. And I encourage you to experiment with other cheeses such as Gruyère or Jack or a mixture. This dish is really hard to mess up, so go for it!

Serves 6

Sea salt
16 ounces whole-grain macaroni
1 large egg
1 cup whole milk
1 cup Secret White Sauce (page 263)
½ teaspoon onion powder
¼ teaspoon paprika (optional)
¼ teaspoon freshly ground black pepper
¼ teaspoon ground turmeric (optional)
1 pound cheddar cheese, coarsely grated (about 6 cups)

Preheat the oven to 375°F.

Meanwhile, bring a large pot of water to a boil and salt it. Add the macaroni and cook until al dente according to the package directions. Drain and return to the pot.

In a large bowl, whisk the egg with the milk and white sauce, then whisk in 1 teaspoon salt, the onion powder, paprika (if using), the pepper, and turmeric, (if using). Add the liquid mixture and 4 cups of the cheese to the macaroni while it is still hot and mix well to fully coat it.

Transfer the mixture to an 8 x 11-inch baking dish and sprinkle the remaining 2 cups cheese over the top. Bake for 25 to 30 minutes, until bubbling hot and browned in spots. Let sit for 5 minutes, then serve.

PICKY EATER'S TURKEY PATTIES

These mini burgers are always a hit with kids, and if there were a parents' clever chef award, you would win it for serving up this recipe! The patties are a complete meal, with added fiber from the zucchini (which becomes invisible after peeling and grating) and flax and a hit of whole grains from the quinoa. Serve with Skinny Fries (page 181) or Zucchini Fries (page 203), and bigger kids will love them made into full-size burgers nestled into a bun. You can double or triple the recipe and freeze batches of patties unbaked (freeze them on a baking sheet for about an hour, until solid, then put them in freezer bags) for a no-stress, no-fuss anytime meal. *Makes about 12 patties*

1 small zucchini (about 5 ounces)
1 pound ground turkey
½ cup cooked quinoa, millet, or brown rice (see page 219)
2 tablespoons grated Parmesan cheese
1 tablespoon golden flax meal
1 teaspoon onion powder
1 teaspoon garlic powder
1 teaspoon sea salt
¼ teaspoon freshly ground black pepper
Unrefined coconut oil
Big-Batch Marinara Sauce (page 203), for serving

Peel and finely grate the zucchini (save the skins to make Zucchini Skin Chips; page 191). Take small handfuls of the zucchini and wring out as much of its liquid as you can (add it to a soup or smoothie or pour it into a shot glass, add a pinch of salt, and bottoms up!).

Put the zucchini in a large bowl and add all the remaining ingredients except the oil and marinara. Wearing disposable gloves or using just-washed hands, mix very well to incorporate all the ingredients. Form the mixture into about twelve 2½-inch patties, placing them on a plate or baking sheet as they are formed.

Heat a large skillet over medium heat. Add just enough oil to coat the bottom of the pan. Add half the patties and cook for 3 to 4 minutes, until lightly browned on the bottom. Flip and cook for 3 to 4 minutes more, until lightly browned on the second side and cooked through. Transfer to a plate and repeat with the remaining patties.

Serve with marinara sauce.

Next Level, Please!

Add 1 teaspoon dulse granules to the patties for added minerals. Read about dulse on page 76.

ZUCCHINI SKIN CHIPS

Parents of green-fearing kids will peel their zucchini before slipping it into a burger or sauce, but if you take that skin and make it into a chip, your kid might give zucchini chips a chance! These are so tasty, you'll be searching for ways to cook up naked zucchini just so you'll be left with the skins. To make zucchini skin chips, simply toss the skins in a little melted coconut oil or olive oil, sprinkle with salt, lay them out on a toaster oven pan or in a small pan in an oven preheated to 375°F, and toast for about 10 minutes, until crispy. Zucchini chips also make a great soup or salad garnish.

CRISPY BAKED CHICKEN FINGERS

When your kids say no to everything but nuggets, knock these out at home and you'll transform a fast-food favorite to a truly healthy snack or dinner. They're really simple to put together: just give the chicken a soak in yogurt to tenderize it, then coat in bread crumbs, finish with a quick misting of oil, and bake until crisp. To prep your fingers in advance, soak and coat the chicken in bread crumbs, place on a baking sheet, freeze for about 1 hour, until solid, then put them in freezer bags and store in the freezer. Then you can put them in the oven on demand (increase the baking time by about ten minutes) in less time than it takes to get to the drive-thru. *Serves 4 to 6*

1 pound boneless, skinless chicken breasts
1 teaspoon garlic powder
¾ teaspoon sea salt
¼ teaspoon freshly ground white or black pepper
½ cup plain yogurt
1½ cups finely ground Sprouted Wheat Bread Crumbs (page 57), or store-bought whole-grain or gluten-free bread crumbs
Unrefined coconut oil cooking spray
Big-Batch Marinara Sauce (page 203), Rich Ranch Dip (page 152), or ketchup, for serving

Cut the tenders from the chicken breasts, leaving them whole, and put them in a large bowl. Slice the rest of the chicken into 1 by 3-inch "fingers" and put them in the bowl with the tenders. Add the garlic powder, salt, and pepper and toss to coat the chicken with the seasonings. Add the yogurt and stir to coat the chicken well. Leave on the counter for 30 minutes or cover and refrigerate up to overnight.

Preheat the oven to 400°F. Line a baking sheet with parchment paper.

Pour the bread crumbs into a shallow bowl. Remove the chicken fingers one piece at a time from the yogurt, allowing excess to drip off, then dredge them in the bread crumbs. Place them on the prepared baking sheet as they are ready, leaving a little space between them. Lightly coat them with cooking spray and bake until the coating is lightly browned and the chicken is cooked through, about 15 minutes. Place on a plate for grabbing and serve with marinara sauce, ranch, or ketchup for dipping.

Worthy Complements

DELECTABLE SIDE DISHES

A side dish that's worthy of my table can stand on its own but also complements a main dish with class, and that's what this chapter is all about! I've included twists on familiar recipes, such as my light yet creamy spinach (page 207), a mayo-less potato salad made with sweet potatoes (page 208), and a take on coleslaw dressed with a limey peanut butter sauce (page 213). I've shared my reliable way of cooking brown rice (page 219), an introduction to black rice (page 220), and a black-eyed pea dish (page 217) to bring you good luck. You'll find roasted broccoli (page 204) that you don't need to turn the oven on for, winter squash (pages 210 and 212) that you don't need a cleaver to cut into, and a selection of greens, including my famous West Coast Southern Greens (page 197). A cheesy quinoa and rice bake (page 222) sneaks in cauliflower, zucchini, and bone broth in the form of my super-nutritious secret sauce. Roasted potatoes are a family favorite; my recipe (page 221) adds a couple more roots to expand your roasted veggie repertoire. And zucchini fries (page 203) will become an instant family favorite. Nutritious, no-fuss, and convenient, these sides bring some serious flavor to the table!

WEST COAST SOUTHERN GREENS

It is impossible to talk about soul food, cuisine that originated in African American culture, without including Southern greens in the conversation. This dish is a time-honored tradition in Southern kitchens; it is traditionally prepared with a ham hock or salt pork, but I like to use smoked turkey. If you can't find smoked turkey, fresh will do; you'll still get lots of flavor, just not that smokiness. Oftentimes freshly baked cornbread (page 200) is served with greens to sop up the vitamin-filled broth produced by simmering the turkey and greens. And, of course, I had to put my own twist on this recipe to make it fit into a healthy lifestyle. *Serves 6*

1 smoked or plain turkey leg
1 tablespoon extra-virgin olive oil
1 large onion, finely chopped
3 garlic cloves, minced
2 tablespoons Super-Sassy Seasoning (page 117)
½ teaspoon freshly ground black pepper
½ teaspoon red pepper flakes (optional)
½ teaspoon mustard powder
1 teaspoon sea salt, plus more to taste
1 tablespoon smooth natural (no-sugar-added) peanut butter
1 tablespoon tamari or soy sauce
2 teaspoons white wine vinegar
1 bunch mustard greens, stemmed, leaves chopped
1 bunch collard greens, stemmed, leaves chopped
1 bunch kale, preferably curly kale, stemmed, leaves chopped

Pour 8 cups water into a large pot (large enough to hold all the greens). Add the turkey leg and bring the water to a boil over high heat. Reduce the heat to medium-low, cover, and cook until the meat begins to fall off the bone, about 45 minutes. Transfer the turkey leg to a bowl, let cool, then remove and discard the skin and pull apart the turkey meat (save the bones for your next batch of Basic Bone Broth, page 245). Pour the turkey broth into a measuring cup or container.

Wipe out the pot, add the oil, and heat over medium-high heat. Add the onion and cook, stirring often, for about 5 minutes, until softened. Add the garlic and cook for about 1 minute, until aromatic. Add the Super-Sassy Seasoning, black pepper, red pepper flakes (if using), mustard powder, and salt and cook, stirring often, for 1 minute. Add the peanut butter, tamari, and vinegar and stir to dissolve the peanut butter. Stir in 2 cups of the turkey broth (save the rest to start your next batch of Basic Bone Broth or pour it into a mug, add a pinch of salt, and enjoy it as a light sipping broth), bring to a simmer, and cook for 5 minutes to combine the flavors. Add the greens, cover the pan (at this point the pot likely will be too full to stir), and cook for about 5 minutes, until the greens are wilted. Uncover the pan and cook, stirring occasionally, until the greens are well coated in sauce and as soft as you like them, adding more turkey broth if needed. I like to go for about 30 minutes, but if you like your greens more on the steamed side, feel free to go for less. Add the shredded turkey to the pot, stir, and cook to heat through. Taste and add more salt if needed.

OFF YOUR KALE?

Fun fact: So important was kale to the traditional Scottish diet that to "be off your kale" meant you were too ill to eat. Americans have caught on to kale mania, with recipes for kale chips, kale smoothies, and kale salad sweeping the nation. The kale trend is one that's definitely worth following, and I extend my love for leafy greens to collards. Collard greens are Southern comfort food, typically cooked low and slow with a ham hock for flavor. My West Coast way of making collards swaps in turkey and shortens the cooking time for optimal nutrition. And optimally nutritious is a fitting description for these cruciferous family members! They are packed with folate and phytochemicals to support brain function, they are a great nondairy source of calcium, they contain lots of fiber, iron, vitamins C, A, and K, and they are full of cancer-defensive compounds. Most days you'll find me eating a serving of kale, collards, or another leafy green, or I'll combine the two with mustard greens to make my West Coast Southern Greens. The days when I'm off my kale are few and far between!

CORNBREAD DRESSING

This is one of my favorite dishes ever! Cornbread dressing is always a part of my Thanksgiving spread. I enjoy it so much that I would make it on a weekly basis if I were able to exercise self-control and keep myself from going back for seconds, thirds, and fourths! There is something about this cornbread dressing that just keeps calling me back. Maybe it's the sweet-and-savoriness or the mix of the soft and crunchy texture. Whatever it is, I am very proud of this recipe, and I hope you love it just as much as I do!

Serves 8

2 tablespoons unsalted butter or unrefined coconut oil, plus more for the baking dish
1 large onion, chopped
3 celery stalks, chopped
8 ounces ground turkey (not extra lean)
1 teaspoon sea salt
2 teaspoons Super-Sassy Seasoning (page 117)
1 teaspoon paprika
1 teaspoon freshly ground black pepper
1 tablespoon chopped fresh thyme
1 tablespoon chopped fresh sage
1 recipe Skillet Cornbread (recipe follows) or cornbread made from a mix, preferably a day or two old
2 large eggs, beaten
About 2½ cups Basic Bone Broth (page 245) or good-quality store-bought broth

Preheat the oven to 400°F. Grease a 9 by 13-inch casserole dish.

In a large skillet, melt the butter over medium heat. Add the onion and celery and cook, stirring, until slightly softened, about 5 minutes. Add the turkey and salt and cook, breaking up the turkey with a wooden spoon as it cooks, until cooked through with no pink spots remaining, 5 to 7 minutes. Add the Super-Sassy Seasoning, paprika, and pepper and cook, stirring, for 1 minute. Stir in the thyme and sage and remove from the heat.

In a large bowl, break the cornbread into small chunks (some pieces will crumble, which is okay). Stir in the onion-turkey mixture, then add the eggs and stir them in well. Stir in enough broth to make the mixture moist enough to hold its shape when pressed, but not so much that it becomes runny. Transfer the mixture to the prepared casserole dish, cover with aluminum foil, and bake for 35 minutes, then remove the foil and bake for 20 minutes more, or until the top is fully set and nicely browned. Remove from the oven, let sit for 10 minutes, then serve.

Skillet Cornbread

Makes one 10-inch cornbread

1½ cups medium-grind cornmeal
1 cup white rice flour or cup-for-cup
    replacement gluten-free flour blend, such as
    Steve's GF Cake Flour
1 tablespoon golden flax meal
¾ teaspoon baking powder
¾ teaspoon baking soda
½ teaspoon sea salt
2 large eggs
1¾ cups buttermilk
¼ cup honey
½ cup (1 stick) unsalted butter, cut into pieces

Preheat the oven to 375°F and position an oven rack in the middle position.

Put a 10-inch cast-iron skillet in the oven for 10 minutes to heat it up.

In a large bowl, whisk together the cornmeal flour, rice flour, flax meal, baking powder, baking soda, and salt. In a separate bowl, beat the eggs, then whisk in the buttermilk and honey. Add the wet ingredients to the dry ingredients and whisk just until blended. Immediately remove the pan from the oven and add the butter, swirling the pan until the butter is melted. Pour all but 1 tablespoon of the butter into the cornmeal mixture (leave the remaining butter to grease the pan) and gently but quickly whisk it in.

Pour the batter into the skillet and bake for 25 to 30 minutes, until the edges and sides start to brown, the top begins to crack, and a toothpick inserted in the center comes out clean. Allow to cool for about 10 minutes, then serve straight from the pan or turn out onto a wire rack and cool completely.

BAKED ZUCCHINI FRIES WITH MARINARA DIPPING SAUCE

Zucchini is the chameleon of the vegetable world: you can sneak it into red or white sauce (pages 263 and 265) or turkey patties (page 190), blend a little into hummus, even work it into dessert (page 277). Or turn it into this crave-worthy fry that won't break the calorie bank. This recipe is one that will quickly become a favorite for both weeknight meals and entertaining! *Serves 4*

Extra-virgin olive oil or unrefined coconut oil cooking spray
5 small zucchini
3 large egg whites
½ teaspoon sea salt
1 cup fine Sprouted Wheat Bread Crumbs (page 57)
¼ cup grated Parmesan cheese
1 teaspoon Super-Sassy Seasoning (page 117)
¼ teaspoon freshly ground black pepper
Big-Batch Marinara Sauce (recipe follows) or Rich Ranch Dip (page 152)

Preheat the oven to 425°F. Coat a baking sheet with cooking spray.

Quarter the zucchini lengthwise, then cut each wedge in half to make 8 thick fry shapes.

In a shallow bowl, beat the egg whites until frothy. Beat in ¼ teaspoon of the salt. In a separate shallow bowl, combine the bread crumbs, cheese, Super-Sassy Seasoning, remaining ¼ teaspoon salt, and the pepper.

One at a time, dip the zucchini wedges into the egg white, let the excess drip off, then give them a toss in the bread crumb mixture to fully coat. Place the fries on the prepared baking sheet as you coat them and spray with cooking spray. Roast for about 10 minutes, then flip the fries and roast for another 10 minutes, or until browned and crisp all over. Serve with a bowl of marinara sauce or ranch for dipping.

Big-Batch Marinara Sauce

I like to make a big pot of marinara, pack it up, and have it in the freezer for whenever zucchini fries or chicken fingers (page 192) are on the menu. Five minutes active time for several meals' worth of sauce! *Makes about 5 cups*

1 tablespoon extra-virgin olive oil
1 small onion, finely chopped
2 garlic cloves, pressed through a garlic press

2 teaspoons Italian seasoning
1 (28-ounce) can tomato puree
¾ teaspoon sea salt, plus more to taste
½ teaspoon freshly ground black pepper, plus
    more to taste
¼ cup finely chopped fresh basil (optional)

In a large saucepan, heat the oil over medium heat. Add the onion and cook for about 5 minutes, until softened. Add the garlic and cook, stirring often, for about 1 minute, until aromatic. Stir in the Italian seasoning and cook, stirring often, for 30 seconds. Add the tomato puree, then fill the can halfway with water and stir the water into the pan. Add the salt and pepper, increase the heat to medium-high, and bring to a boil. Reduce the heat to low, partially cover, and cook, stirring occasionally, for 1 hour to develop the flavors, adding a little more water if the sauce starts to get too thick. Stir in the basil (if using), then taste and add more salt and/or pepper if needed.

PAN-ROASTED BROCCOLI

You don't have to crank up the oven to achieve the deep, toasty flavors we all love in a roasted vegetable. Broccoli can make a similar transformation on the stovetop, with crisp-tender, well browned, and slightly caramelized results. Trust me, if you find getting in your greens to be a chore, when you cook broccoli this way, you'll find yourself clamoring for more! The trick is to simultaneously sear and steam the broccoli, cooking it at a fairly high heat with the lid on and only stirring once. I throw in half a lime, and when the dish is done, the juice doubles and deepens in flavor, giving the citrus even more gusto. I like to peel the broccoli stems, cut them into matchstick pieces, and add them at the end as a crunchy raw garnish. And don't forget to include the leaves from the broccoli, as they are every bit as nutritious and delicious as the florets.

Serves 4

1 tablespoon extra-virgin olive oil or unrefined
    coconut oil
1 medium head broccoli, cut into florets, stems
    peeled and cut into matchsticks
Sea salt and freshly ground black pepper
½ lime

In a large skillet with a lid, heat the oil over medium-high heat and swirl to coat the bottom of the pan with the oil. Add the broccoli florets to the pan, season with salt and pepper, and lay the lime cut-side down in the pan. Cover and cook for 2 to 3 minutes without stirring, until the broccoli is well seared on the bottom. Turn the broccoli, cover again, and cook for 2 minutes or so more, until the broccoli is well seared on the second side and just tender. Stir in the raw broccoli stems. Squeeze the seared lime over the broccoli, stir until the juice has been absorbed, and serve topped with the broccoli stems.

Swap It Out

- Try cauliflower instead of broccoli; cauliflower is firmer than broccoli, so you'll want to cut it into smaller florets before cooking.
- Add a touch of grated lime zest, some red pepper flakes, or a sprinkling of Parmesan or Sprouted Wheat Bread Crumbs (page 57) to the finished dish.
- Top with a spoonful of Fresh Herb Cheese Spread (page 151) or Rich Ranch Dip (page 152).

Next Level, Please!

- Cook the second half of the lime in the pan in the same way and save it to add a deep lime flavor to your next salad dressing.
- Finish the broccoli with a sprinkling of dulse granules (see page 76) for a mineral boost.

LIGHT-AND-CREAMY SPINACH

I've never been a fan of traditional creamed spinach—it always seems to be overcooked, off-color, and dripping with cream—but some of the "light" versions that skip the fat altogether leave my kids and me less than satisfied. My take on the classic uses half cream, half milk, and is blended with lots of roasted garlic to up the creaminess while adding nutrition, flavor, and a subtle sweetness. The sauce skips a step by requiring no cooking—it heats up when the just-made spinach is blended into the mix. To avoid a watery sauce, drain and press excess liquid from the cooked spinach (the liquid itself is full of flavor; add a pinch of salt and enjoy it as a green drink shot) before adding it to the cream sauce. *Serves 4*

¼ cup milk
¼ cup heavy cream
Cloves from 1 head Toaster Oven Roasted
    Garlic (page 47)
1 teaspoon fresh lemon juice, plus more to taste
½ teaspoon sea salt, plus more to taste
¼ teaspoon freshly ground white or black
    pepper, plus more to taste
¼ teaspoon freshly grated nutmeg
1 pound baby spinach leaves

In a food processor, combine the milk, cream, roasted garlic, lemon juice, salt, pepper, and nutmeg and process until smooth.

Pour ¼ cup water into a large saucepan, place over medium-high heat, and bring to a simmer. Add the spinach, cover, and cook until almost fully wilted, 4 to 5 minutes. Remove the cover and stir until the spinach is evenly wilted. Drain (add a pinch of salt to the fortified spinach juice and drink it, if you'd like), then immediately transfer to the food processor with the milk mixture and pulse until blended to your liking, anywhere from a few seconds for a coarse chop to a minute or two for a fine puree for kids who aren't into chunks. Taste and add more lemon juice, salt, and/or pepper if needed.

SWEET-AND-SALTY SWEET POTATO SALAD

Everyone has their own idea of how a good potato salad should taste. I have enjoyed many different versions, but in coming up with my own recipe, I wanted to create something a little untraditional. So I went with my favorite, sweet potatoes! And because mayo tends to smother a potato salad, I've used a vinegar-based dressing. When you stir the dressing into hot-from-the-pan sweet potatoes, the limey, slightly sweet, and pungent flavors make their mark on the potatoes while the salad remains pleasingly light. Serve hot, warm, or at room temperature. *Serves 6*

FOOD *for* LIFE

1½ tablespoons red wine vinegar
1 teaspoon grated lime zest
3 tablespoons fresh lime juice
1 medium shallot, minced
1 tablespoon brown sugar
1 teaspoon Dijon mustard
½ teaspoon paprika, plus more for sprinkling
1¾ teaspoons sea salt
¼ teaspoon freshly ground black pepper
3 tablespoons extra-virgin olive oil
2 pounds sweet potatoes (3 large), peeled and cut into ½-inch cubes
1 small celery stalk, finely chopped
3 tablespoons thinly sliced fresh chives, plus more for sprinkling
2 turkey bacon slices, cooked until crisp and crumbled (optional)

In a small bowl, whisk together the vinegar, lime zest, lime juice, shallot, brown sugar, mustard, paprika, salt, and pepper. Whisk in the oil until emulsified. Place the sweet potatoes in a steamer basket set over a pot filled with a couple inches of simmering water. Cover and steam until tender when poked with a knife or fork, about 15 minutes. Transfer the sweet potatoes from the steamer to a large bowl and while still hot, pour the dressing over the sweet potatoes and toss to coat. Stir in the celery and chives and serve with the bacon (if desired), and a little paprika and chives sprinkled on top. Let cool slightly and serve warm, or cool completely and serve at room temperature.

Swap It Out

- Try half sweet potatoes, half white potatoes, or all white potatoes. If you find red or purple heirloom potatoes at your farmers' market, give them a go! Or swap in chunks of butternut squash or another type of winter squash.
- In place of the turkey bacon garnish, finish the dish with slivered toasted almonds.
- To give the salad a little Asian flavor, substitute 1 teaspoon toasted sesame oil for a portion of the olive oil, swap in scallions for the chives, and finish with a sprinkling of toasted black or tan sesame seeds.

SPAGHETTI SQUASH, SEVEN WAYS

Opening up a tough-skinned winter squash can be intimidating at best and near impossible without a well-sharpened chef's knife. But when you roast your squash whole, it collapses into submission and a knife will go through it like butter. Try this method with any winter squash, such as butternut (see the next recipe), acorn, or kabocha. While spaghetti squash tastes more like squash than spaghetti, it's fun to separate into noodlelike strands, and it takes well to many of the sauces that finish a bowl of pasta. Here I've shared seven of my favorites. *Serves 4 to 6*

1 medium spaghetti squash (3 to 3½ pounds)
Topping of choice (see suggestions at right)

Preheat the oven to 350°F.

Wash the squash and place it on a baking sheet. Carefully prick it in a few places with a sharp knife. Bake for 1½ to 2 hours, until the flesh is easily pierced with a knife and the squash starts to collapse. Set aside until cool enough to handle, then cut the squash in half and scoop out the fiber and seeds. Use a fork to scrape the flesh from the skin into strands; discard the skin. Transfer to a serving bowl and top with the sauce of your choice.

SEVEN TOPPING SUGGESTIONS

1. Green Salsa (page 28)

2. Roasted Tomato Salsa (page 34)

3. Big-Batch Marinara Sauce (page 203)

4. Super-Sassy and Simple: Extra-virgin olive oil, a little Super-Sassy Seasoning (page 117), and sea salt

5. Garlic Butter: Melt 2 tablespoons unsalted butter and add 2 minced garlic cloves, ½ teaspoon dried oregano, and ¼ teaspoon red pepper flakes. Squeeze in a little lemon juice. Season with salt and sprinkle with Parmesan cheese if you like.

6. Cinnamon Coconut: Melt 2 tablespoons unrefined coconut oil and add 1½ tablespoons shredded coconut, ½ teaspoon ground cinnamon, 1 tablespoon pure maple syrup, and sea salt

7. Toasted Sesame: 1 tablespoon toasted sesame oil, 1 minced scallion, and sea salt

PURE AND SIMPLE SQUASH PUREE

Silky, creamy, and smooth are the words that best describe this fall comfort side dish. Just a touch of coconut milk brings the puree together while allowing the pure flavor of the squash to shine through. If your kids would like a little more sweetness, add a small amount of maple syrup or honey. And while the oven's on, why not toast some nuts (see page 261) or throw in a second squash? Or be really efficient and fill up a second baking sheet; your oven will comfortably hold four squash. Puree everything or leave some in chunks; pop it all into the freezer and have it ready to thaw when you need a side to serve with almost any supper. *Serves 4 to 6*

1 medium butternut squash (about 3 pounds)
½ cup unsweetened coconut milk
½ teaspoon sea salt, plus more to taste
Splash of fresh lemon juice (optional)

Preheat the oven to 350°F. Line a roasting pan or baking sheet with parchment paper.

Wash the squash and place it on the prepared pan. Carefully prick it in a few places with a sharp knife. Bake for 1½ to 2 hours, until the skin is papery, the flesh is easily pierced with a knife, and the squash starts to collapse. Remove from the oven and set aside until cool enough to handle, then peel away the skin, cut the squash in half, and scoop out the fiber and seeds. Break the squash into rough chunks and put the chunks in a food processor. Add the coconut milk and salt and process until very smooth, about 2 minutes, stopping to scrape down the sides of the processor bowl a couple of times. Taste and add more salt if needed and a splash of lemon juice for a hit of brightness if you like.

Swap It Out

- Swap in heavy cream for the coconut milk or half cream and half milk for a lighter puree.
- Add a touch of cinnamon, cardamom, or pumpkin pie spice to flavor your puree.
- Swap in the squash for the sweet potato in my Pecan Sweet Potato Pie Oatmeal Parfait (page 29).

Next Level, Please!

Thin your puree out with some Basic Bone Broth (page 245) or Very Veggie Broth (page 248) to make a simple creamy butternut squash soup.

PEANUT BUTTER CITRUS SLAW

Crunchy cabbage slathered in a slightly sweet, limey peanut butter dressing sets this salad apart from your basic picnic fare. And without the mayo, there's no worry about spoilage on the buffet table on a hot summer's day. If peanut allergies are a concern, swap in almond butter for the peanut butter and toasted almonds for the peanut garnish. *Serves 4*

1 small green cabbage (about 2 pounds)
3 tablespoons fresh lime juice, plus more to taste
1 tablespoon natural (no-sugar-added) smooth peanut butter
1 tablespoon pure maple syrup
2 garlic cloves, pressed through a garlic press
Pinch of ground turmeric
Pinch of cayenne pepper
½ teaspoon sea salt, plus more to taste
3 tablespoons extra-virgin olive oil
¼ cup chopped fresh mint
1 scallion, thinly sliced
¼ cup chopped roasted peanuts (page 261; optional)

Halve and core the cabbage, then very thinly slice it (or slice it in a food processor with the slicing blade) and place it in a large bowl.

In a small bowl, combine the lime juice, peanut butter, maple syrup, garlic, turmeric, cayenne pepper, and salt and whisk to dissolve the peanut butter. Whisk in the oil until emulsified. Add the dressing to the cabbage and mix very well (you can use your hands if you don't mind getting a little messy) to coat the cabbage. Stir in the mint, scallion, and peanuts. Taste and add more salt and/or lime juice if needed.

Swap It Out

- Add 1 tablespoon unsweetened shredded coconut for a hint of the tropics.
- Use half red cabbage, half green cabbage, or all red cabbage. Or try a different type of cabbage such as napa or savoy.
- Add grated carrot for color and a bit of beta-carotene.

GREEN BEANS WITH TURKEY BACON

Green beans have always been one of my favorite vegetables. When I visited my grandmother's house as a kid, I would always ask her to open up a can of green beans for me. Well, times have changed and I no longer eat them out of a can now that I know how much tastier and more nutritious fresh beans are. Here's my trick for par cooking green beans to crisp-tender perfection: Add them to boiling water, turn off the heat, cover, leave for five minutes, then drain. For their final sear in the skillet, resist the urge to stir the green beans for the first two minutes so they can get good and browned in spots. Vegetarians can skip the turkey bacon or swap in tempeh bacon. *Serves 4*

Sea salt
12 ounces green beans, ends trimmed
2 turkey bacon slices
2 teaspoons extra-virgin olive oil
1 teaspoon Super-Sassy Seasoning (page 117)
¼ teaspoon sea salt, plus more to taste
2 teaspoons sherry vinegar or white balsamic
   vinegar, plus more to taste
2 tablespoons slivered almonds, toasted
   (optional)

Bring a large saucepan of water to a boil and salt the water. Add the green beans, turn off the heat, and cover the pan. Leave for 5 minutes, then drain; shake the strainer to remove as much water as possible.

While the beans are cooking, place the turkey bacon in a large skillet over medium heat. Cook for 8 to 10 minutes, to desired crispness, turning a few times. Remove the turkey bacon from the pan, let cool slightly, then cut it into ¼-inch matchstick strips down the length of the bacon strips.

In the same pan, heat the oil over medium-high heat. Add the green beans and cook, without stirring, for 2 minutes. Add the Super-Sassy Seasoning and ¼ teaspoon salt and cook, stirring, for about 2 minutes, until the green beans are crisp-tender and browned in spots. Add the vinegar and cook, stirring, for about 30 seconds, until it is fully soaked into the green beans. Taste and add more salt or vinegar if needed. Top with the bacon and almonds, if desired.

Swap It Out

- Try yellow wax beans instead of the green beans, or use a mix of the two.
- If you don't have my Super-Sassy Seasoning handy, swap in ¼ teaspoon garlic powder, ¼ teaspoon onion powder, ¼ teaspoon dried thyme, and ¼ teaspoon freshly ground black pepper.

BLACK-EYED PEAS AND SAUSAGE

In the South, black-eyed peas are traditionally served on New Year's Day to bring good luck. Well, I feel fortunate any day that this high-protein side dish makes its way to my dinner table. It's a cinch to make—if you've got frozen or canned beans in the house, you're halfway there, and if you double it up, serve with a grain and a salad such as my Simple Red Cabbage Salad (page 59), you've got a full spread. Sometimes I'll finish the dish with a poached egg or two: when the dish is done, crack the eggs on top, cover the pan, and poach until the whites are just set. *Serves 4*

2 teaspoons extra-virgin olive oil
1 large fresh chorizo or other sausage (about 5 ounces)
1 small yellow onion, finely chopped
1 medium carrot, cut into ¼-inch cubes
2 garlic cloves, minced
½ cup Basic Bone Broth (page 245), Very Veggie Broth (page248), or good-quality store-bought broth
½ teaspoon sea salt, plus more to taste
¼ teaspoon freshly ground black pepper, plus more to taste
1¾ cups thawed frozen black-eyed peas, or 1 (15-ounce) can, drained and rinsed
1 teaspoon apple cider vinegar or red wine vinegar, plus more to taste
1½ tablespoons chopped fresh flat-leaf parsley
1 teaspoon chopped fresh thyme

In a large skillet, heat the oil over medium-high heat. Remove the sausage from its casing and crumble it into the pan. Add the onion, carrot, and garlic and cook, stirring often, until the sausage is cooked through and lightly browned and the vegetables are slightly softened. Add the broth and salt and pepper, bring to a simmer, then reduce the heat and cook for about 10 minutes, until the vegetables have softened and the broth has reduced slightly. Add the peas and cook for 5 minutes to heat them through and bring the flavors together. Add the vinegar, parsley, and thyme. Taste and add more vinegar, salt, and/or pepper if needed.

Next Level, Please!

- Use dried, cooked black-eyed peas instead of frozen ones. To learn how to cook beans from scratch, see page 107.
- Add a handful of kale, chard, or spinach leaves at the end and stir until wilted.
- When you add the broth, add 1 teaspoon dulse granules for extra minerals and a slightly smoky flavor accent.

BAKED SWEET POTATOES WITH CINNAMON AND VANILLA

You won't believe what a sprinkling of cinnamon and a drizzle of vanilla do to pop the flavor of a sweet potato. This simple but decadent-tasting recipe always makes me thank God for creating sweet potatoes! *Serves 4*

4 medium sweet potatoes
1 teaspoon pure vanilla extract
½ teaspoon ground cinnamon
2 tablespoons unrefined coconut oil or grass-fed butter, melted
Sea salt

Preheat the oven to 400°F. Line a baking sheet with parchment paper.

Scrub the sweet potatoes and prick them in several places with a fork. Place them on the prepared baking sheet and bake for 40 to 50 minutes, until thoroughly soft and beginning to ooze. Remove from the oven.

In a small bowl, whisk the vanilla and cinnamon into the oil. Cut the sweet potatoes down the middle and pour the flavored oil onto the hot sweet potato flesh. Sprinkle with salt and serve.

Swap It Out

- Swap yams for the sweet potatoes. Yams can look like sweet potatoes but are generally white or cream colored on the inside and starchier than sweet potatoes.

CINNAMON, NO SUGAR

Though it's commonly mixed with sugar, cinnamon on its own has been shown to help *control* our sugar by lowering fasting blood glucose levels. Cinnamon can also help digestion, relieve gas, lower blood pressure, and work as an anti-inflammatory in relieving pain and stiffness of muscles and joints. Its flavor—aromatic, pungent, and warming—makes this spice equally at home in sweet and savory dishes. And as cinnamon aids absorption of nutrients, I encourage you to use it liberally, in dishes as diverse as my Sweet-and-Salty Cinnamon Pecans (page 234), Baked Sweet Potatoes with Cinnamon and Vanilla, and North African–Inspired Chickpea Bowl (page 83). And instead of sugar, mix cinnamon with a little honey to make a bowlful of Cinnamon-Swirl Greek Yogurt (page 231).

30-MINUTE BROWN RICE

Believe it or not, it has taken me some years to figure out how to get good results when I make brown rice. Brown rice is fussy and can easily turn out sticky, mushy, or tough. So instead of cooking it the standard way, which takes about forty-five minutes, I boil it pasta style and have it on the table in thirty minutes. You'll save an extra five minutes or so (and make your rice more digestible) if you take the extra step of soaking your rice the night before—just put the rice in a bowl, add water to cover by a couple of inches, cover with a kitchen towel, and set aside to soak for 8 to 24 hours, then drain.

Brown rice freezes well, so you can cook up extra, portion it out into freezer bags, store in the freezer, and thaw one whenever you're in need of a grain for dinner. *Serves 4*

1 cup brown rice
1½ teaspoons sea salt

In a large saucepan, bring 2 quarts water to a boil over high heat. Add the rice and salt, return to a boil, then reduce the heat to medium-high and boil for 30 minutes, or until cooked to al dente (reduce the cooking time to 25 minutes if you soaked your rice the night before). Drain the rice in the strainer and give it a few good shakes to remove excess water. Return the rice to the pan, cover, and set aside for about 10 minutes to steam and absorb the last of the moisture. Fluff with a fork and serve.

SOAKING GRAINS

Soaking is a simple way of making grains (and legumes) more digestible. The outer layer or bran of whole grains contains a substance called phytic acid, which can bind with a number of minerals to block their absorption in the body. Enzyme inhibitors, which can interfere with digestion, are also found in whole grains. Soaking your grains (eight to twelve hours is ideal, but a little less or a little more is fine) and then discarding the soaking water works to neutralize the phytic acid and breaks down those enzyme inhibitors. Soaking grains takes a little forethought, but in the end it makes you a more efficient cook, as it cuts down on cooking time.

COCONUT BLACK RICE

This rice dish, a stunning deep purplish-black color with a satisfying nutty flavor, turns an everyday side into a showstopper. Equally impressive is the nutritional profile of black rice: it's rich in iron, contains a high level of an antioxidant class called anthocyanins (the same one that gives red cabbage, blueberries, açaí berries, and grapes their purplish color and superfood status), and has its fiber-rich bran intact, just like brown rice. And as an added bonus, black rice has an alkalizing effect on the body (brown rice is slightly acid-forming). Black rice can be found at natural food stores and Asian grocery stores.

Serves 4

NOTE: Avoid cooking black rice in a white enamel pot, as it could stain the enamel.

1 cup Chinese black rice (also known as Forbidden rice)
½ teaspoon sea salt
½ cup unsweetened coconut milk

Place the rice in a strainer and rinse it well under cold running water.

Bring 4 cups water to a boil in a medium saucepan over high heat. Add the salt, then add the rice and return the water to a boil. Reduce the heat to medium-high and boil, pasta-style, for about 30 minutes (or about 25 minutes if you've soaked your rice in advance; see sidebar, page 219), until the rice is al dente. Drain in a sieve and shake the sieve a few times to remove excess water.

Return the rice to the pan, add the coconut milk, and place over medium-high heat. Cook, stirring continuously, until most of the liquid has been absorbed, about 3 minutes. Turn off the heat, cover, and leave for 10 minutes, then uncover, fluff the rice with a fork, and serve.

ROASTED ROOT VEGGIES

Roasted potatoes are a classic, family-pleasing side, but I like to venture beyond the spud by studding my potatoes with roots of various colors such as carrots and yellow, purple, or candy-stripe beets. Yellow and pink beets won't stain your potatoes, but purple beets will; if you're including them, dress them and set them on a separate part of the pan to keep your colors clean. Much of the nutrition in potatoes is found in their skin, but that's also where pesticides concentrate; if your potatoes are organic, leave the skin on, but peel conventional potatoes. This recipe easily doubles to fill up two baking pans. *Serves 4*

1½ pounds red or Yukon Gold potatoes, scrubbed but not peeled, cut into bite-size wedges
1 medium beet, peeled and cut into bite-size wedges
1 large carrot, cut into ½-inch half-moons
3 tablespoons extra-virgin olive oil
¾ teaspoon sea salt
¼ teaspoon freshly ground black pepper
4 to 6 garlic cloves, unpeeled (optional)
2 teaspoons minced fresh rosemary, thyme, or oregano, or a mix

Preheat the oven to 425°F. Line a baking sheet with parchment paper or a silicone baking mat.

Place the potatoes, beet, and carrot in a large bowl and toss with the oil, salt, and pepper to evenly coat. Spread the vegetables out on the prepared baking sheet and toss in the garlic (if using). Roast for about 45 minutes, stirring a few times, until the vegetables are well browned, crisp, and tender when pierced with a knife. In the last 3 minutes of the roasting time, sprinkle the herbs over the vegetables. Remove from the oven and place in a serving bowl. If you added the garlic, carefully squeeze the soft flesh from the skin (it will be very hot), mix it into the vegetables, and serve.

Swap It Out

- Add a squeeze of lemon juice and a sprinkle of grated lemon zest at the end. Or throw a couple of lemon wedges into the roasting pan; squeeze the concentrated roasted lemon juice over the vegetables before serving.
- If you don't have fresh herbs, substitute 1½ teaspoons dried herbs.

CHEESY QUINOA AND RICE BAKE

Warming, just a little creamy, and with a pleasing crunch on top, this casserole gets a toss with my Secret White Sauce to add comfort-food appeal while keeping it light.

I promise your whole family will love this one, but you'll be the only one who knows the secret ingredients (bone broth, cauliflower, zucchini!) that make it both nutritious and super delicious. This dish is great for using up leftover grains. *Serves 6 to 8*

Extra-virgin olive oil cooking spray
3 cups cooked quinoa
3 cups cooked brown rice (page 219)
2 cups Secret White Sauce (page 263)
½ teaspoon sea salt
1½ cups grated Gruyère cheese (about 4 ounces)
¼ cup grated Parmesan cheese
2 teaspoons Super-Sassy Seasoning (page 117)

Preheat the oven to 375°F. Coat an 8 by 10-inch baking pan with cooking spray.

In a large bowl, combine the quinoa, rice, white sauce, and salt and mix well to coat the grains with the sauce. Stir in the Gruyère. In a small bowl, mix the Parmesan with the Super-Sassy Seasoning. Top the casserole with the Parmesan mixture. Bake until the cheese has melted and the top is lightly browned in places, about 40 minutes. Remove from the oven and let sit for 5 to 10 minutes before slicing and serving.

Swap It Out

- Choose another grain such as millet or spelt for the quinoa or rice. Or try black rice in place of the brown rice.
- Use any melting cheese you like, such as cheddar, Monterey Jack, mozzarella, or Gouda.

On the Move

EASY, SATISFYING SNACKS

Snacks need to be quick to grab, but as an athlete and a health-conscious person, I like to know exactly what's in the food I eat. It's easy to pick up something from the store—a protein bar, granola bar, or bag of roasted nuts—that seems healthy enough, right? Not so fast . . . upon closer inspection, you may find that they are made with artificial ingredients, unhealthy oils, or refined sugars. That's why it's best not to make a habit of purchasing packaged snack products. I do my best to stay prepared, with bags of freshly roasted nuts (pages 233 to 235), individually wrapped energy bars (page 237), and little containers of yogurt (page 231), hummus (page 228), or guac (page 227), along with a sidekick of raw veggies for dipping. These are the snacks that energize my family and keep us happy till the next meal is on the table. Your kids are going to love the peanut butter granola bar (page 241), and they'll have fun making the fruit leather (page 239) with you. While putting together your own snacks does require a little advance prep, having them on hand will keep you moving with the energy and grace you need to make your way through your day.

GOCHUJANG GUACAMOLE

When I competed on *Chopped*, a hard-core cooking competition on Food Network, we were given four ingredients to work with—chicken tenders, avocado, vanilla cupcakes, and gochujang. I had no idea what the heck gochujang was (I soon learned that it's a sweet-and-spicy Korean condiment), but after I tasted it, I figured out how to make the best use of it. I made a guacamole and added a kick of spice with the gochujang, which served as a dip for my crispy vanilla chicken tenders. If you're wondering how it all turned out, let's just say that my dish advanced me to the final round, where I won the competition! Gochujang can be found in Asian markets, usually in a red tub. Without the four-ingredient restriction I had on *Chopped*, you have the option to go with the gochujang or keep to tradition and spice your guacamole with jalapeño. *Serves 6*

4 medium avocados
1 small tomato, chopped
½ small red onion, minced
1 tablespoon gochujang (Korean chile paste), or to taste, or ½ jalapeño, minced
½ teaspoon sea salt, plus more to taste
¼ cup chopped fresh cilantro leaves
1½ tablespoons fresh lime juice, plus more to taste

Slice the avocados lengthwise around the pit and carefully remove the pit. Using a large spoon, scoop out the avocado flesh and place it in a large bowl. Using the back of a fork, mash the avocado until as chunky or smooth as you like it. Mix in the tomato, onion, gochujang, salt, and cilantro. Stir in the lime juice. Taste and season with more salt and/or lime juice if needed, and serve.

CLASSIC HUMMUS

Classic, real-deal hummus is made with lots of tahini and spends a good amount of time in the food processor to achieve its signature smoothness. Making your own hummus is simple, saves money, and allows you to come up with your own hummus flavors. I've shared a couple of my favorite creations—hummus with pickles and pink beet hummus—here to get you started. Most supermarket brands use refined canola oil in their hummus; try using extra-virgin olive oil and you'll taste and feel the difference.

If you're cooking chickpeas from scratch, boil them a little longer than usual, until they are very soft, almost falling apart, so they break down easily. If possible, process them while they are still hot. If you're using canned chickpeas, drain them, rinse them well under cold running water, then simmer them in water to cover for ten minutes to further soften them and remove their tinny taste. If you're not serving your hummus right away, taste it again just before serving it, adjust the flavors with more salt and/or lemon juice if needed, and add a little water or oil if it has thickened up more than you like it. *Makes about 4 cups*

2½ cups cooked chickpeas (see page 107)
½ cup water
3 garlic cloves, fresh or roasted (page 47), chopped
¾ cup tahini (sesame seed paste)
⅓ cup fresh lemon or lime juice, plus more to taste
¼ cup extra-virgin olive oil
1 teaspoon sea salt, plus more to taste
½ teaspoon freshly ground black pepper
3 tablespoons chopped fresh flat-leaf parsley or cilantro
Vegetable sticks, crackers, or flatbread (page 153), for dipping

Place the chickpeas, ¼ cup of the water, and the garlic in a food processor and process to a thick paste, about 1½ minutes, scraping down the sides of the processor bowl once or twice and adding a little more water to get the blade moving if needed. Add the tahini, lemon juice, oil, salt, pepper, and the remaining ¼ cup water and process for 5 to 7 minutes, until silky smooth, stopping to scrape down the sides of the processor bowl a few times and adding more water if needed. Remove the lid, add the parsley, and pulse it in briefly to combine (or let it go further to color it green for fun!). Taste and add more lemon juice and/or salt if needed. Transfer to a bowl or box it up and take it to go with your choice of dippers.

Swap It Out Variations

- Dill Pickle and Cracked Black Peppercorn Hummus: Finely chop 1 dill pickle (page 257) and blend most of it into the chickpeas, leaving a small amount to stir in at the end. Reduce the salt to ½ teaspoon, add a little of the pickle juice in place of some of the lemon juice, substitute fresh dill for the parsley, and finish with coarsely ground black pepper.

- Beet, Chard Stem, and Thyme Hummus: Chop the stems from 1 bunch of chard, place them in a pan with water to cover, bring to a simmer over medium heat, and simmer for about 10 minutes, until very tender. Add the stems to the chickpeas along with the juice of 1 beet (grate the beet, then squeeze the pulp through your hands wearing disposable gloves to extract the juice) in place of some of the water (add the chard stem cooking water in place of the rest of the water). Substitute 2 teaspoons fresh thyme leaves for the parsley.

CINNAMON-SWIRL GREEK YOGURT

Cinnamon swirl doesn't have to come in a 500-calorie bun or French toast breakfast. A simple drizzle of cinnamon-infused honey turns a plain bowl of yogurt into an irresistible treat, especially when you pretty up the presentation with a fancy-looking swirl. Let your kids get in on the fun by creating their own edible artwork in their cups. *Serves 2*

1 cup plain Greek yogurt
1 tablespoon liquid honey
¼ teaspoon ground cinnamon, plus more for sprinkling
½ teaspoon pure vanilla extract

Divide the yogurt between two small cups or containers. In a small bowl, whisk together the honey, cinnamon, and vanilla and pour it over the yogurt. Draw the tip of a knife or toothpick through the honey to create a swirled pattern. Sprinkle with cinnamon and serve or pack up to enjoy later. It's perfect popped into a lunchbox.

Swap It Out

- Use another spice, such as pumpkin pie spice, nutmeg, or cardamom.
- Add dried or fresh fruit and/or nuts.
- Whisk a quick splash of orange flower water or rose water (available at international markets, Middle Eastern markets, and some supermarkets) into the yogurt before adding the flavored honey. If you've made my peach cobbler (page 279), you'll already have some!

SMOKY CITRUS PUMPKIN SEEDS

Munch on them out of hand or sprinkle a few on a soup or salad. Or for something completely different, pulse them in a food processor to a powder and use as a dairy-free alternative to Parmesan, perfect for finishing a salad or bowl of pasta. *Makes 2*

2 cups hulled raw pumpkin seeds
4 teaspoons extra-virgin olive oil
1 teaspoon smoked paprika
2 teaspoons fresh lime or lemon juice
1 teaspoon sea salt

Place the pumpkin seeds in a large bowl. Add the oil and toss to coat, then add the smoked paprika, lime juice, and salt and toss to coat. Heat a large skillet over medium heat. Reduce the heat to low, add the pumpkin seeds, and cook, stirring very often (continuously would be better for the most even toasting), for about 5 minutes, until lightly browned all over, watching carefully to make sure they don't burn. Transfer to a plate and let cool. Store in an airtight container or individual snack bags at room temperature for up to 1 week.

Swap It Out

- Substitute ½ teaspoon ground chipotle chile for the smoked paprika for smoky, spicy pumpkin seeds.
- Substitute hulled raw sunflower seeds for the pumpkin seeds.

SWEET-AND-SALTY CINNAMON PECANS

These hit that perfect salty-sweet sweet spot, so I recommend bagging them up immediately or they'll be gone before the kids come home! *Makes 2 cups*

2 cups pecan halves
6 tablespoons dark brown sugar
½ teaspoon ground cinnamon
½ teaspoon sea salt

Line a baking sheet with parchment paper or a silicone baking mat.

Heat a large skillet over medium heat. Add the pecans and toast, stirring often, until lightly browned, 3 to 4 minutes. In a small bowl, whisk together the brown sugar, cinnamon, and salt. Sprinkle the mixture over the pecans and cook, stirring continuously, until the brown sugar has melted and darkened in color (take care,

as the pecans can quickly go from deep brown to burnt), about 3 minutes. Spread the pecans in a single layer (it's okay if some of the nuts stick together) on the prepared baking sheet and let cool completely. Break up any clumps with your hands. Store in individual snack bags for up to 1 week.

Swap It Out

- Use walnuts or chopped almonds in place of the pecans.
- Swap in pumpkin pie spice for the cinnamon.

SUPERFOOD NUTS AND SEEDS

Nuts and seeds are superfoods.

Walnuts, as their shape might indicate, are excellent for brain health, and they contain the amino acid l-arginine, which is beneficial to the heart. Pecans are a rich source of vitamin B6 to support the nervous system and heart. Almonds are an excellent source of vitamin E, manganese, and magnesium; the greatest health benefits are in their skins. They're a great salad or stir-fry topper, and almond flour provides structure and protein to pastries (and is gluten-free to boot). Cashews can help lower the risk for gallstones and improve blood circulation, and they become creamy when blended to make a rich-tasting dip (page 152) and a dairy-free cheesecake (page 291). Pistachios have been shown to reduce blood pressure and lower oxidized LDL cholesterol. Pumpkin seeds are high in iron, zinc, magnesium, chlorophyll, and tryptophan, which promotes restful sleep. Little flax and chia seeds are too small to snack on, but they add their omega-3 goodness and belly-filling fiber to smoothies (page 25 and their binding powers to baked goods (pages 269 and 295), burgers (page 190), and meatballs (page 182). Note that peanuts are legumes and not true nuts, which means they must be cooked before consuming.

ROSEMARY AND SPICE ALMONDS

I like to use my Super-Sassy Seasoning wherever I can, because it makes everything it touches so darn tasty! Rosemary adds a savory accent, but could easily be swapped out for another dried spice such as oregano, thyme, or Italian seasoning. *Makes 2 cups*

1 tablespoon extra-virgin olive oil or unsalted butter
2 cups raw almonds
2 teaspoons Super-Sassy Seasoning (page 117)
½ teaspoon dried rosemary
1 teaspoon sea salt

In a large skillet, heat the oil over medium heat. Add the almonds, Super-Sassy Seasoning, rosemary, and salt, reduce the heat to low, and toast, stirring very often (continuously would be better for the most even toasting), until lightly browned all over, about 5 minutes, watching carefully to make sure the spices don't burn. Transfer to a bowl and let cool. Store in an airtight container or individual snack bags at room temperature for up to 1 week.

Swap It Out

- Swap in thyme, oregano, or Italian seasoning for the rosemary.
- Add ¼ teaspoon cayenne pepper for some heat.
- Try cashews in place of the almonds.

CLEAN GREEN ENERGY BARS

If you can drink a green smoothie, why not eat a green bar? Some of my favorite smoothie ingredients—spirulina, maca, and flax—go into this energy bar. You can stash one in your purse, car, or office or keep a few in your gym locker for an on-the-spot boost, bypassing the unnatural ingredients found in many commercial energy bars. Read about spirulina and chlorella on page 22 and maca on page 20. *Makes about 8 bars or 16 mini bars*

7 ounces pitted dried dates
2 tablespoons pure maple syrup
1 tablespoon spirulina or chlorella powder
½ teaspoon maca powder
½ teaspoon matcha tea powder (optional)
½ teaspoon grated lemon zest
½ teaspoon fresh lemon juice
¼ teaspoon sea salt
¼ cup flax meal or ground chia seeds
1 cup raw cashews
¼ cup currants
¼ cup unsweetened shredded coconut
2 tablespoons mini chocolate chips (optional)

In a food processor, combine the dates, maple syrup, spirulina, maca powder, matcha tea powder (if using), lemon zest, lemon juice, and salt and process until well broken down and almost smooth, about 2 minutes, stopping to scrape down the sides of the processor bowl if needed. Add the flax meal and process until well incorporated, about 1 minute. Add the cashews and process for 30 to 45 seconds, until the cashews are broken down into small pieces. Add the currants, coconut, and chocolate chips (if using), and pulse for about 15 seconds, until incorporated. Remove the mixture from the food processor to a bowl, scraping the sides to get it all out, gather it in your hands, and form it into a firm ball. Pull out pieces of the mixture with your fingers and roll them into balls. Continue to roll them in your hands until the mixture is smooth, uniform, and glossy. Form the balls into bar shapes about 2½ inches long, 1 inch wide, and ¾ inch thick, or half the length for mini bars. Wash your hands between bars if they start to stick. Place the bars in a storage container or individually wrap them and store in the refrigerator for up to 2 weeks or in the

ANY BERRY FRUIT LEATHER

When berry season shows up, roll up your sleeves and roll up some fruit! Sure, you can find fruit leather in any grocery store, but homemade tastes so much fresher and allows you to decide which fruit and flavor combos you like. Choose ripe fruit and taste it to know how sweet it is, adjusting the amount of sweetener up or down to taste, keeping in mind the flavors and sweetness will concentrate when your fruit turns into leather. The cooking time varies widely according to how low your oven goes and how much moisture the fruit contains. If your oven's lowest temperature is 200°F, open and close the oven door once every twenty minutes or so, so the fruit doesn't cook too fast and brown around the edges. Check it often and take it out when it is still barely tacky to the touch but peels away easily from the parchment paper. If you overbake your fruit leather, it will become crisp, but don't despair—turn it into fruit chips to snack on or top ice cream or yogurt with. You can also make your fruit leather in a dehydrator set to 170°F (line the shelves with dehydrator sheets and spread the fruit mixture over the sheets).

Makes 2 sheets of fruit leather

2 pounds berries (about 6 cups)
¼ cup honey or pure maple syrup, or to taste
2 tablespoons fresh lemon or lime juice
Flavorings of choice (see page 240)

Preheat the oven to its lowest setting; 170°F is ideal, but no higher than 200°F. Line two baking sheets with parchment paper or silicone baking mats.

In a blender, combine all the ingredients and blend until smooth. For completely smooth fruit leather, strain the puree through a fine-mesh strainer into a bowl, pressing on the solids to extract all the liquid.

Pour the puree onto the lined baking sheets, make a loose rectangular outline around the pan with it, and then fill it in. Tilt the pan to form a thin layer (but not so thin that it's transparent—if that happens, make your fruit leather smaller) that is as even as possible. Use a silicone spatula to make any final adjustments to the layer. Bake until the roll-ups are only very slightly tacky to the touch but peel fairly easily from the parchment, anywhere from 2 to 5 hours, depending on the type of fruit you use and its moisture content. Cut the roll-ups right through the parchment into strips (any size you like) and test one to see if it pulls off the paper easily. If it's still a little tacky, return them to the turned-off oven (tape the handle to the door to remind yourself not to turn it on!) and leave for up to 5 hours more, or simply leave them to dry on the counter. Roll up the strips, tie them with kitchen string, and store in a sealed bag at room temperature for up to 2 weeks, in the refrigerator for up to 1 month, or in the freezer for up to 1 year.

Swap It Out

Spices and extracts set your roll-ups apart from the kind you buy in a box. Go lightly, as whatever you add will intensify in flavor as the fruit concentrates. Here are some ideas to get you started:

- Strawberry, cinnamon, and vanilla
- Strawberry and orange blossom water
- Raspberry and cardamom
- Blueberry and rose water
- Blackberry and cloves
- Any berry and beet (add the juice of 1 beet to the puree)

NO RECIPE REQUIRED! SEVEN SIMPLE SNACK SUGGESTIONS

1. Whole-grain bread with nut butter, peach slices, and cinnamon

2. Pear halves, blue cheese, and toasted pistachios

3. Salted avocado chunks folded into a sheet of nori seaweed (the "wrapper" used for sushi)

4. Warmed corn tortilla with honey

5. Celery sticks with goat cheese, nut butter, or hummus

6. Frozen grapes, cherries, or blueberries

7. Hard- or soft-boiled eggs (keep a few in the fridge) with a sprinkle of salt and Super-Sassy Seasoning (page 117)

NO-BAKE PEANUT BUTTER GRANOLA BARS

The majority of no-bake granola bar recipes I've seen have one thing in common: they contain no granola! Instead they are made with raw oats, which can be hard to digest. I use actual granola in my bars, and I make sure to choose a brand made with unrefined oils and a wholesome sweetener such as honey or brown sugar. Mix in some protein-rich peanut butter, omega-3-rich chia, crunchy nuts, and puffed rice, and you've got a granola bar to fuel your on-the-move lifestyle! *Makes 12 bars*

⅓ cup honey
¾ cup salted natural (no-sugar-added) smooth peanut butter
2 tablespoons unsalted butter or unrefined coconut oil
2½ cups granola (see headnote)
2 cups plain puffed rice cereal
¼ cup ground chia seeds or flax meal
⅓ cup dried unsweetened cranberries, raisins, or goji berries
⅓ cup chopped toasted almonds or peanuts
⅓ cup mini chocolate chips

Line an 8 by 12-inch baking pan with parchment or waxed paper.

In a medium saucepan, combine the honey, peanut butter, and butter. Place over medium heat and stir until the butter has melted and the ingredients are well combined and smooth. Turn off the heat, add the granola, rice cereal, ground chia seeds, cranberries, and almonds, and stir to combine. Stir in the chocolate chips.

Transfer the mixture to the prepared pan and spread it into an even layer. Line with a second sheet of parchment or waxed paper and press the mixture down firmly to set it. Place in the refrigerator for 1 hour, then carefully cut into bars, wrap them individually in plastic wrap, parchment paper, or waxed paper, and store in the refrigerator for up to 2 weeks or in the freezer for up to 3 months.

Next Level, Please!

Increase the nuts to ⅔ cup and omit the chocolate chips.

Next Level, Please!

LIFE-ENHANCING CONCOCTIONS

Ready to up your healthy lifestyle game? Then this chapter is for you! Health and healing is a full-time passion for me with a never-ending quest to reach new heights. I was healthy back when I was undefeated in the ring, but I'm even healthier now because I'm learning more and more every day. Throughout the book I've been supplementing recipes with "Next Level, Please!" sidebars, small ways you can make my recipes even more nutritious. Now my hope is to inspire you to take it even further. Today you might buy a packet of bones from the butcher and simmer them in water all day, and by the evening you'll have made your first pot of bone broth (page 245). Or learn how to pack your everyday sauces with veggies (pages 263 and 265) to secretly upgrade your family's nutrition without sacrificing a bit of flavor. You might start making super drinks, simple beverages tailored to how you feel on a given day, whether it's to combat inflammation (page 249), jump-start your metabolism (page 251), alkalize your body (page 252), or pack in the greens (page 252). Or you could decide to bring fermentation (pages 254 to 260), a powerful way of adding nutrition and probiotics to your food, into your life. You don't have to do it all right now: start slowly, see what works for you, and take note of the results. You'll be happy you did!

BASIC BONE BROTH

If you've ever cooked a whole chicken into chicken soup, you are well on your way to making bone broth! Bone broth has become a new trend, but its roots go far back, with most cultures keeping a tradition of throwing bones and water into a pot, tossing in vegetable scraps, and simmering them all day. Adding a splash of vinegar and long cooking extracts essential nutrients and releases healing compounds, including collagen, glutamine, and proline and easily absorbable calcium and magnesium and other minerals.

Bone broth counters colds and flu and is healing for the gut, which supports the immune system and the whole body-mind system. There's a whole lot of health in a simple mug of broth, and the flavor enhances any recipe you use it in! I add a little turmeric to up the antioxidant content and for the lovely golden color it adds, but if your recipe calls for a clear stock, you can omit it. And sometimes I'll swap in broth for water when I cook up a pot of rice, quinoa, or another grain. Note that peeling your onion will result in a lighter broth; onion peels tend to color the broth. *Makes about 3½ quarts*

2 to 3 pounds chicken, beef, or lamb bones
4 quarts water
1 large onion (peeled or unpeeled), quartered
1 large carrot, coarsely chopped
1 celery stalk, including leaves, coarsely chopped
2 garlic cloves
1 bay leaf
2 tablespoons apple cider vinegar
½ teaspoon ground turmeric (optional)
1 teaspoon fine sea salt, plus more to taste

Place the bones in a large stockpot. Add the water and bring just to a boil; boil for 5 minutes, skimming off any foam that rises to the top. Add the vegetables, bay leaf, vinegar, turmeric (if using), and salt. Bring to a simmer, then reduce the heat to very low, cover, and cook at a bare simmer for 12 hours. Alternatively, combine all the ingredients in a slow cooker, cover, and cook on low for 12 to 24 hours.

Remove the bones with tongs or a slotted spoon, then strain the broth through a fine-mesh strainer lined with cheesecloth into a heatproof bowl. Taste and adjust the seasoning if needed. Use immediately, or cool, pour into containers, and store in the refrigerator for up to 1 week or in the freezer for up to 4 months. You can reuse the bones for a second batch of broth.

BONE BROTH WITHOUT A RECIPE

If making your own broth seems intimidating, forget about a recipe and go about it this way: buy a packet of bones from the butcher counter (whatever type of bones are available will do the trick) or save the remains of last night's roasted chicken; throw them into a pot with a few veggies, if you have them; add water, a splash of vinegar, and a little salt; and simmer all day. The measurements don't need to be exact, so you really can't go wrong! If you have a slow cooker, it becomes even easier: take the couple of minutes to set it up before you go out in the morning, set it to low, and soup's on when you return.

EVERYDAY HEALING SOUP

On days when I want to give my body a break and do some light cleansing, I'll cook seasonal veggies in a pot of simmering bone broth with a good pinch of turmeric and enjoy mugs full of this healing elixir throughout the day. I'll drink lots of purified water and sip on my Coco Green Dream drink (page 252), and that's all that's needed to give my system a well-deserved break!

VERY VEGGIE BROTH

Want to become a better cook? Here's something you can do right now: make your own broth! Just as bone broth extracts minerals from bones, vegetable broth brings out the best in your vegetables, concentrating nutrients and flavor and improving the taste of anything you cook with it. Making broth at home lets you control the flavors and salt level so you can tailor it to the recipe you're using it in, and it saves money over store-bought. I include a sheet of kombu seaweed for its added minerals and shiitake mushrooms for their powerful healing properties and earthy, umami flavor. Feel free to add or omit any vegetables, favoring those in your crisper drawer that are threatening to wilt, and save vegetable and herb scraps in the freezer to add to your next pot of broth. *Makes about 3 quarts*

6 fresh or dried shiitake mushrooms, sliced if fresh
2 tablespoons extra-virgin olive oil
2 large onions, coarsely chopped
2 large carrots, coarsely chopped
2 large celery stalks, including leaves, coarsely chopped
4 garlic cloves, smashed
2 handfuls of fresh flat-leaf parsley or cilantro stems or sprigs
1 bay leaf
1 piece kombu seaweed (about 3 by 4 inches)
½ teaspoon ground turmeric (optional; omit for a clearer broth)
1 teaspoon sea salt, plus more to taste
1 teaspoon whole black peppercorns
3 quarts water

If you are using dried shiitake mushrooms, soak them in enough hot water to cover for 30 minutes while you prep the rest of the vegetables.

In a large stockpot, heat the oil over medium-high heat. Add the onions, carrots, celery, garlic, and fresh shiitakes (if using) and cook, stirring frequently, until the onions are well browned, about 10 minutes. Add the remaining ingredients and bring to a boil. Reduce the heat to very low, cover, and cook at a bare simmer for 45 minutes. Strain the broth through a fine-mesh strainer into a heatproof bowl, pressing on the solids to extract all the flavorful liquid. Taste and adjust the seasoning if needed. Use immediately, or cool, pour into containers, and store in the refrigerator for up to 1 week or in the freezer for up to 4 months.

NOTE: Don't add crucifers such as cauliflower and broccoli; their sulfurous aroma will overtake your broth.

SPICY INFLAMMATION-BUSTER

Who would have known bone broth and green tea could be so tasty together? You'll just have to try it to see how good it is! While we might picture superdrinks as cold and thirst-quenching, when it's cold-and-flu season and inflammation fighting is in order, there's nothing more powerful than a steaming mug of bone broth. Steep a green tea bag in the broth, add warming ginger, cayenne, and a little turmeric, and you're on the road to restoring your immunity! *Serves 1*

1½ cups Basic Bone Broth (page 245)
1 green tea bag
¼ teaspoon fresh ginger juice (see Note)
Pinch of cayenne pepper
Pinch of ground turmeric
Pinch of sea salt

In a small saucepan, bring the broth to a simmer. Pour it into a mug over the tea bag.

Steep for 3 minutes, then remove the tea bag. Add the ginger juice, cayenne, turmeric, and salt and serve.

NOTE: Finely grate a small piece of ginger (no need to peel it first) and squeeze it in the palm of your hand to extract the juice.

MAPLE WATER: THE NEW COCONUT WATER?

. . . .

Enjoying the water from a cracked-on-the-spot coconut is natural . . . when you're in Thailand or India. But folks in New England have been enjoying maple water—the sap of the maple tree before it's boiled down to syrup—for as long as maple syrup has been around. Maple water is light and slightly sweet (with about half as much sugar as coconut water and about a third of the calories), with a refreshing, very light maple flavor, and in recent years several companies have started to bottle it. While there are differences between coconut water and maple water, both are high in minerals, antioxidants, and electrolytes, and I enjoy them equally. But I love that maple water is the more local choice!

WATER: WE ARE WHAT WE DRINK

. . . .

Our bodies are more than half water, so I like to have a constant supply of pure water coming in to flush out my system. Fruits and veggies contain even more water than we do—typically 80 to 90 percent—so I make a point to include them in liberal quantities in my daily meals and snacks.

As an athlete, I know firsthand the importance of keeping hydrated. Drinking lots of water keeps me at my best: sharp, clear-minded, and at the top of my game. When you consider the consequences of dehydration—fatigue, irritability, muscle cramps, constipation, and bloat from water retention—it's worth the effort to keep a bottle of water handy at your desk, in the car, and at the gym, and to bring one to the movies or ballgame to avoid the temptation of sugary drinks. Dehydration can even make you think you're hungry when you're really thirsty. So if you feel unsatisfied after you've eaten, try drinking a glass of water, waiting a few minutes, then checking if those hunger pangs have subsided. In addition to water drinking, herbal teas (but not caffeinated teas, as they can act as a diuretic) and bone broth are excellent ways to hydrate, as are coconut water and maple water. Soda is not! Drinking a smoothie hydrates you while you enjoy a quick, nutritious meal. Filtering your water through a pitcher filter or faucet filter is a convenient and cost-effective way of hydrating the whole family with pure, clean water. Reusable steel or glass containers are excellent to transport your water, but if you're grabbing a plastic bottle at the store, make sure it's a BPA-free bottle (learn more about BPAs on page 53).

SUPER-SAVVY METABOLIZER

Drinking green tea is a great way of revving up your metabolism, a gentler pick-me-up than coffee, and cold-brewing your tea results in a less-astringent, less-caffeinated, light-flavored cup. Coconut water and maple water are super hydrating, so I steep the tea in one or the other instead of plain water to further jump-start my metabolism. Berries—also known to stimulate metabolism—get muddled into the tea, cocktail-style, then the mix infuses in the fridge for a few hours. A little honey sweetens the brew; lemon juice and a pinch of cayenne and cinnamon add a pop of flavor. Tiny chia seeds absorb about thirty times their weight in water, so you might add a spoonful at the end to take your drink to new heights of hydration! To speed things up, hot-brew your tea in plain water rather than coconut water, let it cool, then proceed with the recipe, adding ice to the cocktail shaker to put a chill on it. *Serves 1*

1½ cups coconut water or maple water
1 tablespoon raw liquid honey
Tiny pinch of cayenne pepper
Tiny pinch of ground cinnamon
1 tablespoon fresh lemon juice, plus more to taste
10 fresh raspberries, blackberries, or blueberries, or 4 hulled strawberries
8 fresh mint leaves, plus a small sprig for garnish
1 green tea bag
2 to 4 drops of liquid stevia (optional)
1 teaspoon chia seeds (optional)

Pour ¼ cup of the coconut water into a cocktail shaker or jar. Add the honey, cayenne, cinnamon, and lemon juice and whisk to dissolve the honey. Add the berries and muddle them with a muddler or fork. Add the remaining 1¼ cups coconut water, the mint leaves and tea bag. Cover and shake. Refrigerate for 6 to 8 hours to cold-brew the green tea. Remove from the refrigerator, remove the tea bag, and strain into a glass, pressing on the berries to extract all their liquid. Taste and add a little stevia if you'd like your drink a little sweeter. Add the chia seeds, if desired, and refrigerate for about 15 minutes to let the chia seeds swell. Serve over ice with a mint sprig garnish, if you like.

ALMIGHTY ALKALIZER

Interesting fact: While the sour taste of citrus makes your mouth pucker, the effect it has on your body is alkalizing rather than acidifying. And the same is true for apple cider vinegar. Highly processed foods and refined sugar can throw the body's pH off balance to the acidic side, and in an acidic environment, disease has more chance of taking root. So when I need a little alkalizing boost, I turn to the Almighty Alkalizer: citrus and cider vinegar in a base of ruby-colored rooibos tea are just the thing to equalize my system. Almost all herbal teas are alkalizing, and this is especially true for rooibos, an antioxidant-rich, noncaffeinated alternative to green tea. *Makes 1 drink*

1 cup brewed rooibos tea, cooled
¼ cup fresh grapefruit juice
1½ tablespoons fresh lime juice, or to taste
1 teaspoon apple cider vinegar
4 drops of liquid stevia, or to taste
Sprig of fresh mint

In a glass, whisk together all the ingredients. Add ice if you like, and serve with the mint sprig.

COCO GREEN DREAM

When I want to get some greens into my system fast, I turn to chlorella or spirulina.

Light and refreshing cucumber and slightly sweet coconut water or maple water serve as the liquid base, with a generous hit of lemon and a pinch of salt to offset any grassiness from the greens. Cooling, refreshing, and downright dreamy! Read more about chlorella and spirulina on page 22, and turn to page 250 to learn about maple water. If possible, use organic cucumber and leave the peel on. *Makes 1 drink*

1 medium cucumber (about 8 ounces), peeled (if not organic) and chopped
1 cup coconut water or maple water
½ teaspoon chlorella or spirulina
1 tablespoon fresh lemon or lime juice
Pinch of sea salt

If you have a juicer, pass the cucumber through the juicer. If you don't have a juicer, combine the cucumber and coconut water in a blender and blend until smooth, then strain into a glass, pressing on the cucumber pulp to extract all the liquid. Whisk in the chlorella, lemon juice, and salt and serve, over ice if you like.

KEFIR

When we hear the word *probiotics,* yogurt with its live and active cultures is what comes to mind. But kefir, yogurt's tangy, drinkable cousin, contains an even greater variety of probiotic strains, with the probiotics in kefir working to directly colonize your gut. *Kefir* means "to feel good" in Turkish, and on days when I don't have time for a full breakfast, a glass of kefir gives me some feel-good fuel to jump-start my morning. And I'll often include kefir in my smoothies (pages 21 to 22).

You can find kefir at the grocery store (typically next to or in the yogurt section), but you'll save money by making your own, and homemade gives you the most potent probiotic power-punch. Once you purchase kefir starter grains, making kefir takes just a couple of minutes of active time. See Resources (page 305) for where to find kefir starters online (they're not yet widely available in stores). With each batch of kefir, your starter multiplies, so you can share your culture with friends and family. Makes a unique host or hostess present! *Makes 4 cups*

4 cups milk
About 1 tablespoon kefir starter grains

Pour the milk into a wide-mouth jar or pitcher and add the kefir starter. Cover the jar with a clean dishtowel and secure it with a rubber band or loosely cover with the lid (do not tighten the lid).

Leave at room temperature in a cool spot away from direct sunlight for 12 to 48 hours, depending on the season and kitchen temperature (kefir ferments more quickly when it's warm out), until thickened and tangy to your liking. Feel free to taste it along the way; it's ready whenever it tastes best to you. Strain the kefir into another jar, pour into glasses, and drink. Whatever you're not drinking right away, you can cover and refrigerate for up to a couple of weeks.

To make your next batch of kefir, take the starter grains from the strainer (no need to rinse them), put them in another jar of milk, and proceed as directed above. If you aren't ready for another batch of kefir, store the starter in a small jar with enough milk to cover in the refrigerator; change the milk every week or two until you're ready to start making kefir again.

NONDAIRY KEFIR

As with yogurt, the live cultures in kefir help break down the lactose in dairy milk, so many people with lactose intolerance are able to drink kefir. But for those of you who completely avoid dairy or just want to change up your kefir-drinking experience, try making your kefir with almond milk or coconut water. Note that you can use your kefir culture over and over again for nondairy kefir, but it will not multiply.

Almond Milk Kefir: Substitute an equal amount of almond milk for the dairy milk. It will culture quicker than other milks, normally in less than 12 hours. It will separate and come out thinner than dairy kefir and taste a little like buttermilk. Shake before drinking.

Coconut Water Kefir: Substitute an equal amount of coconut water for the dairy milk. Coconut water kefir doesn't change much in appearance; it will just make the liquid a little cloudy and will taste less sweet and slightly tangier than plain coconut water.

WHAT IS FERMENTATION?

From sauerkraut in Europe and kimchi in Korea to the classic American dill pickle, fermenting is a traditional way of preserving food common to every country. The flavors of fermentation range from salty to sour, tangy, and tart, and in terms of nutrition, ferments add an unparalleled probiotic punch to your food. Fermented foods soothe the gut, improve digestion, and can even boost your state of mind.

How does fermentation happen? To get technical for a moment: Bacteria and yeast feed on the nutrients in food, which creates lactic acid, a preservative, which in turn transforms the taste and sometimes the texture of the food. In other words, fermentation turns cabbage into sauerkraut, milk into yogurt or kefir, and cucumbers into pickles. It's one of the most health-supporting transformations ever to happen to food, so I highly recommend giving fermentation a try!

My cowriter, Leda Scheintaub, authored a book called *Cultured Foods for Your Kitchen: 100 Recipes Featuring the Bold Flavors of Fermentation*, so the subject is near and dear to her heart. I'm excited to share with you in this chapter three of her go-to ferments: kefir, cucumber pickles, and sauerkraut. It was with kefir that she first fell in love with fermentation, and from there she was unstoppable!

If your busy life doesn't allow you to go DIY, don't let that keep you from reaping the benefits of ferments! A stroll through your local natural foods store, farmers' market, or even grocery store is likely to reveal at least one option for naturally fermented veggies or kefir. How do you know a product is naturally fermented? Look for the words *live*, *raw*, or *contains living cultures* on the label and for products in the refrigerated section. Anything that's on the shelf—pickles made with vinegar or sauerkraut in a can—is likely pasteurized and contains no living cultures. Even if it was fermented to begin with, it is no longer a living food.

SIMPLEST CUCUMBER PICKLES

First-time fermenters, this recipe is for you! Salt, water, and cucumbers are all you need to start a pickle habit that rewards you with more live and active cultures than you'll get in a probiotic pill. That's because traditionally fermented foods like pickles are an even more concentrated source of probiotics, feeding you tasty medicine with every bite you take. (Store-bought pasteurized vinegar pickles, no matter how tasty they are, contain no active cultures.)

The hardest part of pickle making is putting together a brine, and that is no harder than mixing water and salt. A live pickle with your sandwich instantly upgrades your lunch, and I like to chop up pickles and add them to salads such as my tuna salad (page 73) to add a burst of salty, tangy flavor. And when you've eaten your last pickle, save the brine. It's full of flavor and charged with probiotics. Use it in a salad dressing in place of part of the citrus and salt, or pass around shots of it as an after-dinner digestif.

For this recipe, you will need a two-quart wide-mouth glass jar and a weight that fits inside the jar to keep the pickles submerged in the brine. Once you've perfected pickles, why not turn to page 259 and give sauerkraut a try? *Makes 2 quarts*

1 quart filtered water
3 tablespoons sea salt
2 pounds small to medium kirby or pickling cucumbers, rinsed

In a small saucepan, combine 1 cup of the filtered water and the salt and bring to a simmer. Remove from the heat and set aside, stirring occasionally, until the salt has dissolved. Pour into a glass jar, add the remaining 3 cups of water, and let cool completely.

Place the cucumbers in a 2-quart glass jar. Pour enough of the brine over the cucumbers to cover them with at least 1 inch of space left at the top to avoid spilling over. Save any leftover brine for the next step.

Place a small drinking glass that fits comfortably in the jar to weight the cucumbers down into their brine and fill the glass with brine (so if it happens to spill, you'll simply have more brine in the jar). If you don't have the right size glass, try filling a zip-top bag with brine and snuggling it into the jar.

Place the jar on a rimmed plate or baking pan to catch any potential dripping, cover with a clean dishtowel, and set aside in a cool spot away from sunlight to ferment.

Check your pickles every day or two and remove mold if any develops (don't let the word *mold* scare you—because the pickle jar becomes an anaerobic environment, there is close to no chance of harmful bacteria taking root). Your pickles will be ready in 1 to 2 weeks, depending on whether you're going for half sour or fully sour and how warm your kitchen is. Cover and refrigerate for up to 3 months. Note that the brine may start to bubble and become cloudy—this is a good thing. It's a sign that your pickles are fermenting!

Swap It Out Variations

- **Classic Dill Pickles: Add a couple of handfuls of fresh dill fronds and 5 peeled garlic cloves.**
- **Spicy Pickles: Throw in a few dried red chiles with or without the dill.**
- **Beyond Cukes: Swap in another firm or fairly firm vegetable such as green beans or carrots for the cucumbers. The firmer the vegetable, the longer the fermentation time will be.**

BASIC SAUERKRAUT

It's a crowning touch for sandwiches and a condiment as familiar as mustard. But it's so much more: fermenting cabbage into kraut creates a probiotic powerhouse! Make a batch of your own, taste the difference between that and sauerkraut from a can, and you just might get hooked on ferments. Making sauerkraut requires a little more work than making pickles—massaging salt into cabbage and pounding it down a bit—but the process can be a lot of fun and requires just two ingredients. Add a little sauerkraut to accent a soup, salad, or sandwich, even scrambled eggs—anywhere you're looking for a little burst of flavor.

For this recipe, you will need a two-quart wide-mouth glass jar and a weight that fits inside the jar to keep the sauerkraut submerged in its brine. *Makes 2 quarts*

2 small to medium heads cabbage (about 2½ pounds each)
2 to 3 tablespoons sea salt

Remove the outer leaves from one head of cabbage. Cut the cabbage in half and core it. Quarter the cabbage, slice it into thin lengthwise strips, then chop the strips. Put the cabbage and half the salt in a large nonreactive bowl. Massage the salt into the cabbage very well to release liquid from it and start to create a salty brine. To speed up the process, finish by pounding the cabbage with a kitchen pounder. Pack the cabbage into a 2-quart jar a little at a time. After each addition, pound the cabbage down to release more water. Repeat with the second head of cabbage, slicing it and massaging in the remaining salt in the same bowl. Pack the remaining cabbage into the jar a little at a time and leave at least 1 inch of space at the top. When all the cabbage is in, the brine should cover the surface of the cabbage; keep pounding until it does.

Place a small drinking glass that fits comfortably in the jar to keep the sauerkraut in its brine and fill the glass with filtered water and a little salt (so if it happens to spill, you'll simply have more brine in the jar). If you don't have the right size glass, try filling a zip-top bag with salted water and snuggling it into the jar.

Place the jar on a rimmed plate or baking pan to catch any potential dripping, cover with a clean dishtowel, and set aside in a cool spot away from sunlight to ferment. Check your sauerkraut every day to make sure it is covered with brine, pressing down on it to squeeze out more brine if it isn't. Remove mold if any develops (don't let the word *mold* scare you—because the sauerkraut jar becomes an anaerobic environment, there is close to no chance of harmful bacteria taking root). Your sauerkraut will be ready in 1 to 4 weeks, depending on how tangy you like it and how warm your kitchen is. Cover and refrigerate for up to 6 months.

Swap It Out Variations

- **Seedy Kraut: Add 1 tablespoon toasted cumin seeds or caraway seeds to flavor your kraut.**
- **Cabbage and Carrot Kraut: Swap a small amount of grated carrots for a portion of the cabbage.**
- **Ruby Kraut: Use half or all red cabbage or add a shredded beet for a ruby-colored kraut.**

10-MINUTE NUT BUTTER

Once you get a taste of homemade nut butter, you'll see why it's worth the ten-minute (much of it inactive kitchen time) effort to grind your own. The freshness and flavor can't be compared with what you get from a jar, and you get to decide how much salt and sweetener goes into yours. What's more, the kids can have some fun watching: as the nuts break down, they start to stick to the sides of the machine like crazy and ultimately gather into a large ball for the grand finale of ready-to-spread nut butter. You can use raw or toasted nuts for your nut butter, but note that peanuts must be toasted and cannot be eaten raw. PB&J aside, I enjoy a scoop of nut butter in my morning smoothie (page 25) for extra protein and body, and a spoonful straight from the jar makes for a satisfying between-meal bite. If you love cinnamon, add ½ teaspoon to the mix, and after you've made nut butter, you might want to try a butter made from pumpkin seeds or sunflower seeds. Or add a small amount of flax or chia seeds to step up the omega-3 content of your nut butter. *Makes about 2 cups*

3 cups raw or toasted almonds or cashews or
   toasted peanuts
½ teaspoon sea salt, or to taste
1 tablespoon safflower oil, plus more if needed
1 to 2 tablespoons honey (optional)

Place all the nuts in a food processor for smooth nut butter; for chunky nut butter, reserve a handful of nuts to pulse in later. Process for about 2 minutes, stopping to scrape down the sides of the processor bowl a couple of times, until broken down into a crumbly, dry powder. Add the salt and oil and process for about 8 minutes, to the desired smoothness, stopping to scrape down the sides a few times: as the oils release, the mixture will start to stick to the walls of the bowl, then the whole thing will gather into a large ball. Shortly after, as the oils continue to release, the ball will loosen into a fairly smooth puree. Resist the urge to add more oil in the beginning—wait until the oils from the nuts release before determining if more oil is actually needed. Add the honey (if using) and process until incorporated. If you're making chunky nut butter, add the reserved nuts and pulse a few times, to the desired chunkiness, without pureeing them. Transfer the nut butter to a jar, cover, and refrigerate for up to 3 months.

HOW TO TOAST NUTS

IN THE OVEN: Preheat the oven to 350°F. Spread the nuts over the prepared baking sheet in a single layer and roast for 5 to 10 minutes, shaking the pan once halfway through, until the nuts are lightly browned and toasty smelling. Remove from the oven and transfer to a plate to cool. The nuts will continue to darken slightly after they are removed from the oven. For smaller batches, toast your nuts in a preheated toaster oven.

ON THE STOVETOP: Heat the nuts in a dry, heavy skillet over medium heat, stirring continuously, until they are lightly browned and toasty smelling, 3 to 5 minutes. This method works nicely for small batches of nuts; stirring continuously yields evenly colored and richly flavored nuts.

SECRET WHITE SAUCE

This sauce is one of my secret weapons in the kitchen, and I pull it out often, especially when I'm making meals for my kids. Zucchini and cancer-fighting cauliflower cooked in bone broth add concentrated nutrition with a mild flavor that no one will notice. I like to stir a scoop into soups, stews, and casseroles, and I'll even add some to mac and cheese. The zucchini is peeled to avoid turning the sauce green, but you can cook the peel separately in the pot to extract its nutrition, then scoop it out and discard it before blending. Or save the peel to make Zucchini Skin Chips (page 191). Add more broth to the sauce and perhaps a touch of cream or coconut milk to make an impromptu soup. The sauce freezes well, so you can keep portions on hand for supplementing your recipes. *Makes about 3 cups*

2 cups Basic Bone Broth (page 245) or Very Veggie Broth (page 248)
½ medium head cauliflower, cut into florets and stems chopped
1 medium zucchini (about 8 ounces), peeled and coarsely chopped
Sea salt

Pour the broth into a large sauté pan or high-sided skillet. Bring to a simmer over medium-high heat. Add the cauliflower, return to a simmer, then reduce the heat to medium and cook for 5 minutes. Add the zucchini and cook for 10 minutes more, or until both vegetables are very soft. Strain, reserving the broth. Transfer the vegetables to a blender, add the broth, season with salt, and blend until very smooth.

SECRET RED SAUCE

There's no denying the convenience of opening a can, jar, or box of tomato sauce. But nothing beats the taste of a homemade sauce, and this recipe easily doubles or triples and freezes well to keep your family flush in sauce for a couple of months. But the best thing about making your own sauce is that you get to be in charge of what goes into it: organic tomatoes whenever possible, minimal to no sugar, and extra veggies that make the sauce even tastier but become invisible when blended. *Makes about 6 cups*

2 tablespoons extra-virgin olive oil
1 medium yellow onion, chopped
1 medium red bell pepper, chopped
2 garlic cloves, chopped
1 teaspoon dried oregano
1 teaspoon Italian seasoning
1½ teaspoons sea salt, or to taste
1 large carrot, finely chopped
1 medium zucchini, finely chopped
2 (28-ounce) cans diced tomatoes
Up to 1 tablespoon unrefined brown sugar
  (optional)

In a large saucepan, heat the oil over medium heat. Add the onion and bell pepper and cook, stirring, for about 7 minutes, until softened and starting to color. Add the garlic and cook, stirring, for about 2 minutes, until softened. Add the oregano, Italian seasoning, and salt and cook for about 30 seconds, until aromatic. Stir in the carrot and zucchini and cook for 2 minutes to coat them in the spices and start to soften them. Add the tomatoes and bring to a simmer, stirring to release any of the delicious browned bits stuck to the bottom of the pan. Reduce the heat to low, cover, and simmer, stirring occasionally, for 20 minutes. Uncover the pan and taste the sauce. Add a little salt if needed and some brown sugar if the sauce calls for a little sweetness. Use an immersion blender to blend the sauce directly in the pan until smooth (for a silky-smooth sauce—especially for kids who would otherwise veto the veggies—transfer the sauce in batches to a standing blender and blend until smooth, then return the sauce to the pan). Cook for up to 20 minutes more (the flavors will continue to develop), or as much time as you have to get dinner to the table!

Sweet Benefits

SCRUMPTIOUS, UNBELIEVABLY WHOLESOME DESSERTS

❦

I love dessert! Desserts play a big role in my life, and if there's one thing I simply won't give up, it's sweets. Because I indulge, balance and portion control are my ticket to guilt-free enjoyment. I want my desserts to be as wholesome as possible without sacrificing an ounce of deliciousness. To accomplish this goal, I've enlisted some top talent to bring my vision to life, in particular Patricia Austin of Wild Flour Vermont Bakery, author of *Pâtisserie Gluten Free*, who has had her hand in many of this chapter's recipes. Since I don't feel my best when I eat a lot of gluten and so many people are going completely gluten-free these days, I've made this entire chapter gluten-free. By using a revolutionary new gluten-free flour blend (see page 271), you'd never know the difference. I designed this chapter to bring new life to old classics, like Sock-It-to-Me Honey Cake (page 269) sweetened with honey and raw sugar, Heavenly Lemon Yogurt Cake (page 273) that you might mistake for cheesecake, Key Lime Cheesecake (page 291) actually made with cashews, and Red Velvet Cupcakes (page 287) flavored and colored with beets. The chapter concludes with one of my absolute new and improved favorites, Not Your Mama's Sweet Potato Pie (page 299). I am very proud of what we have accomplished in this chapter!

SOCK-IT-TO-ME HONEY CAKE

Southern-style sock-it-to-me cake is a coffee cake that's moist, buttery, and laced with cinnamon and pecans. It has always been one of my favorite desserts, and I am excited to share this new and upgraded honey of a cake with you! A slice of this all-natural, gluten-free Bundt cake reveals a tempting cinnamon-nut filling, lovely moist texture, and warming cinnamon, cardamom, and honey flavors. A drizzle of chocolate completes the sweet experience but could be omitted for a simpler presentation. When I was boxing, I often had to give up dessert for weeks before a fight for mental toughness and in order to make weight. After every fight, there would be a fresh-baked cake in my dressing room waiting for me to slice into. When there was sock-it-to-me cake on the table, I would vow to go for an early knockout just to get back to my dressing room sooner to enjoy a slice! *Makes one 12-cup Bundt cake or 9-inch tube cake*

FILLING

1 cup pecans, finely chopped
¾ cup raw sugar
¼ cup cup-for-cup replacement gluten-free
    flour blend, such as Steve's GF Cake Flour
1½ teaspoons ground cinnamon
3 tablespoons unsalted butter, melted
Pinch of sea salt

CAKE

1¾ cups cup-for-cup replacement gluten-free
    flour blend, such as Steve's GF Cake Flour
2 teaspoons baking powder
½ teaspoon baking soda
1 teaspoon ground chia seeds
1 teaspoon ground cinnamon
½ teaspoon ground cardamom
1 teaspoon sea salt
¾ cup (1½ sticks) unsalted butter, at room
    temperature, plus more for the pan
½ cup honey

¼ cup raw sugar
4 large eggs, at room temperature
2 teaspoons pure vanilla extract
1¼ cups plain yogurt or sour cream
2 tablespoons chopped dark chocolate

Preheat the oven to 350°F. Lightly butter a 12-cup nonstick Bundt-style pan or 9-inch tube pan.

To make the filling: In a small bowl, combine the pecans, sugar, gluten-free flour, cinnamon, butter, and salt. Rub the ingredients between your fingers until the mixture is well blended and set aside.

To make the cake: Sift the gluten-free flour, baking powder, baking soda, ground chia seeds, cinnamon, cardamom, and salt into a large bowl.

In the bowl of a stand mixer fitted with the paddle attachment, cream the butter, honey, and sugar on medium-high speed until the ingredients are lightened in color, about 4 minutes. The raw sugar will break down, but some sugar granules will remain; this is okay. Add 1 egg and beat for 30 seconds, turn the mixer off, and scrape down the bowl and paddle with a rubber spatula. Add the remaining eggs one at a time, beating on medium-high speed for 1 minute after each addition, then add the vanilla and beat briefly to incorporate. Turn off the mixer and thoroughly scrape down the bowl, then beat again for 30 seconds.

Turn the mixer off, add one-third of the flour mixture, and beat on low speed until just incorporated. Add one-third of the yogurt and mix on low speed until combined. Continue to alternately add the dry ingredients and the yogurt, mixing each until well blended before adding the next addition. When the ingredients have all been added, turn the mixer off, scrape down the bowl and paddle, and beat on medium speed for 30 seconds. Remove the bowl from the mixer and finish mixing by hand with a rubber spatula.

Scoop half the batter into the prepared cake pan and, using a small metal spatula, evenly distribute the batter to the edges of the pan and smooth the surface. Using a butter knife or metal spoon, scrape a ½-inch-deep circular indentation into the center of the batter and sprinkle the nut-sugar filling onto the batter. There will be lots of filling, but this is okay. Top the filling with the remaining batter and, using the metal spatula, smooth the top so it's level. Use the spatula to dip into the center of the cake and run a single wavy line through the batter to distribute the filling, then smooth the top so it's level again.

Bake for 35 to 45 minutes, until a cake tester inserted into the center of the cake comes out clean.

Remove the cake from the oven and let cool in the pan on a wire rack for 15 minutes. Release the cake from the pan by flipping it upside down onto the rack. Set the rack over a baking sheet lined with parchment paper and let the cake cool completely.

Put the chopped chocolate in a heatproof bowl and set it over a pan of simmering water, making sure the bottom of the bowl doesn't touch the water. Stir the chocolate often, using a rubber spatula until it has fully melted, then use a large spoon to scoop up the chocolate and drizzle it over the cooled cake.

Serve the cake immediately or wrap well in plastic wrap and store in the refrigerator for up to 1 week or in the freezer for up to 1 month. Let the cake come to room temperature or wrap in aluminum foil and heat in a preheated 350°F oven for 10 minutes before serving.

Swap It Out

- The filling can be switched up by choosing a different kind of nut, adding ½ cup mini chocolate chips, or using coconut oil in place of the butter.

- Add 1 teaspoon ground ginger to expand on the warming effects of the cardamom and cinnamon.

GLUTEN-FREE FLOUR BLENDS

Your choice of gluten-free flour blend is crucial to the outcome of whatever baked goods you make with it. For best results, use a blend that acts as a cup-for-cup replacement for wheat flour. And to ensure that your baked goods are as wholesome as possible, make sure the blend you choose is also gum-free, as xanthan gum and guar gum, used as additives in many blends, can cause digestive upset to some people. The recipes in this chapter recommend a specific flour blend: Steve's GF Cake Flour from Authentic Foods, which is not only gluten-free, but gum-free and GMO-free as well, and its uses go well beyond cake. I absolutely *love* this brand because I've found that baked goods made with this flour most closely resemble their wheat-containing originals. You've got to try it to believe it! To find it, see Resources (page 305).

HEAVENLY LEMON YOGURT CAKE

This cake is so moist, you might mistake it for cheesecake! Yogurt gives it an airy lightness and almond flour provides structure without adding gluten. A golden brown almond crust adds crispy contrast and makes a stunning presentation.

Note that almond flour and almond meal can be used interchangeably in this recipe. Almond flour is made from raw blanched (skins removed) almonds that are finely ground to a flour consistency, while almond meal is made from raw skin-on almonds that are also finely ground but will have a heavier texture due to the skins. Almond flour will produce a slightly lighter cake than almond meal. While this cake takes a little extra effort, the end result is so worth it! *Makes one 8-inch cake*

ALMOND CRUST
1 tablespoon unsalted butter, at room
    temperature
½ cup raw sliced almonds
1 tablespoon raw sugar

CAKE
3¼ cups almond flour or almond meal (see
    headnote)
¼ teaspoon baking soda
½ cup (1 stick) unsalted butter, at room
    temperature
⅓ cup raw sugar
⅓ cup honey
½ teaspoon sea salt
3 large eggs, at room temperature
1 cup plain Greek yogurt
Zest of 1 lemon
2 tablespoons fresh lemon juice
1 teaspoon pure vanilla extract

Preheat the oven to 325°F.

To make the almond crust: Generously butter the bottom and sides of an 8-inch round cake pan. Scatter the sliced almonds into the pan. Shake the pan to distribute the almonds across the bottom and inside edges of the pan. Add the sugar and shake the pan in the same way to distribute it across the bottom and inside edges of the pan. Set the pan aside.

To make the cake: In a large bowl, whisk together the almond flour and baking soda.

In the bowl of a stand mixer fitted with the paddle attachment, cream the butter and sugar on medium speed until light and fluffy, about 4 minutes. Add the honey and salt and beat until combined. Reduce the speed to low, add the almond flour mixture, and beat until the dough comes together. Divide the mixture in half and return one half to the mixer bowl. Break the remaining half into walnut-size pieces and set them along the bottom of the pan over the almond-sugar crust. Place a large piece of plastic wrap over the dough in the pan and, using your hand, press and smooth the dough flat and evenly across the bottom of the pan. Work gently and try not to disturb the sliced almonds because they are important for the creation of the cake's outer crust.

With the remaining dough in the mixer, turn the mixer to medium speed and add the eggs one at a time, beating until each one is incorporated before adding the next. Add the yogurt, lemon zest, lemon juice, and vanilla and beat for 1 minute. Scrape down the bowl with a rubber spatula and mix again briefly to thoroughly combine. The batter will be creamy and somewhat loose.

Pour the batter over the prepared base in the pan and, using a small metal spatula, smooth out the surface.

Bake for 30 to 35 minutes, until the cake is golden brown and the center is set.

Remove the cake from the oven and let cool completely in the pan on a wire rack. To release the cake from the pan, run a thin metal spatula around the inside edge of the pan. Place a plate over the top of the pan and flip the pan and plate together to release the cake onto the plate. Slice and serve, or store, well wrapped in plastic wrap, at room temperature for up to 3 days or in the refrigerator for up to 1 week.

BREAKING THE SUGAR HABIT

If after a meal you find you're consistently craving "a little something," try making the food you eat more satisfying. The less satisfied you are, the more you want to eat, and it becomes harder and harder not to follow a meal with a sugar-filled treat. Sugar has addictive qualities, as it causes a release of dopamine in the reward center of the brain. The cycle continues, and more and more sugar becomes needed to reach the same satisfaction level. Sugar is a major cause of obesity, and it's been found that sugar, more than fat, is a key culprit in heart disease. Sugar causes insulin resistance, and constantly elevated insulin levels can progress to type 2 diabetes and contribute to cancer. Sugar is an empty-calorie food, so the more sugar you eat, the less room there is for nutritious food. You'll find sugar in places you might not suspect, from soup to bread to processed meats and even in condiments such as ketchup. All this adds up to the typical American eating more than twenty teaspoons of sugar a day.

You'll be ahead of the game by decreasing the amount of sugar you eat in non-dessert foods, which is easy to do when you pay attention to package labels and cook your meals from scratch. Find your true appetite by making whole grains, vegetables, and good-quality meats and fats the foundation for your meals, and you're on the road to kicking the sugar habit.

We all need a little sweetness in our lives, which is why this chapter is so important to me. "Sweet Benefits" means giving desserts we know and love a wholesome makeover without sacrificing flavor or satisfaction. None of my desserts contain refined sugar; instead I use complex sweeteners with their trace nutrients intact. Honey, pure maple syrup, and raw, unrefined sugar are my favorites. I back that up by eliminating white flour, another source of empty calories, from my desserts in favor of whole-grain and gluten-free flours. The result is desserts for life, desserts for those who want it all!

GERMAN CHOCOLATE CHIP ZUCCHINI CAKE

Did you know that German chocolate cake isn't actually German? Its name comes from the brand of chocolate originally used in the cake—German's Baking Chocolate—developed by Samuel German, an English American chocolate maker. I love the taste of German chocolate cake, but I find the sticky coconut pecan frosting overly sweet. This lighter version skips the frosting, adds nuts and coconut to the batter, and includes zucchini to make the cake super moist. An accent of chocolate, in the form of mini chocolate chips, completes this stunning gluten- and dairy-free remake of an American favorite. *Makes one 9-inch loaf*

¾ cup unrefined coconut oil, melted and cooled, plus more for the pan

1½ cups cup-for-cup replacement gluten-free flour blend, such as Steve's GF Cake Flour

2½ teaspoons baking powder

¼ teaspoon sea salt

½ cup honey

2 large eggs

1 teaspoon pure vanilla extract

2 cups grated zucchini (from about 1 medium zucchini)

½ cup mini chocolate chips

½ cup raw pecans

½ cup shredded unsweetened coconut

Preheat the oven to 350°F. Lightly grease a 9 by 5-inch loaf pan with coconut oil and line the bottom with parchment paper.

Sift the gluten-free flour, baking powder, and salt into a medium bowl and set aside.

In the bowl of a stand mixer fitted with the paddle attachment, beat the honey on high speed until it lightens in color, about 3 minutes. Reduce the speed to medium, add the oil, and beat until combined, about 1 minute. Add the eggs one at a time, beating until each is incorporated before adding the next, then add the vanilla and beat briefly to combine.

Turn the mixer off, add the flour mixture to the bowl, and mix on low speed until the ingredients just come together. Turn the mixer off, add the zucchini, then beat on low speed for 30 seconds. Add the chocolate chips, pecans, and shredded coconut and beat on low speed for 1 minute. Remove the bowl from the mixer, scrape down the bowl with a rubber spatula, and mix again briefly with the spatula to thoroughly combine so the batter is creamy and somewhat loose.

Pour the batter into the prepared loaf pan and, using a small metal spatula, smooth out the surface.

Bake for 50 to 60 minutes, until the cake is golden brown on top, and the center cracks but holds its shape when lightly pressed with a finger.

Remove the cake from the oven and let cool completely in the pan on a wire rack. To release the cake from the pan, run a thin metal spatula around the inside edge of the pan. Place a plate over the top of the pan and flip the plate and pan together to release the cake onto the plate, then invert it so it's upright. Slice and serve, or store, well wrapped in plastic wrap, at room temperature for up to 5 days.

Swap It Out

- If dairy isn't a concern, you can use melted butter instead of the coconut oil.
- Use walnuts instead of pecans.

SWEETER THAN SUGAR

Sweeter than sugar but much more complex, honey is among the oldest sweeteners known and one of my favorites because of its host of healing benefits. It's common sense that honey soothes a sore throat and cough, but did you know that honey can treat burns and ulcers and protect against cancer and heart disease? Some varieties can even provide immune-strengthening probiotic bacteria when eaten in their raw state. For these compelling reasons and because I love the flavor, I've opted to use honey in several of my dessert recipes in place of plain table sugar. If you'd like to do the same, try swapping in honey for sugar in some of your favorite white sugar–based recipes: use a little less honey than you would sugar (½ to ⅔ cup honey for each cup of sugar) and reduce the liquid a little. Note that light-colored honey is generally best for baking. Darker honeys such as buckwheat tend to have a stronger flavor and can dominate whatever they're added to; they are perfect paired with a mild cheese for a dessert course!

ORANGE BLOSSOM PEACH COBBLER

There is nothing like the smell of fresh peaches, cinnamon, and vanilla baking in the oven! In this more nutritious version of a classic cobbler, the fruit bakes on its own a bit, and then the biscuit dough is added to the hot filling, which helps cook the biscuits into fluffy, light, and satisfying deliciousness. The cobbler is perfect with a scoop of ice cream, a touch of yogurt, or just as is. Peaches are low in calories and a good source of vitamins A and C and fiber, making this a dessert you can feel good about (in moderation, of course!). And for you romantics out there, here's a fun fact: peaches are actually a member of the rose family. Orange blossom water can be found in international or Middle Eastern markets and some supermarkets. *Serves 8*

FILLING
2 pounds peaches, peeled, pitted, and sliced ¼ inch thick
2 tablespoons honey
1 teaspoon orange blossom water
½ teaspoon grated orange zest
1 teaspoon fresh lemon juice
3 tablespoons cornstarch or potato starch
Pinch of sea salt

BISCUIT TOPPING
¾ cup cup-for-cup replacement gluten-free flour blend, such as Steve's GF Cake Flour
¼ cup almond flour or almond meal (see headnote, page 273)
¼ cup plus 2 teaspoons raw sugar
2 teaspoons baking powder
½ teaspoon baking soda
1 teaspoon ground cinnamon
¼ teaspoon sea salt
⅔ cup buttermilk
6 tablespoons (¾ stick) unsalted butter, melted and cooled
1 teaspoon pure vanilla extract

Preheat the oven to 375°F.

To make the filling: In a large bowl, combine the peaches, honey, orange blossom water, orange zest, and lemon juice. Sift in the cornstarch and salt and stir well to evenly distribute the ingredients. Pour the mixture into an ungreased 8 by 8-inch square or 8 ½ by 6 ½-inch rectangular baking pan and bake for 30 minutes, or until the fruit is bubbling and the juices begin to thicken.

Meanwhile, to make the biscuit topping: In a large bowl, whisk together the gluten-free flour, almond flour, ¼ cup of the sugar, the baking powder, baking soda, ¾ teaspoon of the cinnamon, and the salt and set aside.

In a small bowl, whisk together the buttermilk, melted butter, and vanilla. In a separate small bowl, whisk together the remaining 2 teaspoons sugar and ¼ teaspoon cinnamon.

About 5 minutes before you remove the peaches from the oven, finish making the topping by adding the wet ingredients to the dry ingredients and stirring briefly with a wooden spoon until the dough comes together into a soft, cohesive mixture.

Remove the peaches from the oven and increase the oven temperature to 425°F.

Using a large spoon, place dollops of dough on top of the hot peach filling, spacing them about ½ inch apart. Sprinkle each mound with cinnamon sugar. Bake for 20 minutes, or until the filling is bubbling and the dough is golden brown and firm on top. Remove from the oven and let cool on a wire rack for about 20 minutes, until the juices set up, then serve.

Swap It Out

- To make an almond peach cobbler, substitute ¾ teaspoon pure almond extract for the orange blossom water and omit the orange zest. Sprinkle ½ cup finely chopped almonds along with the cinnamon-sugar onto the top of the biscuits before baking.
- Swap coconut oil for the butter, if you like.

COCOA MACA-ROONS

These little cookies, slightly sweet and super moist, get their name from one of my favorite superfoods, the energy- and stamina-boosting plant maca. (Read more about maca on page 20.) This unbaked take on macaroons requires just five minutes to put together, perfect for impromptu entertaining or to satisfy sweet cravings on the spot! Take care to process the ingredients briefly, just to combine; otherwise, your macaroons will become dense rather than light. *Makes about 16 macaroons*

1 cup almond flour
2 cups unsweetened desiccated coconut
¼ cup unsweetened cocoa powder
6 tablespoons honey
¼ cup unrefined coconut oil, melted and cooled
1 teaspoon fresh lemon juice
1 teaspoon maca powder
1 teaspoon ground cinnamon
1 teaspoon pure vanilla extract
¼ teaspoon sea salt

In a food processor, combine all the ingredients and process for about 15 seconds, until just combined, scraping down the sides of the processor bowl once if needed. Transfer the mixture to a bowl and, using a 1½-inch cookie or ice cream scooper, scoop out the mixture and pack it in to form macaroons (if you don't have a scooper, roll the mixture with your hands into rounds and flatten them on the bottom). The macaroons will keep in an airtight container in the refrigerator for up to 2 weeks or in the freezer for up to 2 months.

FATS ARE BRAIN FOOD

Getting good-quality fats into your diet and eliminating refined oils are some of the most important steps you can take for your overall health. Healthy fats are brain food, providing energy for the cells in our brains, nourishing our hearts, and supporting our complete body systems. It's crucial for kids to get ample good fats into their bodies as they are learning and growing, and adults need fats to stay sharp, focused, and full of energy.

There's a lot of conflicting information as to what constitutes a healthy fat, but you'll be ahead of the game if you remember to look for the words *unrefined* or *extra-virgin* on the label. Other oils are refined, which means they are stripped of nutrients, flavor, and color. Ever wonder why vegetable oils like canola are considered heart-healthy but are also remarkably cheap? It's because they have been refined, and any omega-3 fatty acids they once contained have been denatured, which is worse than simply losing their benefits because the denaturing can lead to the formation of carcinogenic free radicals. To refine an oil, the oil-containing food is crushed or pressed, heated beyond the smoke point, then treated with chemicals to extract as much oil as possible. The result is an oil with the same bland taste and greasy mouthfeel regardless of which vegetable or seed it came from. Instead, favor oils that smell like the foods they're made from, like my favorites, heart-healthy extra-virgin olive oil and unrefined coconut oil. Grass-fed butter adds incredible flavor and health benefits you might not be aware of. See page 98 to learn more about butter.

CHUNKY CHOCOLATE CHIP COOKIES

Chocolate chip cookies are the cookie of choice for many Americans, my family included! They are quick and easy to make, and there are lots of ways of giving the classic a nutrient boost, such as using gluten-free flour, raw sugar, and organic, grass-fed butter. You choose whether or not to add nuts (my husband likes his with walnuts), or for families with mixed preferences, add nuts to half the dough and keep the rest plain.

Makes 24 cookies

1⅔ cups cup-for-cup replacement gluten-free flour blend, such as Steve's GF Cake Flour
1 teaspoon sea salt
½ teaspoon baking soda
1 cup (2 sticks) unsalted butter, at room temperature
1½ cups raw sugar
2 large eggs
1 teaspoon vanilla extract
12 ounces semisweet chocolate chips
1 cup chopped walnuts (optional)

Preheat the oven to 350°F. Line two baking sheets with parchment paper.

In a large bowl, whisk together the flour, salt, and baking soda.

In the bowl of a stand mixer fitted with the paddle attachment, cream the butter and sugar on high speed until the mixture is light and fluffy, about 2 minutes (or beat by hand in a large bowl with a wooden spoon for about 4 minutes; the raw sugar may not break down as much, but this is okay). Beat in the eggs, one at a time, until well blended, about 1 minute. Add the vanilla and beat to combine. Using a rubber spatula, scrape down the sides of the bowl and the paddle attachment. Turn the mixer to low speed and add the dry ingredients in three additions, beating until combined. Add the chocolate chips and walnuts (if using), and mix until the ingredients are blended and well distributed.

Working in two batches, using your hands, form balls of dough, about 2 tablespoons for each (or use an ice cream scoop), setting them on the prepared baking sheets with 2 inches of space between them. Keep a small bowl of cold water handy and dip your hands in it as needed to keep the dough from sticking. (At this point, the individual portions of dough can be chilled until firm, then bundled into a freezer bag and frozen for up to 2 months. To bake, simply set them on the prepared baking sheets, set aside for 1½ hours to come to room temperature, and then bake.) Using the heel of your hand, flatten each dough ball onto the baking sheet so it is ⅓ inch thick.

Bake for 8 to 10 minutes, until the

cookies are golden brown around the edges and firm in the center, rotating the pans from top to bottom and front to back halfway through baking to ensure even browning. Transfer the baking sheets to wire racks to cool for 5 minutes, then transfer the cookies from the baking sheets to the racks to cool. Cool the baking sheets and repeat with the remaining dough. The cookies will keep in a storage bag at room temperature for up to 2 days or in the freezer for up to 2 months.

Next Level, Please!

- Add 1 teaspoon maca powder, flax meal, or ground hemp seeds to the dough when you add the dry ingredients.
- Add a different type of nut, raisins, dried cranberries, or dried cherries.

RED VELVET CUPCAKES

Who wants a cupcake that doubles as an immune booster, blood pressure regulator, stamina booster, and is a fantastic source of fiber, vitamin C, and potassium? I do! These little red velvets get their subtle red hue and impressive nutritional profile from crimson-colored beets and are completely free of food coloring. Beets can also lend their pretty pink coloring to the honey cream cheese frosting. The lemon juice and cider vinegar help to set the red coloring, which will be at its strongest within a few hours of baking and then slowly begin to fade. But don't let all that health talk fool you—these cupcakes are just as delicious as they are nutritious! *Makes 18 cupcakes*

CUPCAKES

2 large red beets

1¾ cups cup-for-cup replacement gluten-free flour blend, such as Steve's GF Cake Flour

3 tablespoons unsweetened Dutch-process cocoa powder

1¼ teaspoons baking powder

½ teaspoon baking soda

1 teaspoon sea salt

¾ cup buttermilk

1 tablespoon fresh lemon juice

2 teaspoons apple cider vinegar

1½ teaspoons pure vanilla extract

¾ cup unrefined coconut oil, melted and cooled

1¾ cups raw sugar

3 large eggs, at room temperature

FROSTING

1 cup (2 sticks) unsalted butter, at room temperature

2 (8-ounce) packages cream cheese, at room temperature

½ cup honey

2 teaspoons pure maple syrup

2 teaspoons pure vanilla extract

To make the cupcakes: Scrub the beets and quarter them. Bring a medium pot of water to a boil over medium-high heat. Add the beets and boil until they are tender and can be easily pierced with the tip of a knife, about 1 hour. Drain, let cool slightly, then place the beets in a container and refrigerate for about 30 minutes to cool completely.

Preheat the oven to 350°F. Line 18 muffin cups with paper liners.

Sift the gluten-free flour, cocoa powder, baking powder, baking soda, and salt into a large bowl and set aside.

Peel the beets, put them in a food processor, and puree. Measure out 1 cup of the beet puree and set aside 2 tablespoons in a small bowl for the frosting (if you plan to tint it pink). Transfer the remaining puree to an airtight container and refrigerate for another use, such as in a smoothie or to color your hummus pink (see page 229).

Return the 1 cup beet puree to the food processor. Add the buttermilk, lemon

juice, vinegar, and vanilla and process until smooth. Set aside.

In the bowl of a stand mixer fitted with the paddle attachment, combine the oil and sugar and beat on medium-high speed for 5 minutes, or until the mixture lightens in color and the sugar granules have slightly broken down. Beat in the eggs one at a time, scraping down the sides of the bowl after each addition. Turn the mixer off, add one-third of the flour mixture, and mix on low speed until incorporated, then add one-third of the beet mixture. Alternately add the flour mixture and beet mixture, ending with the dry ingredients. Turn off the machine, then use a rubber spatula to scrape down the bowl and beat again for 30 seconds. Remove the bowl from the mixer and give the batter a thorough final mixing by hand.

Fill each cupcake liner three-quarters full and bake for 15 to 20 minutes, until a tester inserted into the center of a cupcake comes out clean.

Remove the cupcakes from the oven and let cool in the pan on a wire rack for 5 minutes. Use the tip of a paring knife to gently flip each cupcake out of the pan. Let cool completely before frosting. (At this point, the cupcakes will keep, well wrapped in plastic wrap, in the refrigerator for up to 1 week or in the freezer for up to 1 month.)

To make the frosting: If you choose to color your frosting pink, put the reserved 2 tablespoons beet puree into a fine-mesh strainer set over a small bowl and press

against the puree to extract all the liquid. Measure out 2 teaspoons and set aside.

In the bowl of a stand mixer fitted with the paddle attachment, combine the butter and cream cheese and beat on medium-high speed until creamy and well blended, about 2 minutes. Reduce the speed to medium, add the honey, maple syrup, vanilla, and beet juice (if using), and beat for about 1 minute, until fully incorporated.

Immediately frost the cooled cupcakes.

Swap It Out

- Swap out the coconut oil for butter.
- Add 3 ounces melted chocolate to the frosting for a chocolate cream cheese treat.

Next Level, Please!

Add a splash of the beet cooking water or extra beet juice to fruit juice or punch to give a vitamin and mineral boost that the kids will never notice.

KEY LIME CHEESECAKE

Cheesecake is a guilty pleasure, but not when you make yours from cashews and coconut! Cashews are incredibly creamy when soaked and blended; coconut cream adds even more creaminess, and pistachios contribute their rich flavor and vibrant green color. This cheese-free cheesecake can be made vegan by sweetening it with maple syrup rather than honey. This recipe requires planning in advance, first to soak the nuts and then to freeze the cheesecake for a few hours before serving. *Makes one 10-inch cheesecake*

2 cups raw cashews
1 cup raw shelled pistachios, plus chopped pistachios for garnish
Date-Nut Piecrust (page 299)
4 teaspoons grated lime zest
¾ cup fresh lime juice, preferably from key limes
⅔ cup unrefined coconut oil, melted and cooled
1 cup unsweetened coconut cream or coconut milk
1 cup honey or pure maple syrup
⅛ teaspoon sea salt

Place the cashews and pistachios in two separate bowls and add warm water to cover by a couple of inches. Cover with dishtowels and leave to soak for at least 4 hours or up to overnight (to shorten the soaking time to 1 hour, use hot water), until the pistachio skins have loosened. Drain the nuts and peel and discard the pistachio skins.

Meanwhile, press the crust into the bottom of a 10-inch springform pan (the bottom of a flat dry-measuring cup would be a good tool for the job).

In a high-speed blender or food processor, combine the drained cashews and pistachios, the lime zest, lime juice, oil, coconut cream, honey, and salt and blend until very smooth, about 3 minutes, stopping to scrape down the sides of the processor bowl if needed. Pour the filling over the crust and smooth it with a rubber spatula. Cover the pan with aluminum foil and freeze until solid, at least 4 hours or up to overnight.

Remove the cheesecake from the freezer about 20 minutes before serving, but do not let it thaw completely (the goal is a semifreddo consistency; if the cheesecake thaws completely, it loses its wonderful silky, rich texture). Run a butter knife along the edges of the springform to loosen it, then remove the springform ring. Run a smooth, sharp knife under hot water and slice the cheesecake, re-warming the blade between slices. Sprinkle the slices with chopped pistachios. Store leftovers in the freezer; remove slices from the freezer about 20 minutes before serving. I like to slice the whole cake, freeze the slices individually and wrap in plastic wrap, and thaw them as needed.

Swap It Out

Omit the pistachios and use 3 cups cashews total. You'll sacrifice a little of the green color but save time on peeling the pistachios.

CARDAMOM SPICE BAKED APPLES

Just like peaches, apples are a member of the rose family, and more than 2,500 varieties are grown here in the United States. For this recipe, choose a cooking-type apple that will stand up to long baking with soft and tender results. Good choices include Braeburn, Gala, Fuji, Golden Delicious, or Rome. Baked apples are a reliable, comforting, not-too-sweet dessert option with any number of filling and flavoring options. My favorite is to stuff the apples with dates and nuts, sweeten them lightly with maple syrup, and flavor them with warming cinnamon and cardamom. These apples are perfect served warm with a scoop of ice cream or frozen yogurt. If you don't have a food processor, chop the dates and walnuts into small (¼-inch) pieces and squeeze the ingredients together to make the filling. *Makes 6*

12 dried dates, pitted
½ cup walnuts
2 tablespoons pure maple syrup
2 tablespoons plus 1½ teaspoons unrefined coconut oil

2 teaspoons ground cardamom
½ teaspoon ground cinnamon
1 teaspoon pure vanilla extract
1 teaspoon fresh lemon juice
Pinch of sea salt
6 large apples
1 cup no-sugar-added apple juice or water

Preheat the oven to 350°F.

In a food processor, combine the dates, walnuts, maple syrup, 2 tablespoons of the oil, 1½ teaspoons of the cardamom, the cinnamon, vanilla, lemon juice, and salt and process the mixture into a thick paste. There will be small bits of nuts and dates remaining; this is okay.

Core the apples almost all the way through, leaving the very bottom intact to form a cup to hold the filling. Using a vegetable peeler, peel away one strip of apple skin from the top of each apple. (This will prevent the apples from bursting while they bake.) Using a small spoon or butter knife, stuff the center of each apple with the date filling. Smooth over the top of the filling and set the apples into an 8-inch square baking pan or 9-inch pie plate. Top each apple with ¼ teaspoon of the remaining coconut oil. In a small bowl, whisk the apple juice with the remaining ½ teaspoon cardamom, then pour the liquid into the bottom of the pan with the apples. Cover the pan with aluminum foil, being careful not to let the foil touch the tops of the apples.

Bake for about 1 hour, until an apple can be pierced through easily with the tip of a paring knife, the skin is wrinkled, and the top of the date filling is dark brown. Remove the pan from the oven, place on a wire rack, and let cool for 20 minutes. Serve drizzled with the juices from the pan.

Swap It Out

- Simple Baked Apples: Place 1 teaspoon butter, 1½ teaspoons pure maple syrup, and 1 teaspoon chopped nuts into an apple cored as described, sprinkle with a light dusting of ground cinnamon or cardamom, and bake as directed.
- Substitute butter for the coconut oil, honey for the maple syrup, or use another kind of nut.

BANANA CAKE WITH MACADAMIAS AND VANILLA WHIPPED CREAM

The three layers of this moist and light banana cake are sandwiched with a subtle vanilla cream and finished with a sprinkling of buttery, rich macadamias. Serve with berries on the side—blueberries are brilliant here—or include berries in the layers to add a fruity accent. To go the minimalist route, eat the cake without the cream as banana bread. Add nuts or raisins to the filling and bake in a standard loaf pan. Or try the sour cream chocolate ganache option I've shared at the end. *Makes one 9-inch cake*

BANANA CAKE

¾ cup (1½ sticks) unsalted butter, at room temperature, plus more for the pan
1 cup mashed ripe banana (about 2 large)
¼ cup plain yogurt
2 large eggs, at room temperature
1 teaspoon grated lime zest
1½ teaspoons pure vanilla extract
1½ cups cup-for-cup replacement gluten-free flour blend, such as Steve's GF Cake Flour
¾ cup plus 2 tablespoons raw sugar
1½ teaspoons ground chia seeds
1 teaspoon baking soda
¾ teaspoon baking powder
½ teaspoon sea salt
½ cup macadamia nuts, chopped
Fresh blueberries or other berries (optional)

VANILLA WHIPPED CREAM

2 cups heavy cream
2 teaspoons pure vanilla extract
1 tablespoon pure maple syrup

Preheat the oven to 350°F. Butter a 9-inch round cake pan and line the bottom with parchment paper.

To make the cake: In a food processor, combine the bananas and yogurt and process until smooth. Add the eggs, lime zest, and vanilla and process for about 30 seconds, until the ingredients are well blended.

Sift the gluten-free flour, sugar, ground chia seeds, baking soda, baking powder, and salt into the bowl of a stand mixer fitted with the paddle attachment. Add the butter and three-quarters of the banana mixture to the dry ingredients and mix on low speed until the ingredients are blended. Increase the speed to medium-high and beat for 1 minute, or until the batter is fluffy and lightened in texture. Add the remaining banana mixture and beat for 30 seconds to incorporate. Turn off the mixer and scrape down the bowl and the paddle using a rubber spatula. Beat on medium speed for 30 seconds, then remove the bowl from the mixer and use the rubber spatula to finish mixing the batter by hand.

Scrape the batter into the prepared

cake pan and, using a small metal spatula, smooth the surface so it's level. Sprinkle the macadamia nuts, and berries (if using), evenly over the top of the cake batter and gently press them onto the batter so they adhere. Bake for 30 to 40 minutes, until the cake springs back when pressed lightly in the center. Remove from the oven and let cool in the pan on a wire rack for 10 minutes. Release the cake by running a small metal spatula around the inside edge of the cake, then flip the cake over onto the rack. Let cool completely before assembling.

To make the whipped cream: In the bowl of a stand mixer fitted with the whisk attachment, whip the cream on medium-high speed until it just begins to hold soft peaks. Add the vanilla and maple syrup and whip until the cream holds medium-firm peaks.

Slice the cake horizontally into thirds and set the bottom third on a flat plate. Using a metal spatula, spread half the whipped cream over the bottom cake layer in a thick, even layer, then gently press the second cake layer onto the cream. Spread the remaining whipped cream over the cake layer and top with the macadamia nut cake layer. Using the metal spatula, smooth any excess cream around the sides of the cake. Garnish with fresh berries, if desired, slice, and serve. The cake is best assembled just before serving but can keep for up to 1 hour before serving.

Swap It Out Variation

SOUR CREAM CHOCOLATE GANACHE FILLING

1½ cups finely chopped bittersweet chocolate
1½ cups sour cream

Place the chocolate in a heatproof bowl and set it over a pan of simmering water, making sure the bottom of the bowl doesn't touch the water. Stir the chocolate often until it has melted, then remove the bowl from the pan. Stir the sour cream into the melted chocolate until well blended. Assemble the cake as directed, using the ganache in place of the whipped cream.

NOT YOUR MAMA'S SWEET POTATO PIE

Traditional sweet potato pie is made with white flour, refined sugar, shortening, and cream. Although this type of pie is truly mouth-watering, I usually don't feel too great after indulging in a slice or two. This recipe, which happens to be both gluten- and dairy-free, has a winning combination of goodness and wholesomeness with pure and simple sweet potato flavor.

My go-to piecrust is made from dates and nuts, making it more nutritious and flavorful than a flour crust, and requires no special pastry-making skills. Note that this type of crust browns quickly, so you'll need to cover it with a piecrust shield (available at kitchen supply stores) or a strip of aluminum foil ten minutes into baking so it doesn't burn.

This pie tastes even better the next day, after the flavors have had some time to mingle and chill in the fridge. Remove it an hour or so before serving to come to room temperature. A dollop of plain Greek yogurt or Vanilla Whipped Cream (see page 295) would be a fitting finish for a slice. *Makes one 10-inch pie*

2 pounds sweet potatoes (2 large)

DATE-NUT PIECRUST
1½ cups walnut pieces
½ cup pitted dried dates
½ teaspoon fresh lemon juice
½ teaspoon pure vanilla extract
⅛ teaspoon sea salt

FILLING
⅔ cup pure maple syrup
½ cup unrefined coconut oil
3 large eggs
1 teaspoon pure vanilla extract
1 teaspoon grated lemon zest
¾ teaspoon ground cinnamon
½ teaspoon ground turmeric
½ teaspoon freshly grated nutmeg

¼ teaspoon sea salt

Plain Greek yogurt or Vanilla Whipped Cream
    (see page 295), for topping
Sprinkling of freshly grated nutmeg, for topping
    (optional)

Peel the sweet potatoes and cut them into roughly 1-inch chunks. Place them in a steamer basket set over a pot filled with a couple of inches of simmering water. Cover and steam until tender when poked with a knife or fork, 20 to 30 minutes. Remove from the steamer and let cool.

Preheat the oven to 350°F.

While the sweet potatoes are steaming, make the crust: Combine all the crust ingredients in a food processor and process until broken down into a rough puree that holds together, leaving small pieces of nuts visible for texture. Transfer the dough to the center of a 10-inch pie plate and loosely form it into a ball (set the processor bowl aside, no need to rinse). Press the dough evenly over the bottom of the pie plate and up the sides (the bottom of a flat dry-measuring cup would be a good tool for the job), but do not make a rim over the top of the plate.

To make the filling: Combine all the filling ingredients in the food processor and process until smooth, about 2 minutes, stopping the machine to scrape down the sides once or twice as needed.

Pour the filling into the crust and use a rubber spatula to spread it out evenly, making sure the filling reaches the sides of the crust in all places. Bake for 10 minutes, then carefully place a piecrust shield or a strip of aluminum foil over the crust and bake for 40 minutes more, or until the pie is mostly set but still a little jiggly and a cake tester inserted into the center comes out mostly wet (*not* dry). Place on a wire rack to cool completely before slicing and serving.

A PINCH OR TWO OF TURMERIC

From scrambled eggs to soup, I've been including a pinch or two or more of turmeric in the recipes throughout the book. Its brilliant color and anti-inflammatory properties inspire me to cook with it in unconventional ways. My love for turmeric even extends to dessert, as in this sweet potato pie, as it doesn't change the flavor but adds nutrition and helps pop the golden-orange color of the sweet potatoes. See page 50 to learn more about the healing benefits of turmeric.

IN CLOSING

Thank you for opening my book and entering my kitchen! I hope you enjoyed *Food for Life* as much as I enjoyed creating it. I truly believe that we are all meant to be happy and healthy, and what we choose to eat makes all the difference. I am passionate about taking the foods we love and turning them into recipes that are nutritious, delicious, and satisfying. I encourage you to do your own research on the power of food and how it can improve your health! Use my recipes as inspiration to experiment in your own kitchen, and from there turn your healthy lifestyle into a tradition your family will enjoy for many generations to come.

Acknowledgments

I would like to thank the amazing team of people who contributed to making my cookbook idea into a reality! A tremendous amount of work went into creating *Food For Life,* and I appreciate every single person involved!

Celeste Fine and Sarah Passick of Sterling Lord Literistic, you gals were my book whisperers. You have given me perfect guidance along the way and your expertise is second to none! You ladies are truly amazing at what you do, and I look forward to creating many more books with you at my side.

To my cowriter, Leda Scheintaub, you have been an amazing partner. Your attention to detail and excellent time management skills are what got this book done on time. The thought of taking the recipes I have been cooking for years and putting them down on paper seemed like a daunting task and gave me anxiety, to say the least! But you made the process seamless. Whether you were making small changes to my recipes in order to elevate them or developing my recipe ideas into a complete dish, you did it with creativity and perfection. Thanks for making my first cookbook a delightful experience!

Patricia Austin, you're a true artist when it comes to gluten-free desserts! You took my dessert ideas and turned them into recipes that surpassed my expectations. Thank you for collaborating with Leda and me to create healthy desserts that we can all feel good about eating.

To my editor, Elizabeth Beier, thank you for believing in my vision from the start and for making a home for me at St. Martin's Press. I am grateful for your unlimited enthusiasm!

Also on the St. Martin's team: editorial assistant Nicole Williams, for ushering my manuscript through with grace; Brant Janeway and Erica Martirano in the marketing department; Tracey Guest and Jessica Preeg in publicity, cover designer Lesley Worrell; Lisa Davis and Cathy Turiano in production, Kathryn Parise and Susan Walsh for their interior design; and Ivy McFadden for her copyediting. Without you all this book would not be as fabulous as it is!

Matt Armendariz, you photographed my recipes beautifully. I wanted the photos of my dishes to jump off the page, and you made it happen. Your talent and warm personality made my ten-day food shoot a breeze. Thank you for enthusiastically adhering to my creative direction and capturing the perfect cover shot to represent what this book is all about! I would also like to extend my appreciation to photo assistant Byron Gamarro. Your hospitality skills did not go unnoticed!

I had an amazing team of food stylists. Adam Pearson and Carrie Purcell, you are exactly what I hoped for. Thanks for arranging my recipes artfully while keeping them true! Food stylist assistants Hristina Misafiris and Aubrey Devin—many thanks for your professionalism and attention to detail.

Allen Cooley, thank you for capturing me and my family spending time together at home, surrounded by food and love. You always make me look great, so I'm keeping you around! I would like to also thank Keith Taylor and Nikki Richardson for assisting Allen with photography.

I had a serious glam squad for the multiple photo shoots required for this project! Autumn Moultrie, Robbi Rodgers, Ki Williams, Tai Young, and Kya Bilal, you all know that I think your talent is top notch, but what I appreciate most is that I can call you my friends! You have always come through for me, and I love you gals.

Ché Graham, you are my secret weapon. Thanks for so delicately retouching all of my photos, making them look perfectly un-perfect!

A special shout-out to my neighbors Keith and Laura Meadows. I truly appreciate your willingness to let me and my entire crew invade your home and shoot in your beautiful newly remodeled kitchen—I can't thank you enough. Anytime you want me to bring a pot of gumbo across the street, just text me!

A big hug and thank-you to my wonderful recipe testers Lizi Rosenberg and Janice Baldwin. And to Rebecca Wood, author of *The Whole Foods Encyclopedia*, who did a review of the manuscript for me.

I have tons of appreciation for Giovanni Clark for going back and forth to the grocery store to buy ingredients for me. They knew your name at the store by the time we were done!

Amber Noble Garland, my big-hearted business partner and friend, you have given me constant guidance and support from the day I met you. I appreciate all of your knowledge, wisdom, and friendship!

To my publicist, Lisa Perkins, at Fifteen Minutes—you have always cheered me on and shown me support. I respect that you handle your business with integrity and authenticity. I am glad to have you in my corner!

Grandma, you have given me cooking direction and recipes over the phone that have developed into some of my favorite dishes over the years. Thanks for teaching me how to cook with flavor and soul!

Mom, I would like to thank you for indirectly inspiring me to become a cook—due to the fact that you didn't spend much time in the kitchen, coupled with my constant desire to eat. LOL! You have always encouraged me to do my best and gave me self-confidence through your consistent belief in me and love for my cooking.

To my husband, Curtis, and my two children, Curtis Jr. and Sydney, you are my joy and my inspiration. All I need in this life is you three and my health. I created many of the recipes in this book with you in mind, and I look forward to making many more for us to enjoy together!

RESOURCES

Ingredients and Products

AUTHENTIC FOODS
www.authenticfoods.com
Steve's GF Cake Flour
Cup-for-cup gluten-free replacement flour (for general gluten-free baking, not just for cakes)

CULTURES FOR HEALTH
www.culturesforhealth.com
Kefir starters

FRONTIER CO-OP
www.frontiercoop.com
Large selection of organic spices and seasonings

GEM CULTURES
www.gemcultures.com
Kefir starters

GOLD MINE NATURAL FOOD CO.
www.goldminenaturalfoods.com
General natural foods, including grains, beans, nuts, seeds, dried fruit, seaweed, and sweeteners

MAINE COAST SEA VEGETABLES
www.seaveg.com
Dulse granules, kombu, nori seaweed

MOUNTAIN ROSE HERBS
www.mountainroseherbs.com
Organic herbs and spices, maca, spirulina, chlorella, chia seeds, flaxseeds, matcha tea, seaweed

NATURESPIRIT HERBS
www.naturespiritherbs.com
Kombu and nori seaweed

THRIVE MARKET
www.thrivemarket.com
Large selection of organic and non-GMO products at discounted prices

TROPICAL TRADITIONS
www.tropicaltraditions.com
Organic coconut oil

Further Reading

Cultured Foods for Your Kitchen: 100 Recipes Featuring the Bold Flavors of Fermentation by my cowriter, Leda Scheintaub (Rizzoli, 2014)
The inspiration behind my recipes for pickles, sauerkraut, and kefir; how to make ferments and use them in your everyday cooking.

The Flavor Bible: The Essential Guide to Culinary Creativity, Based on the Wisdom of America's Most Imaginative Chefs by Karen Page and Andrew Dornenburg (Little, Brown and Company, 2008)
A comprehensive reference of ingredients with compatible flavors; will motivate you to play with taste and texture pairings and make you a more confident cook.

The Food Lab: Better Home Cooking Through Science by J. Kenji López-Alt
(W. W. Norton & Company, 2015)
Simple new cooking techniques for familiar foods, introduced through an understanding of the science behind cooking.

The New Whole Foods Encyclopedia: A Comprehensive Resource for Healthy Eating
by Rebecca Wood (Penguin Books, 2010)
An A-to-Z of whole foods with detailed information on their selection, preparation, storage, uses, and healing properties.

Pâtisserie Gluten Free: The Art of French Pastry
by Patricia Austin, who contributed to the dessert section of this book (Skyhorse Publishing, 2017)
French pastry recipes made gluten-, gum-, and GMO-free.

INDEX